To my best
friend, and
brother...
Son

**CHIANG KAI-SHEK**

# BOOKS BY EMILY HAHN

CHIANG KAI-SHEK

LOVE CONQUERS NOTHING

PURPLE PASSAGE

A DEGREE OF PRUDERY

ENGLAND TO ME

MISS JILL

RAFFLES OF SINGAPORE

HONG KONG HOLIDAY

CHINA TO ME

MR. PAN

THE SOONG SISTERS

# CHIANG

# KAI-SHEK

an unauthorized biography

by Emily Hahn

DOUBLEDAY & COMPANY, INC.
GARDEN CITY, NEW YORK, 1955

Library of Congress Catalog Card Number 55-5582

951.04
C 532 h

## AUTHOR'S NOTE

Generalissimo Chiang Kai-shek did not co-operate on this book; on the contrary, he doesn't want anything published about himself as long as he is kept off the mainland. He feels that in these circumstances he is not worth attention. The author doesn't agree.

# CONTENTS

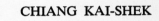

CHIANG  KAI-SHEK

# 1 FLASHBACK 1887–94

That night in Takata, near the northwest coast of Japan, there was a dinner party in a restaurant. Uniformed men with shaved heads and stockinged feet sat cross-legged on the matting floor and toasted each other, and laughed a good deal and sang marching songs. They were young and cheerful. It wasn't an elaborate or expensive party; just a routine dinner, a farewell gesture from the Japanese officers of the town garrison for three Chinese brothers in arms. These Chinese had been with them for several years, training in the Imperial Army by special arrangement with the War Office in Peking. Now they were going home. Their plans, like many other Chinese plans, had suddenly been changed by an accident, due to some clumsy unknown, miles away in Hankow. There, a bomb had gone off in a cellar and blown the lid off the latest revolution against the Ching Dynasty. It was October 1911.

Somebody filled one of the tiny cups with water instead of rice wine, and with a sweeping gesture handed it to his neighbor, a Chinese. "Military people don't drink sake," he said. "Please drink water instead. According to the *bushido* spirit of Japan, drinking water means that the soldier won't return alive."

All the Japanese nodded approvingly and in silence watched the little ceremony that followed. Two of the guests took a sip, but the last one to hold the cup, a solemn young man named Chiang Kai-shek, swallowed all the water that was left.

"Gentlemen, thank you for the honor you have done me," he said.

"And as he drank his face was red with emotion," said General Nakaoka, trying valiantly in 1928 to recall whatever he could of the long-forgotten incident. "Whoever dreamed that the student of those days would ever be chairman of the Chinese Government? None of us thought that Mr. Chiang was going to be a historic personality."

Still less, he might have said, did anybody in the regiment think that some day the Japanese, above all people, would have violent reactions to Chiang's name. In 1911 he was one of the most obscure Chinese students that had ever been sent over to finish his military training in Asia's up-to-date army. Most youths in his category were related to the noble families of China and had got their places through political pull, but Chiang Kai-shek was a nobody.

The officers were sorry later on that they had neglected to notice him. By the time Nakaoka gave his newspaper interview the Japanese had developed a keen interest in that all but forgotten young man, and were even proud of him. In 1928 he was famous as the Chinese leader who had suddenly broken with Russia and taken the new Republic out of Communist clutches. Still, there it was; nobody among the Japanese in his old regiment remembered him except in a vague way, in that scrap of the general's reminiscence. Only a sergeant, a man named Shimoda, could add more to the picture.

"The only thing remarkable in him," said Shimoda, "was the impressive and forbidding expression which would instantly come upon his face when he was ordered to clean the stables."

The twenty-four-year-old Chiang sailed to Shanghai in a state of elation that his code of manners made it necessary to conceal.

It was against his philosophy of self-control to exhibit emotion, but he had waited a long time for this moment. This, he felt, was *it* at last; this time the revolution would succeed. He liked the Japanese well enough after all these years of arduous training; he admired their endurance, and he had long since got used to their scanty diet of cold rice garnished with a little fish and pickle. He knew he had been lucky to get the chance of training with the only modern army in the Far East. Most of the boys sent over from home on the government training scheme were naturally pro-Manchu. But Chiang was different. Already, in spirit, he was a seasoned revolutionary. Nor was it only in spirit that he knew his way around that dimly lit world of the fugitive in which his revered leader, Sun Yat-sen, had lived his adventurous life. Already he felt like a veteran. He didn't look like one—he looked like a boy of sixteen—but it is the feeling that counts.

Chiang knew Shanghai well; the foreign settlements, the great walled estates, the hotels, and the drab Chinese city full of pig-tailed workers. It looked normal when he landed, but something was going on behind the humdrum façade of streets and people. Not only China had been rocked by that amateurish little bomb. The world was following developments.

The French Concession and the International Settlement offered the conspirators who were Chiang's friends their only safety in all the country. Protected by the flags of Europe, Sun Yat-sen's followers had for years been holding their meetings and taking up collections for armaments.

As soon as his ship had docked, the young soldier hurried to the house of his good friend Chen Chi-mei. Whatever was happening, Chen would know the true story. There had been other alarms and they had always turned out to be false or abortive, but this time, Chiang knew, things were better prepared than they had ever been before. There would be popular support in widespread districts. This time, revolution against the Manchus couldn't be quelled. That was why he had insisted upon coming back to his country instead of staying on in the hope of more training. One couldn't go on forever just preparing. A keen young soldier must find his place in the sun; he need not forever accept a role in the background, giving way to spoiled scions from the higher social circles of Peking. There had been a lot of that already—too much. Chiang had suffered a long, long time from resentment and a feeling of neglect. He had a passionate and jealous nature.

He was born in Chikow, a village near the town of Fenghua, in Chekiang. Chekiang is a small province on the Chinese seacoast, south of Shanghai. The land is fertile, and it is counted a wealthy province. Chikow is inland among the hills, where farms are tip-tilted, in a mountain range that runs north and south along China's edge. We have seen its mountains, or their prototypes, in Chinese paintings; austere, jagged outlines against the sky, softened here and there by floating scraps of mist.

He could not have been more widely separate from our country if he had been born in 1587 instead of 1887; his people knew almost nothing about America or any other land, though Americans knew a little—not much, but a little—about China. There were stories of the East told in America: there were pictures painted by Chinese, and missionaries' stories, and there were live Chinese, too, quite a few of them living in California cities or wandering inland to set up shops and laundries. Americans, if they were interested, learned a good deal about China and her people—the black-haired women who wore trousers, and the men's long pigtails. But in Chekiang, America was only a vague name.

From his birth the baby was never out of hearing distance of rushing water. A brook flowed along the foot of the bluff where his house stood. Like the neighbors, his family farmed bits of ground in the nearby valley, but Kai-shek's father Chiang Su-an was also a shopkeeper. (As a child, Kai-shek had another name;

as he grew older and went to school the name was changed, and later he took yet another. But the unfamiliar syllables are confusing enough without this added elaboration, and we had better ignore it.) Su-an was the local salt merchant. Salt was a government monopoly and Chiang held a license to trade in it; his income was steady if modest. Just how modest it was is difficult for a Westerner to estimate.

Were the Chiangs poor? We might think so. But Chiang Kai-shek in his memoirs speaks of his grandfathers as having been wealthy men. The Chiang grandfather had been a salt merchant like Su-an, and the maternal grandfather, Wang, had moved into Chekiang from Anhwei and become a landowner. "After the fall of the Taiping kingdom," says Chiang, "he felt heartbroken . . . and traveled to the west of Chekiang . . . In a few years the rice fields increased and the estate became very rich. For scores of *li* the property was all his."

Chiang's official biographers have been victims of a conflict. They want to prove that their hero has illustrious family connections, if only because it would be discourteous not to say that he has. Yet there was a new fashion, even before the Communist conquest, to emphasize the virtues of the simple life—Lincoln is very well thought of in China. The nearest thing to Lincoln that can be found in their history is the Confucian sage Mencius, and they have worked hard to show parallels between his life and Chiang Kai-shek's. Mencius had a wise, self-sacrificing mother who brought up her son admirably, in spite of abject poverty, and Chiang's chroniclers point out the things he can claim in common with the sage—the widowed mother, the poverty . . . Perhaps they overdid it; he wasn't as poor as all that.

Chiang Kai-shek himself is taciturn about his background. If he hadn't become a Christian and joined the Southern Methodist Church, the notion of being ashamed of his history might never have entered his head. He did become a Methodist, though, and he is ashamed; and it is possible, as a matter of fact, that anybody in China would have been affected to a certain extent in the twenties by our opinions on morality, no matter what religion he held. It may be irrational of Chiang to criticize his Buddhist family for not living according to Christian ideas of propriety, but in these matters few of us are governed by reason. The particular fact he does not wish to dwell on is that his mother, twenty-two years younger than her husband, was not Su-an's first wife, the "big mistress" of the house. She was the "little mistress," the second wife—a concubine, we would call it. This worries the Generalissimo.

No blame attached to Miss Wang for assuming this relationship. There was nothing illicit about a concubine's status. She had her place in the family, by law and custom, and her children enjoyed equal rights with those of the first wife. She was considered as good a woman as any in the community: the rank of concubine did not connote immorality. Before Chiang was converted he must have accepted the general Chinese opinion on such matters: indeed, no other attitude could possibly have occurred to him. It is different now.

In an attempt to compensate for this fact, which he considers a blemish, the log-cabin fanciers talk a good deal about his mother's virtues, and Chiang's memoirs are enthusiastic on this subject. "Alas!" he wrote, "my mother endured thirty-six years of hardship. She swallowed much bitterness and never refused any kind of toil, all for her unfilial son, who, she hoped, would establish himself. But I was unworthy. . . . Not only have I been unable to achieve deeds of virtue or do work of importance so as to fulfill my mother's ambition for me, but I have also failed utterly in the filial duty of a son to look after his mother's health constantly and in making her happy even for a single day. On the contrary she had been allowed to drag on with some kind of a serious illness for over ten years. . . ." This was written in 1921, when her son was thirty-four years old and had done quite a lot of important work. It is the way polite Chinese talk: it is not to be taken literally.

Other narrators are not so modest on his behalf or hers. One story current among his underlings is that Mrs. Chiang, in order to support her fatherless children—Chiang Su-an died when the boy was eight—went out to work as a housemaid. It is not true. She belonged to a large clan, and Chinese families look after their own. She found it hard to manage financially, but there were brothers-in-law and cousins and uncles who helped. She worked embroidery and sold it: she did this work among her own people.

Su-an's first wife had borne two children, and when she died their care was entrusted to Kai-shek's mother. She herself had four children: Kai-shek was the eldest and he had a brother and two sisters. The boy and one of the girls died in infancy, so Kai-shek did grow up, like Mencius, the only son of his widowed mother. Mencius or no Mencius, however, we must not think of him as dwelling in a miserable hovel, in lonely poverty. The Chiangs could afford to indulge in a certain amount of ambition. It was taken for granted, for example, that the boy be educated. He was too bright and lively to be wasted.

The spirit of the West was slowly percolating through the country. Politically, everything seemed stagnant, but politics are never static. The Manchu Dynasty was in the saddle again after years of Taiping rule in the South, but Manchu energy had been ebbing for generations, and would have died out naturally if outside influences hadn't kept it going.

The powers of the West supported the Manchus because they profited by the arrangement, and so a rotten government was aided to hang on for years beyond its normal span. If the Chinese had not feared the West they would have thrown off the Manchus. As it was they smoldered and watched in impotent hatred while foreign powers grabbed one concession after another from them.

Unable to take out their feelings in direct action, they waited and reminded each other that the Manchus, like the Westerners, were foreigners. In later years when the main cause of irritation was removed, Chiang Kai-shek was to take a more moderate and characteristically Chinese viewpoint, declaring that Manchus and Chinese are of the same race. Even then, Chinese had become accustomed to the same Manchu laws that seemed tyrannical three hundred years before, when the Ching Dynasty first promulgated them. There was the queue, for example. When the Court issued the original order that all Chinese men must wear their hair in this fashion, there had been weeping and wailing, yet in the 1880s queues were the convention, and were even cherished. But other grievances were not so trivial: the Manchus were detested and blamed for every misfortune. Taxation was oppressive, corruption was extreme even for people accustomed to venality, and the government was blamed when crops were disappointing, for heaven rewards a country or punishes it according to the virtue or wickedness of its emperor.

The ordinary man had always been content to accept the comfortable fact that he was Chinese and therefore the salt of the earth. Now he was beginning to question this axiom.

Every military convulsion seemed to bring another European country into the picture, ostensibly to watch her nationals' interests or to protect China from herself, and the result was always the same: more and yet more foreigners arrived and made claims. From their point of view these incursions were justified. It was the nineteenth-century faith in Europe that trade should be spread throughout the rest of the world, even when it meant forcing Western-made articles upon Orientals who didn't realize what was good for them. But the Chinese didn't agree. They were still smarting from the indignity of the Opium War and its outcome—the establishment of treaty ports, and British management of their Customs. It was cold comfort to be told by bossy British officials, in schoolmistressy accents, that the Chinese Customs Department was the only one in their government free of corruption. Pigheaded people that they were, they actually preferred homemade Chinese corruption to foreign purity.

After an incident in which a British consul was killed in the interior, the British had insisted that the reluctant Manchu Court permit foreigners to travel anywhere in the Empire under protection of the authorities, in 1875. Barely a year after this humiliation, Russia legalized her occupation of the Ili Valley to the north. In 1882 there was more foreign trouble, this time in Korea. China claimed Korea as a tributary, but the relationship was a loose one. No objections came from Peking when Korea signed a commercial treaty with Japan. But then the King of Korea quarreled with his new friends and Japan moved in troops. Then the Manchus sat up and took notice, and nearly became involved in all-out war with the Japanese. They managed to steer clear of it; an agreement was signed in 1885; the armies of both countries were evacuated from Korea, but the peninsula was to remain a sore point.

Eighteen eighty-seven, the year of Kai-shek's birth, was marked by another flurry over the same country, this time between Great Britain and Russia, both of whom attempted to occupy Port Arthur. The two nations finally withdrew their troops and promised each other to leave Korea alone. China, the nominal sovereign state, was completely ignored in the exchange.

With all this, the most effective infiltration of the West was neither military nor commercial, but religious. There are qualities in the Chinese character that work both for and against missionaries. Most Chinese are not mystic. They are attracted by philosophy rather than the religious spirit, and are not prone to sudden exaltation or emotional conversions. On the other hand, they are not averse to new religions; they are interested and tolerant. The Catholics who came into China in the sixteenth century had found themselves befriended and hearkened to but did not succeed in convincing many of their hearers that the old ways of filial piety and Confucianism or Buddhism were not best. And even the early toleration of Christianity disappeared after Emperor K'ang-hsi expelled the missionaries. It took courage and wit for a Chinese to cling to Catholicism after that, though there were some who did.

The Protestants entered at the beginning of the nineteenth century, and they persisted in spreading the gospel, often at considerable risk, through the troubled years that followed. As treaty after treaty was forced upon China by the Western powers, the missionaries marched farther and farther into the country with their compatriots, the traders. They found more hostility than friendship.

Yet the Christians from the West played an important part in reconciling East and West points of view. Missionaries spent much more time in the country, as a rule, than did the foreign government officials, and when people live in one place for a long time, especially if they behave circumspectly and with good will, friendship with the neighbors is bound to develop. Many of them took eagerly to the ways of the educated Chinese and became Sinologues, a sure way of winning the respect of the locals. Through mission money, schools were built. Missionaries brought in Western books and medicines. Their influence cannot be overrated. They played an essential part in the education of Sun Yat-sen and other revolutionaries. Even Chiang, though he didn't join the Church until middle age, felt their presence long before his conversion.

Meanwhile the Manchu Court at Peking, walled off from the vast country it professed to govern, carried on in medieval splendor in complex conditions. The Emperor, Kuang Hsu, was only a boy, and his claim to the throne was shaky, but he had been placed there by the Dowager Empress Tzu Hsi, who was Regent, and no one attempted to question it. Tzu Hsi had everything under control. She was a redoubtable character with great tenacity and a greedy ambition. Also, she possessed all the prejudices of her class. In this respect Manchus and Chinese were alike: they hated Western innovations.

There were no state schools for young children. Education was the responsibility of the villages or of private persons, but since in China there has always been a tradition of respect for learning, most communities managed somehow to provide a teacher for their young. Chinese have always honored scholars above all other men, paying their learned gentlemen every courtesy except that of a living wage. This remark is not as cynical as it sounds, for honor means much in China and not only the scholars, but most other people, were poor. If a man's son showed a talent for books he was not pushed into a more profitable occupation. His father would make great sacrifices to obtain an education for him.

As Americans we applaud the sentiment, but our teachers would look with horror on the school system that was the result of it. At the age of four little Kai-shek had fearsome tasks to accomplish. He was expected to start off with Confucius.

"The first little book which the scholar has put into his hands," wrote Arthur Smith, a missionary contemporary in China, "is probably the 'Trimetrical Classic,' so called from its arrangement in double lines of three characters above and three below, to a total number of more than 1,000." Reasonably well-educated people aspire to the knowledge of two or three thousand characters, but a truly learned man knows at least six thousand. ". . . The very opening sentence of this initial textbook in Chinese education contains one of the most disputed doctrines in the ancient heathen world: 'Men at their birth, are by nature radically good; in their natures they approximate, but in practice differ widely.' "

Try that out on your own four-year-old.

Of course a child that age wasn't expected to take in the philosophical connotations of the text. The system was aimed solely at developing the memory, a most important function when you consider the complications of Chinese writing. Nevertheless there was a secondary hope that the boy, babbling such pious precepts in singsong, would ultimately imbibe their meaning by a process of osmosis. And so he did. At least, Chiang has not forgotten his first textbook maxims: he is never at a loss for some historical example or improving proverb with which to illustrate his oratory, and for this he is much admired in China. (Though he bores people, too.)

His lessons must have been unutterably wearisome. Children were expected to begin their studying before breakfast and carry on until the end of daylight, and Kai-shek was not considered too young for this routine. For two years he concentrated on reading Confucius's *Great Learning* and *The Golden Mean*.

"These two works . . . are in classical style," says S. I. Hsiung. "Rarely could a boy in his early teens really understand their meaning." (Chiang Kai-shek had to tackle them at five.) ". . . they are the first two volumes of the Four Books of the Confucian Classics, which are invariably imposed upon any youthful beginner who is intended for a scholastic career."

The Chiang child finished memorizing his first two classics by the age of seven. He was now attending school in the village, a place which was not luxurious. It took little preparation to open a Chinese classroom; any empty room in a temple or an unused house would do, and the scholar provided his own table and stool. Discipline was severe and from our viewpoint unconstructive. It was assumed that a scholar who didn't know his lesson was being deliberately naughty, and a forgetful boy was roundly beaten. Every day the pupil would be given a line of characters to learn in his book. The teacher ran through them with him once or twice so that he might hear the right pronunciation, and from then on for the rest of the day the child was left to study, shouting aloud at the top of his voice, committing the sounds to memory. When he was word-perfect and could chatter the line, parrot-like, at top speed, he was given another selection.

We are in no position to patronize; our own system at that time was not much better. Our schools too favored the committing to memory of catalogues, lists of kings and battle dates. But in self-defense we can at least lay claim to an alphabet of only twenty-six letters, which is not much tax on the memory. Chinese students had to remember vast numbers of ideographs, and from this exercise they developed extraordinarily retentive visual memories which served them well in examinations, but let them down when they had to show initiative. Even today, Chinese are slow in developing their talent for independent reasoning: it becomes almost ossified during their youth.

The adult Chiang Kai-shek is austere: he has much respect for discipline, and no wonder. It took a long time to instill that respect, however. Nature kept breaking in: the boy was often boisterous.

# 2 IDEALS AND REVOLUTION 1905–12

Chiang got into trouble with the authorities when he was about eighteen. He was no gangster: he had the most exemplary reasons. All boys with any gumption, he might well have protested, got into trouble with the authorities sooner or later, especially when they were southerners like himself. Take it all in all he was a pretty solid citizen by that time, and a married man to boot. His mother had found a suitable girl in the village, a Miss Mao, and married him off when he was fourteen. As was customary in his country, the marriage made little difference in his life. He had changed schools some time before and was now living with his mother's family in nearby Fenghua, helping out in the shop when he wasn't studying. Miss Mao remained in Chikow in the Chiang house.

Chiang was a grave youth according to all accounts, and a photograph taken in 1905 bears this out: he looks repressed and humorless. Of course, sitting for a photograph in those days was no joke, but we know that he really worked at being grave and inscrutable. "He would stand with his eyes closed and his mouth tightly shut," says Chiang Hsing-hai, "for a quarter of an hour or more as if he were going through some exercise to strengthen his will power." That is exactly what he was doing, as a matter of fact; his diary confesses it. He had, and still has, several heroes in history; chief among them is Chu-ko Liang, nicknamed Wo Lung, or Sleeping Dragon. Wo Lung was a great military strategist and sage of the Three Kingdoms, who lived in the third century A.D. It was said of him that he was so free of wrinkles that his face was like a piece of white jade. No Confucian gentleman gives rein to his emotions; emotions are what wrinkle the face.

Hollington Tong, whose life has since been mingled with Chiang's to an intense degree, knew him then as a student; Tong was English teacher in the Fenghua school. "A certain aloofness—that has since been mistaken for pride—manifested itself," he says. "Although he was ready to join any game in which physical fitness was a requisite—he ran third in a race at the first international school athletic meeting in Ningpo—he was averse to spending his time in empty talk. Often, while others were engaging themselves in the 'tremendous trifles' that preoccupy schoolboys, he wandered away by himself and was evidently ruminating deeply."

Chiang had gone to Hangchow to investigate the possibilities of continuing his education in a law school there. That was his mother's idea: his own tastes were already formed: he preferred military science. Hangchow, the capital city of Chekiang Province, is one of China's famous beauty spots. The lake has been landscaped; a charming series of zigzag pathways on piles, like bridges going nowhere, lead out over the water to pavilions. Ornamental flat-bottomed pleasure boats drift about, and gentle hills fade away in the distance across the lake, giving an illusion of size and space. There are famous Hangchow dishes of fresh-water fish and shrimps; there are innumerable walks and pine-forested temples and tombs of heroes. It seems that Chiang was sitting in one of the lakeside restaurants eating his lunch and bothering nobody when the waiter asked him to move to another place. The table he had, explained the waiter, was the best in the place and was wanted by a couple of important officials.

Chiang took umbrage. He had—perhaps—drunk a little wine; in any case he was easily inflamed by any show of authority on the part of Manchu-appointed officials. He refused to give up his table. He made a scene. The outcome of the story is rather vague; some people say that the police followed him back to his lodgings and kept an eye on him after that, but this is doubtful. If it were true he would probably never have got into a government military academy as he later did. However, the incident became famous in a small way, and it led him to acquaintanceship with older men who were genuine revolutionaries.

It would have been strange if he hadn't been implicated in some conspiracy. He was an impressionable boy when the Japanese trounced China's forces and chased them out of Korea, when the Manchu Court had to sue for peace and sign the humiliating Treaty of Shimonoseki. Chiang heard furious talk about this in the teahouses of Fenghua. He was thirteen at the time of the Boxer rising, and there was more humiliation for China in that. By the time he had grown up he was spoiling for great deeds to do and his mind was full of the heroes of old he had read about at school and seen on the stage, who had freed their country from tyrants. When he wasn't seeing himself as the smooth-faced Wo Lung, he dwelt lovingly on the story of Yo Fei.

Yo Fei was a twelfth-century general of the Sung Dynasty, who at the age of twenty-five, when China was overrun with barbarians from the north, delivered Hangchow from bondage and chased the enemy back to Shantung. He would have pushed them beyond, into Manchuria, if plotters at Court had not falsely accused him of treason and brought him to account. There was a splendidly dramatic moment during the trial when Yo Fei snatched off his clothes to exhibit his back, on which his mother, presumably in nursery days, had branded the words, "Be loyal to your country." But he was dishonored in spite of this proof, and died in prison. The statues of the wicked Minister Chin Kuei and his wife, who conspired against the hero, stand near his tomb in Hangchow, where people still spit on them in passing. The story of Yo Fei was heady stuff for Chiang Kai-shek.

And a modern hero was not wanting, for there was also Sun Yat-sen. Sun was a Cantonese doctor, a southerner like Chiang, poor too—even poorer than Chiang—and a born rebel. He was twenty-one years older than the Chekiang boy. Emigrating to Hawaii as a child to live there with an older brother, he had been converted to Christianity and promptly sent home by his scandalized relatives. Back in Choyhung he was so faithful to his new religion that, though a gentle man ordinarily, he deliberately damaged the idols of the village temple, and had to be shifted out of town again, this time to Hongkong.

British Protestant missionaries helped him attend the Hongkong College of Medicine, where he took his degree. Joining the political struggle was inevitable for a man of Sun's temperament. He soon founded a secret society, with branches abroad, aimed at collecting funds to promote reform for the people of China. As its representative he traveled about furthering the cause. He brought about revolutions, many of them, and all but one abortive. The first failure sent him into exile, and at that time he made a gesture familiar among people of his persuasion: he cut off his queue. (Among the purchases made and smuggled into China for the revolt—gunpowder and rifles for the most part—was a most hopeful item; a pair of scissors intended for everybody's queue. The scissors, and the Day of Jubilo, had to wait.)

The most exciting part of Sun's early history, the incident that made him internationally famous, was his kidnaping by Manchu agents in London in 1896. Thanks to his missionary friend Cantlie and the British Foreign Office he was extricated. After that his name was an inspiration to China's discontented youth, and he continued to be a romantic figure, coming and going in disguise, running the gauntlet of Manchu guards at the seaport.

There were other excitements in the North: the Hundred Days' Reform of 1898 when a scholar named K'ang Yu-wei almost managed to instigate a peaceful change-over to more enlightened government and saw his Emperor disempowered for his pains; then the Boxer rising and its aftermath. All this was a long way from the Fenghua school and the solemn, eager young man who was interested only in military subjects, but he knew every bit of news about local revolts that ever drifted down to Chekiang. He had his sources.

The Hangchow project had not worked out, but Mrs. Chiang, after scraping and saving and coaxing her brothers and in-laws for enough money to send her son somewhere for a higher education, did not intend to drop her ambition for him. For some time before the final decision they wrangled, if wrangled is the word for Chiang's respectful discussions with his mother, as to what he should do with that money instead of training himself as a lawyer. He wanted to be a soldier. Mrs. Chiang opposed the idea strongly because in China soldiers were thought to be low morally, intellectually, and socially. Chiang wanted to be like Yo Fei, the gallant martyr, delivering his country from tyrants, but his mother saw him, if such a catastrophe as a military career should actually overtake her darling son, as a down-at-heel hangdog mercenary, a bogey of country children, a second-string bandit, a permanent landless wanderer. Nevertheless he had his way. Circumstances helped. While he was still smoldering with rebellious fervor after the Hangchow restaurant scene he had a run-in with the local authorities about something that was not his fault at all. A neighbor failed to pay his taxes, the taxgatherer held the whole village responsible, and Chiang Kai-shek was summoned to court arbitrarily, to be rated and disgraced. He came home in a fury against Manchu injustice and packed his bag and marched out. As a final sign of defiance, he cut off his queue, like Sun Yat-sen.

Japan was his destination; in Tokyo there was a famous military academy, the magnet for all Chinese would-be generals. Japan's stock in the Eastern world even more than in the Western had been soaring high ever since her defeat of Russia. Every Asian felt vicariously proud of the islanders, and the fame of their newfangled methods in naval and military technique had spread a long way through the countries on the mainland. Yuan Shih-kai, General-issimo of the Imperial forces of China, had made an arrangement by which a number of his young hopefuls crossed the waters every year to enter the Tokyo academy and take lessons from these masters.

Too, Japan was the place where every up-and-coming radical Chinese desired to go; for it was the Eastern capital of ideas, as Paris used to be for young Americans. Sun Yat-sen made his head-quarters there though, admittedly, he never lived long at a time in any one country, and so did K'ang Yu-wei of the Hundred Days. Such serious thinkers gathered around them hundreds of eager youths. Tokyo was stimulating, and—probably chiefly because it wasn't home—it seemed free. There was as yet little national jeal-ousy in Chinese hearts, and not much resentment of the islanders.

Japan was romantic; Japan meant adventure and opportunity. So in 1905 Chiang Kai-shek, his cropped head feeling strangely light and naked, went to Tokyo.

It must have been an exciting journey. He passed through Shanghai and saw his first big modern city, with high foreign-style buildings along the Bund, and hundreds of carriages in the roads, and swarming city-dwelling coolies, and foreigners lounging in busi-ness houses and banks or dashing about in pony traps. Then there was the sea voyage, and after that Japan—smart, sleek, modern, hard-working Japan, with its arrogantly Europeanized cities and its neat little fields crowding the countryside.

Unfortunately, as Chiang soon discovered, he had been too precipitate; the long arm of the Manchu stretched out and reached even this land of promise. Yuan Shih-kai's candidates were sitting in all available posts at the military academy; the Chinese quota was filled. Chiang had been naïve in supposing he could simply walk in with the fee ready in his pocket and take a seat in a lecture hall. A man had to come to Tokyo in the regulation way from an accredited school in China or else be wangled in by way of the War Board in Peking.

In the West, it would have taken an aspiring student one morning or afternoon to find out the situation, accept his fate, and make other plans. It is not like that in the East. Days went by while Chiang talked, argued, listened, and discussed his case and his chances of getting around the difficulty with cronies living in the Chinese community of Tokyo. He was in Japan for several months, during which time he set to work and learned the Japanese language. He also made a lot of acquaintances among aspiring young revolutionaries. One of these men, Chen Chi-mei, became his good friend, and Chen was important in the group. Possibly Chiang had brought with him a letter of introduction to Chen from kindred souls in China. Until then he had not made many intimate friends and he took this encounter all the more seriously for that reason.

Romantic admirers claim that he met Sun Yat-sen at this time and immediately became one of the charmed inner circle, close to the great man, but even if Chiang entered his orbit the meeting could not possibly have come to much. Sun was always meeting new students. He moved in a world of students, and Chiang Kai-shek was as yet only a raw boy from the provinces.

At length it was clear that Chiang would have to make his entry into the academy, if he did it at all, from China, and so he went home. His absence had given Chikow time to settle down after the affair of the tax collector. Possibly he wore a false pigtail pinned to his skullcap. Many revolutionaries did just that, since Sun Yat-sen had set the style. He was now a father. His wife had given birth to the son who is known today as Ching-kuo, and the very young man was proud of his baby.

Inquiries made in sober mood, without his former impetuous haste, brought the information that he might possibly get into the Tokyo academy by examination if he did a preliminary course at Paoting Military College near Tientsin. The entrance test for this school was suited to his talents and he soon got a place in the ordinary way, without "pull." I say in the ordinary way, but actually it was extraordinary that he should have succeeded in doing so in circumstances where almost everything usually depended upon knowing the right man or having the right cousin. Forthwith, he went to Paotingfu.

This town is in the North, and northerners in China feel superior to southerners. So do southerners, of course, consider themselves superior to northerners, but Chiang had to live among hostile students who vastly outnumbered the boys from his region. There were a lot of Manchu students, who went about snubbing all the others, and to add to this list of discomforts was the fact that Chiang had no queue. He was the only man in the place who didn't wear one, and few of his colleagues failed to mention the deficiency at every opportunity.

He was always on the defensive, and one of Dr. Tong's anecdotes shows how greatly he was under a strain. One day during a lecture on hygiene, the Japanese instructor put a lump of the local clay on the desk and said with heavy jocularity:

"This piece of dirt, roughly a cubic inch in volume, can contain as many as four hundred million germs, like China with her population of four hundred million."

Furiously, Chiang walked up to the desk and broke the clod into eight pieces, saying, "Japan's population is fifty million, like the fifty million germs in one eighth of this mud."

The Japanese made the obvious retort in pointing to Chiang's head. "Are you a revolutionary?" he demanded. He complained to the chancellor, and Chiang was duly reprimanded for impertinence.

When the time came for Paoting men to take e
for the Japanese academy, Chiang found himself left
list of candidates. He had to struggle for the right to participate.
Competition was keen, but he won out in the end by proving he
could already speak Japanese, and he did well in the test. So in
1907 he sailed for the island, this time properly accredited, and
after that it was plain sailing.

He applied himself dutifully to his studies in Tokyo, but he was
more interested in the friendships he made and the earlier acquaintance that he was able to refresh. Chen Chi-mei was still there—
indeed, he couldn't very well have returned to Shanghai, being
under a cloud with the Imperial authorities—and Sun Yat-sen was
back. It wasn't long before Chiang was introduced to the chief
secret society among Sun's followers, the League of Brothers or
Tung Meng Hui that was in future to become the Kuomintang. In
an obscure Japanese house, with the intense solemnity that befitted
the occasion, he took the oath of initiation:

"I swear under heaven that I will do my utmost to work for the
overthrow of the dynasty, the establishment of the Republic and
the solution of the agrarian question by equitable distribution of
the land. I solemnly undertake to be faithful to these principles. If
I ever betray my trust may I be submitted to the severest possible
penalties."

For the next two years Chiang lived in Japan, passing out of the
city's academy in due course and moving on to Takata, where he
served first as an ordinary soldier, then as a non-commissioned
officer, and finally as a regular officer. It was an arduous life in
the Japanese Army, but it suited him. Yo Fei, too, had undergone
harsh experiences when fitting himself for his mission, he reminded
himself.

Once or twice in the longer holidays, when finances permitted,
the cadet went home to see his mother in Chikow, and on these
occasions he was given messages to be delivered secretly to a cer-

tain Charlie Soong in Shanghai. Soong, Sun Yat-sen's most valued
friend, was one of the older generation like Sun himself. He was
educated in America, and had returned to China as a Christian
missionary, but he soon gave up preaching and turned instead to a
strange double life. He published religious literature and grew pros-
perous, and bought a house in Shanghai and begat a large family,
and all the time this was going on he also conspired to the best of
his ability for the revolution. The six Soong children were mere
small fry in 1909, too young to be interested in, or to interest, a
serious, dedicated young man like Chiang Kai-shek.

Then it was 1911. The Dowager Empress had died, but the
Manchu Dynasty hung on. Pu-yi, a child, sat on the throne; Regent
was his uncle Prince Ch'un. There was no outstanding tyrant left,
but the old gang of officials hadn't changed; it had merely slowed
down.

The revolutionary party, on the other hand, had speeded up;
years of trial and error were good for its technique. The last failure
worth noting was a throttled rising in Canton in March 1911, and
that was very near to being a success. Everywhere except in Peking
Court circles Chinese knew about the Tung Meng Hui and waited
confidently for crisis. Sun's bright young men had discovered propaganda. The Hui's own paper, *Min Pao,* circulated widely in the
Chinese countryside. Strolling players went from village to village
carrying messages for the rebels cunningly hidden in their lines.

The mouth-filling phrases of Chiang Kai-shek's oath were not
mere rhetoric; those principles he had sworn to abide by were a
genuine three which Sun Yat-sen had evolved after studying a
certain amount of Western socialism, and on which he now based
his reform program. He wrote a book on the subject, *San Min Chu I*
[Three People's Principles]. Other revolutionaries in China had
appealed to the public on political or nationalist grounds—to
philosophical sentiment—but Sun introduced a new idea; social

welfare, the duty of the state to take care of the people in a material way. His Three Principles were:

1. Racial solidarity, or nationalism. This was nothing new in essence, being the familiar cry of liberation from the Manchus, but Sun added to the roster of enemies war lords and foreign exploiters.

2. The people's sovereignty: their right to choose their leaders. Here, Sun was in favor of a preliminary period of tutelage under the rule of the revolutionary party before the Chinese people should use the vote.

3. The people's welfare. In China, livelihood depends directly upon the land, and this principle demanded that land ownership be equalized.

Unfortunately Sun didn't go into detail as to how this last was to be accomplished. Once or twice he mentioned a land tax, vaguely, but no one seems to have pinned him down. The ambiguity of the Third Principle has since given rise to endless argument.

"Our organization is complete," the leader said, early in 1911, but he never expected his modest boast to be proved so violently within the year. In his opinion the hour for revolution would strike around 1913. In the meantime he continued his wanderings, holding meetings in America from west to east, traversing the continent along the southern route. Sun was somewhere near St. Louis when the balloon went up, an awkward fact for the conventional biographer of a hero to glamorize when writing of his proudest hour.

The fact was nobody meant to touch off a revolution just at that moment. The conspirators had decided upon "Wuhan"—the three manufacturing cities, Wuchang, Hankow and Hanyang on the Yangtse—as their next trouble spot, and had gone to work according to routine, manufacturing bombs in a cellar in the Hankow Russian Concession and busily subverting the local Imperial Army troops. Public resentment was already stirred up there in the provinces by the government's recent highhanded action in confiscating, or, as they called it, nationalizing the railways and appropriating the revenues therefrom. In Szechuan disgruntled contractors called a strike, neighbors joined in, and suddenly what started out as a political quarrel turned into a popular revolt.

It wasn't a struggle that the Tung Meng Hui could claim to have stirred up, but any strife was useful to them, and the local ringleaders wondered if the moment hadn't arrived. In any case, events forced action upon them. On October 8 the famous bomb went off by accident in the Hankow cellar, the Viceroy's men investigated, and four conspirators were caught and executed. The Tung Meng Hui waited no longer. The Revolution was on, and the Imperial troops, given the signal on October 10, promptly mutinied. And, as we have seen, a young officer in Takata gave up his command and hurried back to China.

"The Viceroy declares in his report to the Central Government that he has known for several weeks that a strong revolutionary organization existed in the city," said a *Times* editorial in England on the twelfth. "He has certainly known for a very much longer period, as almost everybody in China does know, that profound, widespread, and merited dissatisfaction with the Imperial Government exists over a great part of the Empire. . . . The suppression of the Taiping rebellion . . . saved the Manchus a generation ago. They have not profited by the respite, and Young China, at any rate, thinks that their cup is full."

This severely critical tone was not heard in the *Times* alone. You would never have guessed, reading British papers, that the Foreign Office had been such a stalwart supporter of Peking. On all sides were comments of sympathy for the rebels, delivered in that admonitory, schoolteacherish spirit which always seemed to possess Westerners discussing the affairs of the Orient. Officially the powers still took it for granted that they were on the side of the Manchus, but still the press carped: there was a schizophrenic aspect to the affair which is nothing new in our civilization.

The struggle was difficult for the public to follow. Newspaper readers in foreign lands were still innocent enough to credit the versions of both sides, which alternated and flatly contradicted, each day, what had been said the day before. Usually when the smoke cleared away the rebels' report proved to have been the more accurate, but the fighting dragged on, for Peking had on its side a superior armory and the capable General Yuan Shih-kai.

Yuan Shih-kai's name was one to conjure with among the Manchus. The Dowager Empress had employed him to crush the reform movement in 1898. He was hated by liberals, especially revolutionaries. Now the Court sent him to deal with the insurgents, but the authorities were slow and inefficient, as usual, in coming to the decision—it was easier to temporize and tell each other comfortably that everything would blow over—and by the time he drew near Wuhan with his troops, the surrounding country had been swept into the revolt. Yuan Shih-kai, seeing that the situation was awkward, turned back to wait for better conditions.

Chen Chi-mei was in charge of the local branch of the party. They had to work under cover, for the Manchus had taken special precautions with this outpost of Europe, and the concessions and the native city were under heavy guard. But Shanghai of all places was impossible to defend against infiltration, and Chen had the situation well in hand. It was not merely a matter of Shanghai itself that preoccupied him: the city alone was of little value; it must have communication with the interior. The revolutionaries must gain control of Hangchow, a hundred miles from Shanghai, and Chen handed over the responsibility for this part of the campaign to his young friend Chiang. For the first time, the Imperial Army, old-fashioned and corrupt, would be opposed by a Chinese who belonged to the new order of military men trained in the Western tradition, as adopted by Japan.

If Chiang was worried, he didn't admit it. He had propagandized

the Hangchow soldiery during his apprenticeship as a revolutionary, and he knew that the cause numbered many friends among
them. However, he commanded a very small detachment, a mere
hundred men not well supplied with arms, and he had to reckon,
over and above the Chinese soldiers, with a special guard of Manchu bannermen, newly arrived from the North, who had not been
indoctrinated. And it was, after all, his first genuine warlike engagement.

The attack started at two o'clock in the morning of November 5.
Chiang and his "dare-to-die" hundred got as close as possible to
the yamen walls before opening hostilities with bombs. The vigor
of the onslaught carried them through, and with the help of reinforcements they succeeded in capturing control of the building,
complete with its Governor, before dawn. According to custom
they burned the yamen. The bannermen put up more resistance
than the first guard, but even so the job was finished by the end
of the day; Hangchow captured, and Chekiang Province in the
hands of the rebels. The young officer had good reason to be proud,
especially as Chen next sent him on a campaign throughout the
province. It was more like a triumphal tour than a hard-fought war.

In the meantime, all over China the barbershops did a rushing
business cutting off queues.

Any member of the Tung Meng Hui who hoped for paradise as
soon as the Manchus were defeated was due for bitter disappointment. The Chinese have always declared that the Double Tenth
marked the birth of their liberty, but like most fixed points in
historical narrative, this one represents an oversimplification. Certainly it was essential that the Manchu Court be done away with,
but their legacy—backward mentality, traditional corruption, and
constant lack of funds—was yet to give China years of trouble.

The insurgents were careful not to antagonize the West. Sun,
who had been overtaken by his revolution while traveling in

America, was now in London endeavoring fruitlessly to arrange a loan. Whitehall was still skeptical. The only satisfaction he obtained was the assurance that British support of the Manchus would probably cease. It was in London that he received a cable from his loyal followers asking him to accept the presidency.

By the time he got back to Shanghai, and to a wildly enthusiastic welcome led by the Soongs, the triumphant rebels had set up their government in Nanking. "Nanking" means "Southern Capital": the city had served this purpose before in ancient times. The Manchus were still on their shaky throne in the North, still pinning their hopes on Yuan Shih-kai, still refusing to abdicate. Yuan played for time. Of China's eighteen provinces he held only three, but they were the most important part of the country, the heart of the North. He was no longer in open combat with the republicans, but officially he was still the Emperor's champion.

Sun's first few weeks at home were rough sailing. Their sudden success had gone to the heads of the pettier leaders. They squabbled over their respective powers, and as soon as he returned he was seized upon and forced to use all his tact to resolve these conflicts. A man of different type, less gentle, less trustful, could have coped with all this in short order, but that was not Sun's character: he was no iron man.

On New Year's Day, 1912, he was proclaimed President in Nanking, having been hastily elected by delegates from seventeen provinces; and the title was qualified, at his own suggestion, by the adjective "provisional." The business of forming a constitution went forward—a constitution also called "provisional." But the Manchus were still unresolved, still unabsorbed. The war was nearly over, and Yuan, refusing to fight any longer, was in communication with the Nanking group; their messages had become almost friendly, since they were now in the same dilemma. They all needed money. It was the general opinion among foreign bankers that a Chinese Republic governed by an unpracticed set of visionaries was a bad risk. Now if someone they were familiar with should be President—someone who trod the middle way, someone strong and efficient, like Yuan Shih-kai . . .

Besides, Yuan had the Manchus in his pocket, and the final outcome of the war rested with him. Within a few weeks of Sun's installation the northern general made a proposition to the Nanking government: he would depose the Manchus, and then assume the presidency. Strange as it may seem to us, Sun agreed.

Immediately the deadlock was broken. The first evidence of landslide was a message that the Manchus' generals thought it best for the Throne to abdicate. On February 12, 1912, it was done. The little Emperor retired with a large pension. The Manchus were out at last.

Yuan Shih-kai was President of the Republic of China.

Chiang Kai-shek returned to Shanghai with a good reputation. His venture in Chekiang had not been a large part of the revolution, but such as it was he had done it in excellent style. Chen Chi-mei, now Commander-in-Chief of the People's Army in Shanghai, appointed him regimental commander and set him to training the new troops. Chiang was also given the duty of organizing a supply and transport body. He oversaw the purchase and shipping of the food and ammunition supplies demanded by the front lines, and also had to find the necessary funds with which to pay for these commodities. It was not an easy commission. Sun Yat-sen, the revolutionaries had told each other, would bring back money, but they were disappointed on that score.

Chen also appointed Chiang editor of an army periodical, the *Monthly for Military Affairs*. Presumably there were not many articulate brother officers around Shanghai, or perhaps, like other editors, Chiang discovered that he liked the work of composing as well as editing. At any rate he supplied his magazine with at least one long thoughtful piece of his own in every issue, and they make interesting reading today. They were straightforward and professional. His thinking was much influenced by his studies in military strategy; for instance, he prophesied that Japan would soon have another go at taking possession of China's territory. Without rancor, detachedly, he commented in this article on Japan's poverty and her fierce ambition "to wrestle with the Great Empires for a leading position in the world." China's prospects at the moment were not bright, he said, because the Manchus had traded off all her strategical points. An interest in military science must be developed among the people: the old-fashioned concept of militarism must be discarded if China was to survive. He suggested a new law providing for conscription and other modern methods of improving the military potential.

Chiang was an ardent nationalist, but he was also a Chinese. The new philosophy he was advocating conflicted with the sensibilities he had acquired during his traditional education. As an old-fashioned Chinese he wanted peace: as a modern army officer he saw the necessity of building military strength. The exultation of success warred with ancient maxims. One result of the compromise he reached was a passage that was prophetic:

"The world today is a place in which we must be armed to maintain peace. If all the nations would only put humanity before everything else and realize . . . that aggression is not right, then instead of maintaining a balance of power, there would be a universal commonwealth. When we have established a world republic comprising white, red and black races, we shall only need a police force to maintain interior order in those united states, and that would be sufficient to keep trouble away. A central government could be created to deal with greater matters, and should there arise disputes between the states, they could go to the central government for justice, when right and wrong would be declared."

This appeared in 1912. There is no evidence that anybody paid attention to it. All young officers have their dreams.

# 3 "STORMS OF TEMPER" 1912–23

"A republic is the best form of government," Yuan Shih-
kai telegraphed to Sun. "The whole world admits this. That
in one leap we have passed from autocracy to republicanism is
really the outcome of many years of strenuous efforts exerted by
you all, and is the greatest blessing to the people."

Not to be outdone in courtesy, Sun retorted, "Mr. Yuan is a
man of political experience, upon whose constructive ability our
united nation looks forward to the consolidation of its interests."

The long, grueling struggle undergone by Sun and his colleagues
had produced heroes, but they were heroes of a special sort. They
were excellent revolutionaries, but none of them had ever been
part of a legislative body operating in the open, and now that the
chance had come they had no idea how to go about the job. Yuan,
on the other hand, understood such matters.

So it was natural that the republicans should give in to his judgment and relinquish their plan to keep the government in Nanking.
Was it not unwise, asked Yuan, to leave Peking to its own devices
when everything was still unsettled? While the discussion was
going on a street riot took place in Peking, and the republicans
were convinced. Possibly Yuan engineered the riot to make his
point. The new President, therefore, was inaugurated in the North.

A private citizen again, Sun went up to Peking to discuss railway expansion. There were already several good railways operating in the hinterland from the coast, but he visualized more; seventy-five thousand miles of new track to begin with, built and operated by the Chinese Government, within the next ten years. He figured the cost of this development as three billion U. S. dollars, which he proposed borrowing abroad. Yuan agreed to everything, and appointed Sun Yat-sen Director of Railways, putting at his disposal a handsome sum. To his surprise Sun did not pocket the money, but in good faith set to work immediately drumming up interest in the loan among Western countries. He had Japan in mind as one possible creditor. Sun trusted Japan, as he trusted everybody, too much, a mistake the young officer Chiang Kai-shek would not have made.

This same officer was still in Shanghai, where the end of hostilities had left him, an instructor in the military academy General Chen Chi-mei had set up. The situation in China was not yet so settled that the former revolutionaries felt they could relax. They kept their uniforms and continued to recognize the standing army. Chiang was one of the few officers available who had had a modern training. Conscious of this, he began to appreciate himself. He was fully fledged; he was a success. He might even have become a little bit swell-headed. He was only twenty-five.

As a veteran of the revolutionary struggle and an early member of the League, he sat in on the political discussions now taking place. Sun had talked it over with three special friends in the Tung Meng Hui: Huang Hsing, Wang Ching-wei, and Hu Han-min; and they came to the conclusion that their League was out of date. Its aim had been to accomplish a successful revolution; and that aim had been achieved. A new party should be formed to deal with whatever governmental problem might arise in the future—the Kuomintang, or National People's Party. Most members were in favor of enlarging its boundaries to include a few of the other political societies that always abound in China.

Chiang Kai-shek found himself at odds with the majority because he thought it better to keep the membership of the Kuomintang select and small. He was not able to carry his point, and grew angry. At the best, he had a quick and imperious temper, and he was suffering from jealousy of Wang Ching-wei and Hu Han-min. Wang and Hu had edited the *Min Pao* when it carried weight as a subversive journal. They were both known as brilliant revolutionary strategists. Furthermore, Wang had earned great merit in the old days by recklessly attempting to assassinate the Prince Regent and suffering ten months' imprisonment as a result in an Imperial jail. Both these men were far better known than young Chiang Kai-shek, and their opinions had more influence than his. They were civilians, not officers: this fact rankled in the military man's heart. Finally he resigned from the Kuomintang and dropped his interest, temporarily, in political matters.

His other occupations continued, however; he still instructed in the military academy, and his influential friend General Chen kept him busy. His nominal salary was not high. Official salaries in China were mere token payments, but he did not depend on this income. Chen helped. To understand the complications of Chinese day-by-day economics is difficult for Americans because we have a cut-and-dried system of salary for the job. Yet it is not many centuries since our people too followed the feudal custom observed in China of patron and patronized. In the footsteps of Chen Chi-mei, by means of such irregular contributions, Chiang prospered. He was not wealthy, but he was better off than he had ever been before. He sent money home and began to enjoy city life and learned to relax among boon companions.

It was another period in his private life that has been obscured by his conversion to Christianity. Only one book compiled by Chinese, a mere outline of his life, comes to grips with the question, and if the Generalissimo had been able to censor the account it would not exist today. Yet it is mild enough.

"Then came a period of rather riotous living, which few young men can escape," it says. ". . . with a comfortable income which he was receiving there was much chance for moral degeneration. His friends, knowing his temper, and that persuasion would be futile, deplored this; and he would have gone from bad to worse, had it not been for the fact that the second revolutionary war started and kindled again the smoldering ashes of patriotism."

It is rather difficult to figure out just what this means. Did Chiang take to drink and gambling? If he drank, it could not have been for a very protracted period, and if he gambled there is no tale of his having been ruined. The only clue that suggests itself is that it must have been about this time Chiang Wei-kuo was born. Today, Wei-kuo is referred to as Chiang Kai-shek's younger son, the half brother of Ching-kuo. Back in the thirties, he was said to be an adopted son, the child of one of Chiang's close friends and a Japanese teahouse girl. There are always scandalous stories about public figures, especially in China, but again I want to emphasize the point that only the Westerner considers this sort of thing as something shameful. The young man of 1913 was not a monster. He merely behaved like the other men of his world.

Before a year passed, the republicans decided they had been misled about Yuan Shih-kai. Under their jealous gaze the President committed sin after sin of omission, and showed no slightest tendency to put their constitution into practice. The old gang of officials carried on in their familiar way. The people of Peking, watching, began to wonder if there had ever been a revolution at all. The only change that could be seen was in the relations Yuan now maintained between China and the Western powers. These had improved. In 1912 Sun would have rejoiced at this fact; in 1913 he was infuriated. If Yuan should manage to float a substantial loan from Europe and America, as he showed every sign of doing, there would be no holding him; he would go his own way and destroy every vestige of republicanism.

The powers were only interested in the old question that had existed in the time of the Manchus: should they or should they not lend money to help develop China? Would it be a good investment? Yuan was persuasive. On New Year's Day, 1913, he made an optimistic speech to correspondents about his country's financial status. "Plenty of Revenue, Declares China's President," said a New York paper's headlines. Foreign bankers, led by the British, themselves advised by pro-Yuan residents in Peking, talked it over and drew up agreements and wrangled as to projected railways and factories, and drove a hard bargain. In the end, it was too hard a bargain for President Wilson's taste. He suddenly announced that he objected to the conditions of the proposed contract: they would hinder China's development. They provided for a much more stringent control—by the British—over Customs revenue, and a lien on the salt tax as well. Wilson's decision, said his diplomatic representative in China, was "a refusal to join with others in placing on the young republic the fetters of foreign financial control."

This was music to the ears of Sun Yat-sen. As spokesman of the Kuomintang he sent an appeal to Europe imploring the nations involved in the five-power loan not to let it go through. But no one listened. The loan was not only met, it was oversubscribed, and one hundred and twenty-five million U. S. dollars were handed over to Peking. As Sun had bitterly predicted, though it was called a reorganization loan at least half of it went down the drain, divided up among army officials and the other key men who must be sweetened to support Yuan.

The days of happy dreams were over: Sun determined to overthrow Yuan. But the President had consolidated his position to a degree of strength that surpassed the old Manchu Court's. In June there was a brief flare-up of rebellion in Wuchang, but it was suppressed by Yuan's forces. A few weeks later, on July 2, Sun sent a telegram expressing his "ultimatum" to Yuan Shih-kai, calling on him to resign the presidency.

Not very much to the world's amazement, Yuan ignored this suggestion, and the Nationalists forthwith began their second revolution. They were woefully unready, and the results of the attempt make one wonder how genuine a mass movement the 1911 revolution was. But that one, of course, had been prepared for years by dint of patient undercover work. This time, Sun found the enemy better entrenched, strengthened by his own hand, and the new revolution was poorly advertised. Most of the country didn't even hear about it.

At the call to duty, Chiang sallied forth like Achilles from his sulking tent, ready to do battle for his old companions. The story was short and painful. Shanghai was strongly manned by Yuan's troops. Chiang was supposed to lead his men against the arsenal and take it, but the guards stood firm, though the siege continued for several days. On all other fronts the "punitive expedition" met with the same fate: within two weeks everyone involved in the debacle, Sun and Chiang included, fled to Japan. They were back where they had started.

It was a strange, intense, melodramatic existence for that little group in Japan. Generals, millionaires, paupers, politicos of every sort moved about and plotted and carried rumors, and went short of money. In the middle of it all was Sun Yat-sen, a little battered, a little sad, very much disillusioned, but undaunted in his determination. There were his faithful friend Charles Soong, and Charles' wife, grave to the point of severity, and their two beautiful daughters, Eling and Chingling. There was his own wife, who had long adapted herself, as the model Chinese woman must, to fits and starts and uncertainties. The Suns and the Soongs were as close as two families can be when their ideals and interests have co-incided for half a lifetime. Mrs. Sun, Mrs. Soong, and Eling had journeyed to Japan in a friendly party before Sun's break with Yuan Shih-kai for a holiday at a spa. And Eling now helped the Doctor as his secretary, just as her father Charles served as treasurer for the Party. It was all very cozy, at first, but then something interfered in the most awkward way.

The Kuomintang authorities who built up Sun Yat-sen as an idol after his death, taking their technique wholesale from Soviet Russia's treatment of the Lenin story, have always been embarrassed by one aspect of his character which they weren't equipped to camouflage. Lenin's temperament does not seem to have been amorous. Sun's was. He was romantic and naïve, but he was amorous as well. Working day after day in Eling's company, he began to get ideas. At last he put in a formal request to Charles Soong for his daughter's hand. He had not quite forgotten that he was married, but it made no difference, he said; a divorce could be obtained. He also made light of the discrepancy in their ages, and the fact that he was a contemporary of Eling's father and had known her since she was in her cradle.

Charles Soong was shocked and outraged. There was a quarrel, and Eling served no longer as Sun's secretary. Shortly thereafter she married a young man who had already asked for her hand: Dr. Kung Hsiang-hsi, educated in America like Eling herself, and working with the Y.M.C.A. in Japan. Kung came of a banking family in Shansi; he was a Christian, politically sympathetic to the revolutionary cause, and altogether thoroughly suitable. Relations between the Suns and the Soongs continued, on the surface, friendly. Then Chingling upset things again, not only for her unfortunate parents but for those same much-tried historians.

They are unable to relegate Chingling to the background, because she won't stay there: besides, they need her for other reasons; she has been far too useful to hide away. The story had got to be admitted, but it was swaddled and wrapped and softened to such an extent that the writer of this book was definitely taken aback one day by a tactless remark made by W. H. Donald, family friend of the Soongs.

"That was the trouble with the old boy," he said of Sun. "Couldn't keep him off the women."

Chingling took Eling's place as Sun's secretary—Chingling, delicately pretty, ardently absorbed in political questions, obsessed by her ideal of Sun Yat-sen. He had been her courtesy uncle when she was a baby; in America she had heard of his work from her parents; the glorious Revolution of 1911 stirred her blood and made her proud to claim him as a friend. Now she was privileged to serve him. He was in trouble and he confided in her. Hero worship possessed the young girl. Whatever possessed Sun knocked him off balance.

More painful interviews followed. It was a peculiarly difficult situation. Eling had been easily settled because she didn't care for Sun anyway, but Chingling was determined to have her hero. What distressed Mrs. Soong more than anything else was the fact that he was already married to a woman his own age and had had several children by her. Sun was supposed to be a Christian, like Mrs. Soong herself, and Chingling, and all the others. He was no unbaptized heathen. As unChristian Chinese, Sun Yat-sen and Soong Chingling could have lived together without comment from anyone. As unChinese Christians they would have had to suffer a certain amount of obloquy, but Sun could have got a divorce— divorces were becoming common among Westerners in 1913—and his subsequent marriage with Chingling would have been in order. As it was, however, they were Christian Chinese, and so they had to behave in a manner that satisfied neither side of their background. Sun quietly put away his wife, and Chingling moved in with him.

In public the Soongs showed no resentment. Charles continued

to serve the Party as he had done before. Chingling appeared everywhere as Madame Sun. Only the first Madame Sun, to the day
of her death, referred to her successor as the Concubine—and she
used an impolite word for it, too.

There were in the constitution certain checks on a President's
power, chief of which was the National Assembly, which at the
time of the Second Revolution was still full of Kuomintang members. Yuan, on his way up the peak of dictatorship, knew these
men would thwart him if they could. He forced them out, and the
Assembly soon died of anemia. Nothing now stood between Yuan
and his ultimate goal, to be Emperor.

His actions might have been observed with greater attention by
the West had it not been for the date—1914. The powers had no
time to worry about China's government. Japan, however, was
closer to Peking, and the Japanese saw what Yuan was up to.
There was a German naval base at Tsingtao. Japan and Britain
made an alliance, agreeing to attack it. Once it had been won, the
Japanese were left in charge, and then, purely on the strength of
their presence in China—they had no other excuse for such arbitrary action—they presented Yuan Shih-kai with the notorious
"Twenty-one Demands."

In these, Japan claimed first right to finance a northern railway,
monopoly control of trade privileges at Kiaochao Bay, and a
promise that China would restrain all other foreign powers from
digging into Shantung and the coastal islands. She also claimed a
ninety-nine-year extension of Japanese rights in Manchuria, with
a hint of further Japanese expansion in Mongolia. Furthermore,
she wanted control of iron and coal production in Central China
and first rights to the capitalization of practically all future exploitation of natural resources in Fukien. Chinese police and military bodies were to be subject to Japanese authority.

It would give a false impression to say that the Chinese, one and all, immediately became furiously indignant and resentful. The great masses of people were unaware of these matters, or at least indifferent to them, to an extent incomprehensible to our more politically conscious Americans and Europeans. The Chinese peasant was not a dull clod—far from it—but he was cynical after so many generations of Manchu rule, and he deliberately concentrated on the matters which affected him nearly, such as the weather's effect on his crops, local taxation, and the personal affairs of his family.

But educated men understood the significance of the Twenty-one Demands and were much stirred up. Yet Yuan Shih-kai, the best informed of all, could not allow himself to indulge in emotional outbreaks. It would be useless to make a public show of resistance. Europe was in no position to respond to any appeal. He haggled, pointed out in diplomatically gentle language that the demands were really extreme.

The implied acceptance of their terms pleased the Japanese, and Yuan was sure the matter would be straightened out in good time. The West would never let Japan get away with it.

Educated China did not see his reasoning. Educated China cried, "He has surrendered us! He has betrayed us!" and the burden of their complaints was passed on to the illiterate masses. It is always easier to stir up the Chinese, or anyone else for that matter, against foreign interference than their own people.

Watching these events closely from Japan, the republicans kept themselves busy. Chiang Kai-shek was on the revolutionary committee of which Soong was treasurer. He visited Shanghai in 1914, just before the European war, and made an attempt to start a revolt there on the lines of a capture of the city and a *coup d'état,* but the conspiracy was discovered and Chiang slipped away just in time. He next turned his attention to the possibilities of Manchuria, that Chinese territory beyond the Great Wall. There were rumors that the

Manchurians would take kindly to the suggestion of a rising, so Chiang was posted off to Harbin. Unfortunately he found no grounds for supposing that the people there cared a single cash whether Yuan governed China as a republic or a kingdom. Chiang was interested in his surroundings; Manchuria was like a foreign country to him, and he complained later that he was hampered by not knowing much Mandarin dialect. But there was no material there for revolution, and he returned to Tokyo.

After that, he slipped into China and out of it several times, working among the southerners, interviewing cautious war lords, and organizing sporadic demonstrations. His major effort took place in November 1915 in Shanghai. With Chen Chi-mei, Chiang tried to arrange for the assassination of the city garrison commander. The plot involved a cruiser at anchor in the Whangpoo River, the crew of which was to attack just as Chiang and Chen, ashore, led small parties to capture key points of the city government. Everything fell through, and the French police nearly got the two leaders. Then Chiang fell ill and took to his bed, and his mother had to come up from Chekiang to nurse him.

Yuan decided on the end of 1915 as the right time to take his final step and assume the Imperial yellow. To this end he organized a substitute for the disbanded National Assembly, called the People's Representatives Convention. These stooges held a vote in December and declared, unanimously and dutifully, that the form of government should be changed to that of constitutional monarchy, with Yuan as Emperor.

The President could not have picked a worse time to put his plan into action, while the nation was still in the throes of resentment against the Twenty-one Demands, but he had lost touch with public sentiment. Japan sent a warning; Yuan felt he could afford to ignore that; this was a domestic matter. He was a man of manners, a polished courtier, and like Caesar he very properly thrice refused the proffered crown. The fourth offer he accepted in a beautiful speech.

The storm that followed staggered him. On January first, Yunnan Province in the Southwest declared its independence of the monarchy. Yunnan had always been refractory, and without hesitation Yuan sent troops to quell the rising, but other outbreaks followed in rapid succession. One of these, a minor disturbance, was led by Chiang Kai-shek in Kiangsu. It was defeated, but in the ensuing months Kiangsu and eleven other provinces seceded from the monarchy by proclamation and declared their readiness to fight against it. Yuan was forced to reconsider. His term as Emperor had not amounted to three months. On March 22, 1916, he abdicated, and three months later died.

Yuan's death made a difference to the revolutionaries, of course, but it didn't automatically settle all their problems, for the Peking government remained. Vice-President Li Yuan-hung slipped into the presidency to finish out the term, and Sun gloomily told his young men that this was bad. He knew Li, a northern general of pre-revolutionary days, and he didn't like him.

However, the rebels could now live in China again, as long as they were prudent enough to avoid Peking. Their ranks were depleted. To Chiang's grief they had lost Chen Chi-mei. It happened while Chen and Chiang were carrying out one of their conspiratorial missions in Shanghai. Chen had been invited to a meeting with Peking agents and, in spite of Chiang's warning, insisted upon keeping the appointment and was assassinated.

We couldn't expect a man like Chiang not to point out, even to a corpse, that he had been right and the corpse had been wrong. He spared his own sorrow nothing. Why should Chen's spirit escape? He had told Chen, he had warned Chen, and this is what came of ignoring his warnings! He mentioned these facts in his funeral oration.

"I, your younger sworn brother, Chiang Kai-shek, offer this sacrifice to you, the spirit of the late Chen Chi-mei, with these words. Alas! From now on where can be found a man who knows me so well and loves me so profoundly as you did?

"Now that you are gone forever, who is there besides myself to continue your work without changing the aim you had originally in your mind? How about those who tried to flatter you when you were influential and tried to get rid of and slander me? . . . I do not mind that you believed their lies about me when you were living. All I want is that I should have a clear conscience after you are dead.

"Alas! I had no chance to open my mind to you. The treacherous found their opportunity and my good advice was overlooked. . . .

"Your parents, with their gray hair, are still living, while your children are still young. . . . I shall look after the elderly people and support the young ones and shall always keep you in my thoughts.

"Oh, you spirit! If you are here, do come and partake of my offerings."

There were other absences in Sun's ranks. For one thing, disagreement as to party policy had driven Wang Ching-wei to France on leave of absence. The custom of sending men who are out of favor on long voyages is peculiarly Chinese. One tries above all to avoid open breaks or unseemly public quarrels. A refractory statesman or general need not be punished by imprisonment, but merely sent abroad "to study"; an official who doesn't agree with what his leader is doing goes away on his own account. Time heals tempers, or brings about a change in conditions: the quarrel is resolved, and finally the wanderer returns. It is an economical system, conserving trained men who can be used again. It is a pleasing system, avoiding open clashes, which are always ugly. And it is a flexible system, because sooner or later almost every statesman gets his turn in office while the others are away improving their minds.

The world war didn't seem a pressing matter to Chiang: China had her own troubles. Her stresses and strains were divided into halves, with North China struggling around Peking and South China churned up by Sun's Nationalists. But the dividing line was obscured by the private campaigns of war lords who were neither for North nor South, only for themselves. As there is still some confusion as to just what a war lord is—people often say Chiang was one—it seems best to quote Hollington Tong: "a warlord was the governor or the military commander of a province, or group of provinces. He throve when the authority of the Central Government was lax, or uncertain. He derived his power from his control of autonomous military forces and from his ability to appropriate to his own purposes the taxes of his province or area. His role was sometimes predatory . . . at other times benevolent . . . but his distinguishing characteristic was his refusal to recognize the complete authority of the Central Government." Definitely, this doesn't describe Chiang.

Peking, on top of chronic trouble with war lords, was saddled willy-nilly with the responsibility for international affairs. On February 4 Wilson called upon all countries which were still neutral to join the struggle against Germany. Peking held no brief for Germany particularly, but the government could not agree to take the plunge. Neither could the war lords, whose opinions had to be respected because their armies were needed to uphold governmental authority. Dissension tore parliamentary meetings for months, until the war lords had their way and Li Yuan-hung dissolved Parliament. The Kuomintang members who had been holding out against the war lords fled for their lives. Most of them turned up in Shanghai and reported to Sun Yat-sen.

After a lot of switches, Li Yuan-hung got control again, and **Peking** declared war on Germany and Austria, but China's part in

World War I was never to amount to very much. Sun gathered round him the displaced M.P.s and took them to Canton. There he announced that the dissolution of Parliament in Peking had been illegal and that he was re-convening it. A military government was set up, with Sun as Generalissimo and dictator. In spite of his pretensions his domain was woefully small, comprising merely the twin provinces of Kwangtung and Kwangsi. Even over this territory Sun had no real control; he was utterly dependent on the local war lords. His chief support was one of these, a Cantonese general named Chen Chiung-ming, who was now appointed commander of the Kwangtung army.

Chiang Kai-shek was reasonably contented with the new setup, modest though it was. He was back in harness as a military man. Sun sent him North to reorganize an army that they still supported up there, a remnant of the old days. Chiang grimly observed the familiar faults of an old-style military body—lack of discipline, limited loyalties, maladministration—and recommended that the army simply be dissolved and forgotten. When this was done he moved on to Peking and remained there for a few months asking questions and taking notes. Later he sent to Sun an outline for a proposed northern expedition, complete with information on the Peking troops, and even a suggested route for the march.

It seemed a fantastic hope. Peking was actually sending forces against Sun at this time; they had got as far as Hunan. But Chiang's idea was sound enough. Someday when Sun's government was stronger he would undoubtedly have to march against Peking, and one might as well be prepared.

In March 1918 Sun recalled Chiang and gave him a post in the Kwangtung army. The Doctor was trying to consolidate his strength, but he wasn't having much luck. As he grew old and crotchety he was less and less able to control the quarrelsome factions of his group. Soon his opponents managed to ease him out of his top position by replacing the military government with an administrative committee in which Sun was merely one man of seven. This affronted him, and in June he gave up altogether and retired to Shanghai. Though he insisted that he was through forever, his army still fought for him in Kwangtung, and certainly Chiang still considered him the leader. Nor could Sun refrain from meddling. Now and then he sent advice to Chiang or Chen Chiung-ming on military matters, and if they didn't always follow it, they never argued with him.

Instead, all their spare resentment was directed against each other. Chiang had been at outs with Chen Chiung-ming almost from the moment of his appointment. He was still a passionate, opinionated, jealous youth. His advice was always ignored, he said in aggrieved tones, yet it would have saved the day if it had been followed. According to his account—and there is no reason to doubt it—the Kwangtung army was being beaten back and back, until at the end of July it was near final defeat; only then would Chen hand over the problem to Chiang, and an improvement was the immediate result. "Chen Chiung-ming found his hands as good as tied, not knowing what to do," said Chiang in 1931, recollecting. "I forced them not to retreat and altered the plan of operations . . . Luckily the battle brought us a decisive victory, but it also made the other officers jealous of me. When I reflect on it today, I still feel heartache."

National codes of honor are tricky things. An English or American officer would not be so eager to criticize his superiors. But Chiang was not completely typical of his class, either. He stands out because of a certain directness, bluntness, honesty—call it what you will; perhaps it is simplicity. Whatever it is, it can be exasperating even today, when his temper has mellowed, and in youth it must have been maddening to his colleagues, especially on the frequent occasions when he turned out, unforgivably, to have been right. He was like Macartney, the first British Ambassador to China, who "had great pride, and a good deal of conceit, but this arose

rather from a contemptuous opinion of others than from a vain
one of himself."

The stubborn man carried on as best he could, against enemy
and ally alike, for the next few months. He achieved a number of
local victories, and disagreed violently with Chen Chiung-ming
when at the end of 1918 the C-in-C decided to call a halt for the
winter. It was a mistake, argued Chiang, to cease fighting at that
particular moment when he himself, for one, was deep inside the
enemy lines with insufficient men. The letters do not expose Chen
as an unreasonable fellow; as a matter of fact he shows up rather
well, a patient man handling a difficult but talented officer with kid
gloves. Historians on Chiang's side claim that later developments
prove Chen to have been planning treachery the whole time, but
it doesn't necessarily follow. He was certainly out for himself; all
war lords were, but in 1918 he probably thought his best policy
was to support the Nationalists. Chiang disliked him and suspected him of pulling his punches and distrusted him, but that
doesn't mean Chiang had second sight. Chiang didn't trust anybody
very much. It was an attitude that made for a quarrelsome life.

The ins and outs of the sporadic war between the southern
provinces brought out this side of Chiang's character. Nineteen
hundred and nineteen was full of impetuous resignations on his
part, interspersed with returns to the front whenever he had made
his point. By November the complicated situation in Kwangtung
was pretty well cleaned up, with Kwangsi troops driven out and
Sun's army in control. Chiang felt it had been too long a struggle
and too costly, and this also he blamed on the commander-in-
chief, Chen. There was an open quarrel, and Chiang went away,
again, to Shanghai. His temper was even more difficult than usual,
for he had lost one of his good friends in the fighting and he was
possessed by grief.

Sun did his usual gentle best to patch up dissension in the
ranks. He wrote from Shanghai:

"To my dear Elder Brother Chiang Kai-shek,

"When my elder brother Chen Chiung-ming fought back to Canton, he was using all his strength to serve our party and our country. We, on our part, are using all our strength to help him. With only one aim and of only one mind, our co-operation cannot be compared with any ordinary alliance . . .

"The sudden and tragic death of Chu Ta-fu is a loss to me comparable to that of my right or left hand. When I look among the members of our party I find very few who are experts in war and also loyal. Only you, my elder brother, are with us, you, whose courage and sincerity are equal to those of Chu Ta-fu, and your knowledge of war is even better than his. But you have a very fiery temper, and your hatred of mediocrity is excessive. And so it often leads to quarreling and difficulty in co-operating. As you are shouldering the great and heavy responsibility of our party, you should sacrifice your high ideals a little and try to compromise. This is merely for the sake of our party and has nothing to do with your personal principles. Would you, my elder brother, agree with this?"

Chinese are always pointing out to each other just where human nature falls short of the ideal. Their official correspondence is full of artless self-examination, self-condemnation, and—especially when a man like young Chiang is writing the letter—self-justification. But Sun's appeal to his turbulent officer's softer feelings, his evocation of well-loved names and his reminder of the cause, did not suffice. Not pride, Chiang said, but his contemptuous opinion of Chen Chiung-ming made reconciliation impossible. He wrote to Chen:

"You, my Commander-in-Chief, are an expert in strategy and also full of experience; if you had not been ill-advised you would never have done this; if you trusted me, you would never have done this. Even if those who were marching forward with their men at the front had a little common sense, they would not have

done this. . . . I cannot bear those whose minds are full of
jealousy and prejudice and those who have no regard for the
co-ordination of the whole plan, nor any concern about the success or failure of the entire campaign. I am straightforward and
would rather die fighting. I dare not act contrary to my conscience."

No one would have argued with the biographer who said:
"Chiang is by nature obdurate. Not infrequently . . . he would
fly into storms of temper before which few human beings can stand.
Above all, he was self-opinionated, highly so." He added, "No
one could endure him, and by degrees he became more and more
disagreeable to his associates."

The coast was clear, the enemy defeated: Sun went back to
Canton. He appointed Chen Chiung-ming Governor of Kwangtung Province, and Chiang resented this, but it was really none of
his business any more. Chiang was definitely on his own, out of
the Army, facing the necessity of making a living as a civilian.

In Shanghai he found himself among the busiest talkers in the
world. The European war was over. Shanghai swarmed with
foreign businessmen, and there was something else in the picture
—the dispossessed, the White Russians. They flocked across
Siberia to Harbin and Vladivostok, and thence down the coast to
Shanghai in flight from the Bolsheviks. A lot of people talked
about Russia and its revolution.

Chiang did not: he was a military man and no intellectual. His
friends were businessmen who made their money abroad: he was
trying to break into the stock-market world of Shanghai. The fer-
ment in Peking that was intoxicating a librarian's assistant from
Hunan, a young countryman named Mao Tse-tung, did not excite
Chiang Kai-shek. He was broke and simply trying to make a living.
He had been pleased, however, a year before, when the former
rebels in Russia, now firmly in the saddle, sent a fraternal message
to China's revolutionists. These Bolsheviks seemed to have drunk

of the same waters as Sun Yat-sen. They wanted what he wanted, and they had got it, which could not be said for Sun, and in their triumph they did not forget their brothers in other lands. They seemed to wish to help.

"We shall not merely aid the workers, but also wish to aid the people of China," said the Karakhan Manifesto. "Every nation whether large or small should have complete autonomy. We pro-claim that all secret treaties made before the revolution with China, Japan, or the allies are hereby abrogated. . . . We hereby renounce all territory obtained through aggressive means by the former Russian imperial government in China, Manchuria and elsewhere. . . . In short, we hereby renounce all special privileges formerly obtained by Russia in China. . . . If the Chinese people as a result of our proposals wish to become a free people and escape the evil fate of becoming a second India or Korea as has been planned for her at the Paris Peace Conference, we fervently hope that the Chinese people will make common cause with the peasants, workers, and Red soldiers of the Soviet Union and fight for their freedom!"

It was gratifying and astonishing that Europeans should volun-tarily give up something in China which they already possessed. However . . . as long as the northern government was the official one, these international decisions were Peking's job to cope with, not Canton's. So Chiang applied himself to the matter in hand: stockbrokerage.

The time Chiang Kai-shek spent in the wilderness of the Shang-hai Stock Exchange was incongruous. Spiteful comment makes it more conspicuous than it perhaps deserves. Shanghai gossips were later to tell the story over and over, with relish—how Chiang Kai-shek was so poor he had to eat in the cheapest foodshops and buy his hot water by the copper's worth, like any other down-and-outer. The writer has been told by hangers-on around the exchange that

Chiang was "no better than a porter, a janitor. He used to sweep out my father's office."

The tale is exaggerated. Chiang did have a thin time of it; outside the Army he had no regular job. He was for a time without the patron a portionless man had to have in China, but this bad luck was not to last for long. The city was full of friends of the revolution. One of these especially, Chang Ching-kiang, did not allow him to languish.

Chang Ching-kiang, a wealthy merchant with important business connections in Paris, had for years been one of the financial supports of Sun Yat-sen's enterprises. He took an interest in the stiff-necked, bright young officer. The city was enjoying a postwar boom, and fortunes were won and lost every day on the market. Chiang Kai-shek was not exactly a tyro in this world; he came of merchant stock. The gossips say he was staked by his friend and promptly won a fortune; some add that he immediately lost it again and was protected still by Chang. It would not be surprising if both tales are true, as such adventures were commonplace in 1920 Shanghai.

But Chiang's sojourn in the world of finance didn't last long. Sun wanted him back in Canton, and Chang Ching-kiang urged him to go. There was still the enmity, however, between himself and Chen Chiung-ming, and he hesitated. He held long conversations with friends on the subject, especially with a brother officer who like Chiang had walked out of Canton in a huff with Chen Chiung-ming. There are published letters between these two. Chiang apologizes to his friend for having lost his temper: "The other day when the trouble started, you . . . seemed to me to be very stern both in your voice and color: I could not get a word in edgeways, and so felt it unbearable. . . . I have a bad temper and am usually lacking in good manners. When I think that I am overpatient with you, my elder brother, after having had enough of your anger, I become unconsciously rude, bursting out all at once. . . . I feel most ashamed of myself after careful reflection. I know myself that I have been ridiculous."

The friend replied: "You, my elder brother, are extremely self-willed to an almost incorrigible extent. Whenever you are disappointed at some trifle, you let your anger go unchecked. In dealing with people in that way, you run the grave danger of courting calamity; or at least you will find it most damaging to your career."

"The trouble with me in society is that I go to extremes," wrote Chiang. "I have lifelong sworn fast friends but no ordinary boon companions or social acquaintances."

In February 1921 the introspective soldier was coaxed back to Canton. He went with a bad grace, telling Chang Ching-kiang, "It is clearly known that the place is not suitable for me to stay long, that the work is utterly impossible for our party to carry out, yet I am unreasonably made to follow them." Chen was stalling, he was convinced of it. Chiang would go to see Sun merely on a friendly visit. He would definitely not accept an official commission under Chen Chiung-ming.

There are various American newspaper descriptions of Chiang Kai-shek. We would expect these portraits to be slapdash, but their effect is not only sketchy but often definitely misleading. From the war-lord period of 1916–25 the picture that emerged was of a tough, mysterious military man without principle, an unlettered opportunist, self-hewn from hard rock. Later other traits were added to this awe-striking character; it was discovered that Chiang was devious and cunning.

No one who reads his letters can continue to believe it. There is hard common sense as well as naïveté, but the outstanding characteristic of Chiang at thirty-four is earnest innocence. Even his suspicions partake of this quality.

An election, he warned Sun, would be a bad move. (Sun had

proposed one.) People wouldn't understand or accept it. "Today the time is not yet ripe, and our foundation is far from solid. The Kwangsi enemy is still at large and the Southwest unconquered." There were people in the Kwangtung army, he hinted in an elephantine way, who would oppose it. In any case, what good would an election do? What difference did one's diplomatic standing make? Japan hadn't helped them as she was expected to do after recognizing them; neither had England or America. On the contrary. For that matter, look at the new Soviet Russia. That state had had no diplomatic standing, and the European powers and America had gone out of their way to hold her down, but Soviet Russia had not failed because she was strongly united. The lesson was obvious. An election would disunite South China even more than it was already divided and Peking would no doubt leap at the chance to denounce Sun Yat-sen.

"You, my Master, can only hope for Chen Chiung-ming not to do things which are outside his authority, and to pursue the same aim as you do yourself." With this hidden—but not very subtly hidden—barb, Chiang signed off.

His words carried no weight: Sun had himself elected.

Chiang's mother died and he went to Fenghua for the conventional days of mourning. Who would be crass enough to criticize a man for showing his natural filial sorrow in this manner? Nevertheless, some of his friends claimed that the mourning period stretched out inordinately; Chiang stayed in Fenghua for months, coming out now and then in response to an urgent summons from Sun, but always diving back again into Chekiang. In the meantime the scheduled Kwangsi campaign went ahead and Chen Chiung-ming scored successes without Chiang's assistance.

No one could be sure why Sun Yat-sen should have decided on a "Northern Punitive Expedition" early in 1922; certainly not because he felt secure in Canton, for things there couldn't have been in more of a mess. Chen Chiung-ming was feeling his oats and all the officers were squabbling. But Sun was aware that Peking, too, was in a mess, and the time must have seemed propitious for an attack. Impetuously he started off, leaving Chen Chiung-ming in command as Minister for War.

The Army was hardly on its way when Chiang Kai-shek, watching balefully from Chekiang, perceived signs of treachery in Chen's behavior. He sent warning telegrams madly to all his colleagues, and they telegraphed back in an equally reckless manner. The expedition soon slowed down—because money and supplies were held back by Chen, according to Chiang's accusation, but it was probably doomed from the start anyway. The Army had not yet reached the provincial border when Chen's supply arrangements broke down and Sun's troops were stranded. In the interim before the commanders admitted this, Kai-shek's telegraphic correspondence was lively. Liao Chung-kai, one of the officers accompanying Sun, no piker on the wire himself, retorted:

"Your telegram received and understood. Unless rebellion actually broke out in Canton, to call back our forces from the front would never be allowed in any circumstances. . . . There are the Navy and three divisions in the provincial capital; the wretches surely would not dare to rise rashly. You, my elder brother, ought to come soon and go to the front immediately to help. . . . How can you bear to leave . . . the rest of us to suffer all the hardship? How could you?"

I have not been able to discover who paid for military telegrams.

Then Chen moved his forces into Canton and Sun came rushing back to prevent any dirty work, and sacked his deputy governor. Chiang's Cassandra behavior was justified.

Nobody liked to say openly that the Northern Punitive Expedition was fizzling out, but that was the fact. Sun stayed in

Canton to do his own governing and left the management of the campaign to two generals. With Chen out, he might reasonably look forward to the addition to the staff of Chiang, still stubbornly mourning in Chekiang. In the meantime there came something unusual from Peking—a friendly message.

There, the endemic civil war was quiet for the moment. Li Yuan-hung, who had been out and in several times, was again in the presidential chair. An alliance was apparently pending with the new Soviet Union of Russia; at any rate, an agent had arrived from Moscow. The leaders claimed that the Peking government was constitutional. This being so, said the northerners, what was the use of that separate Parliament down in Canton? Let Sun Yat-sen come to Peking and talk over a merger.

Sun refused the invitation. He still didn't like Li Yuan-hung, and he did not trust the party in power. There was a buzz of criticism among some of his followers at this decision: they felt that the Master was letting personal prejudice sway him. The loudest critic was Chen Chiung-ming, still smarting from his demotion and primed for his part. Sun should resign, he said. He wasn't needed any more.

Chen had sympathizers among the Canton merchants, who were liking Sun less and less. At first they had accepted his socialist sentiments with indulgence, assuming that they were demagogic trappings. But the man evidently meant what he said. Taxes were being levied on the wealthy, and valuable slum property had been confiscated in the name of the public good. The merchants were aggrieved. Enthusiastically they agreed with Chen; it was time to get rid of Sun.

Thus encouraged, Chen struck. On the night of June 15, 1922, he brought his troops into the city walls again and made straight for the residency. In their usual lighthearted fashion the soldiers fired and looted as they went, and gangs from the town joined in, until a great horde of shouting, excited people bore down on Sun's house.

No conspiracy ever went completely unheralded in those circles, and Sun was given warning a few hours in advance. He made his way alone through the streets, without interference, to navy headquarters. The residency, with all his books and manuscripts, was burned down.

The admiral in command at the navy yard found his distinguished refugee's presence embarrassing. Pointing out that the place was not built to withstand a siege, he bundled the President aboard the cruiser *Yung Feng* and sent him out into the river off Whampoa. There the cruiser mingled with the foreign craft that rode at anchor, and there it stayed. Chen did not dare to fire anywhere near the European ships.

After one or two days Sun got a telegram out to Chiang Kai-shek calling for help. Chiang was his only recourse: the other generals, who had been at the front, fled into Fukien, and the Navy had turned its back.

Chiang started out immediately. By the twenty-seventh he was aboard the *Yung Feng* with Sun, and he stayed aboard until the end, for nearly two months. He had never shown up so well. He did his job without fuss, looking after his leader like an orderly. He helped the ratings of the undermanned ship. His notorious temper remained cheerful and even, though quarters were cramped aboard and the midsummer weather was cruelly hot. Most Chinese generals would have been too lofty to behave in this manner, waiting personally on Sun, carrying meals, sweeping out the cabin: tradition forbade such sacrifice of dignity, but Chiang's training in the Japanese Army canceled out that foolishness.

They could easily have got away, but they hung on, hoping Chen would lose ground after his initial push. When at last, early in August, it became clear that the war lord had the support of all the Cantonese who counted, Sun and Chiang pulled out and made their way by British gunboat to Shanghai. A number of displaced M.P.s sadly greeted them at the dock. Sun retired to his house in the French Concession, and Chiang went back to Fenghua and that so often interrupted mourning.

In the eyes of the Western world, China still meant Peking. Revolts might come and rebels might go, but in our experience trouble in China always ended with somebody or other running things from the northern capital. Soviet Russia shared this idea at first, and so Communism was brought in by way of Peking, through the intellectuals at the universities.

Europeans and Americans are often puzzled by the student strikes and demonstrations of the East. We too have turbulent scenes in our universities, and look on unruly behavior as a natural part of youth, but we would be outraged if the youngsters attempted seriously to change the law. We have no awe of the educated because we have nearly all been students ourselves. It is different in the crowded East. There, students are the elite; progress and civilization depend upon them. And they know it. From our point of view, they know it far too well.

Students in China have always been the ones who fostered revolt. Most of the revolutionary societies that abounded in China before 1911 were based at universities. Eling Soong's husband, H. H. Kung, was a charter member of one of these as a student in Peking. He is now abused by the Left as a reactionary of reactionaries, but as a boy he plotted the assassination of Imperial tyrants at secret meetings in classrooms in the dead of night.

So, though at first the theory of the Russian Revolution didn't interest the Peking government clique, it sent a ripple through lecture halls and dormitories. It filled a need of the day; faculties and undergraduates were thirsty for reform. A sign of their restlessness was the demand, started by Hu Shih, for the use of everyday language in literature. Chinese writing until then had been confined to the stilted style of the ancients, which after many centuries had become incomprehensible to ordinary people; its only usefulness was that it gave a feeling of superiority to the privileged scholars who could read and use it. Hu Shih's movement stirred up tremendous excitement. Hundreds of students rushed to his support. The classicists were horrified and defended the old ways stoutly, but progress won out, and after 1918 there appeared the first books—fiction, poetry, history—written in the language of every day. Hu Shih's challenge was the beginning of literacy among the people, and that later tied up in its own way with Communism. Much of world importance grew out of that lecture-hall quarrel.

The leading spirits of Chinese Marxism were two men at Peking National University, Li Ta-chao the librarian, who later became a professor of history, and Ch'ên Tu-hsiu, dean of the Department of Literature. They were strongly attracted by the novel concept of a scientific approach to government. Confucianism, Taoism, Buddhism had failed, and the nation, where it was not standing still, was sinking into chaos and poverty. Marx seemed to hold the answer. As early as 1918 Li founded a Society for the Study of Marxism, and one of the keenest members was his assistant in the library, Mao Tse-tung, the peasant of Hunan.

At first neither Ch'ên nor Li appreciated the amount of self-sacrifice demanded of a true Marxist. They behaved as Chinese scholars always did when studying philosophy; they picked and chose and considered themselves free to reject what they did not approve. But by 1920 they were fully fledged, dedicated Communists who showed only the most occasional tendency to argue with the sacred word. That year the Chinese Communist Party was founded. Few people outside Ch'ên's direct circle even noticed it.

The members rode happily on the wave of enthusiasm that everywhere met the Karakhan Manifesto of 1919. Lenin's plan for revolution gratified Ch'ên Tu-hsiu because it stipulated leadership (in the early stages) by the intelligentsia, and he saw himself as the chosen intellectual, the great man of China. Li Ta-chao declared that all theories of history before Marx were mere tools of the ruling class, used to stupefy the people. The new language had caught on.

The Russian who assisted at the birth of the Chinese Communist Party—which hereafter I'll call the C.C.P. for short—came from Moscow to Peking on purpose for the occasion. Moscow still thought of the Peking leaders as the moving force of China, and intended to make an alliance with them. But they flirted with Sun, too, and he responded eagerly. He had sent a telegram of congratulation to Lenin when the Russian Revolution succeeded. No doubt he felt even more interest in the matter because he had known Tchitcherin in earlier days in Paris. He was gratified when Tchitcherin wrote to him—"Your country advances now resolutely, your people enter consciously the path of struggle against the world-suppressing yoke of Imperialism"—though the date of this letter was 1920, the same year the Kremlin was making up to Peking.

Whatever hard-and-fast agreements Sun made with Soviet Russia are obscured, like those with Japan, by his secrecy and the loss of so many papers in the Canton fire. But some points are well known, and have often been cited by Communists to buttress their claims to him and all his works. He was already imitating some of the Soviet methods when he instituted his reform of the Canton government. Moscow's indifference to him vanished in 1922, when a "Russian" calling himself Maring (he was a Dutchman named Sneevliet) came to Canton early in the year to inspect the setup. Maring was so favorably impressed that after reading his report the Kremlin focused its interest on South China, although it continued to play both ends against the middle and did not drop Peking. Clearly, Sun Yat-sen was the best bet.

Sun is often called a blind idealist, but he must have been shrewd, or at least cautious. He was still making up his mind, still hoping for support from someone besides Russia. Nineteen hundred and twenty-two was a time of great anxiety for the foreign powers who had investments in the East—the imperialists, as the Chinese had recently learned from the Russians to call them. In Hongkong a seamen's strike cost the British millions of dollars. Foreigners asked each other worriedly if Russia was behind it with her world revolution. Was this *it?* It looked very much as if it might be, especially when Adolf Joffe came to Peking as envoy from Moscow. For Joffe was one of Russia's best-known diplomats, and the choice gratified the Chinese and frightened the commercial foreign residents. Joffe made a public speech in which he openly pledged Russian aid as soon as China felt the time had come to rid herself of the now infamous foreign imperialism. He was the talk of the country.

If there is any record of Chiang Kai-shek's opinions on this situation, it has not been played up. He had them, but he didn't express them on paper. During the Master's seven months in the Rue Molière, he was in Fukien reorganizing the Army in preparation for a return to Canton: he looked forward to an early engagement with Chen Chiung-ming. His duty was political rather than military; traveling from one section to another, haranguing the officers and flourishing Sun's name like a magic talisman. But we find a good deal about Russia in one of Sun's characteristic letters to Chiang, calculated to soothe the feelings of the prima-donna chief of staff. Sun rallied Chiang:

"I have just seen your letter . . . in which you said, 'If there is no progress at all within ten days then there is nothing for it. . . .' etc. Pooh. What rubbish you talk! . . . Even though we have made no progress, the enemy is losing ground every day. For instance, his officers and men are beginning to see light; his unification is gradually dissolving; the people in Kwangtung are hating him more and more, and thinking of us more and more. . . .

"You had hopes for the West. Recently I have felt the same here, and now the thing is well in hand. But it is very complicated, ten or even a hundred times more so than in Fukien. No wonder all the comrades of our country went to their capital in high spirits, to come back dejected. Luckily I have found the way, and we are coming nearer together every day. But fundamentally we must have a base to rely upon, and then we can make use of it. If we have nothing at all ourselves, we will not be able to do anything, even though we were as agreeable to their principles as the Communist youth of our country. That is why the people in that capital have been urging the Communists to join the Kuomintang. We know we must have a foundation first, and to get that we must recover Kwangtung. . . .

"Now I am moving things outwards, and you and others are in Foochow as my backing. With this backing, my plans are progressing every day. It may turn out that before you can recapture Canton my plan will succeed. You can never tell! . . . The progress here cannot be conveyed on paper with ink. . . . We haven't had such a wonderful opportunity for more than ten years."

All this obviously refers to Joffe. The Ambassador had arrived in Shanghai and was devoting a lot of time to the Doctor. It is a fair guess that he had promised that the Russians would send aid on demand; the same promise he had made to Peking. All camouflage was abandoned a few weeks later, when Joffe and Sun came into the open with a joint statement, a "manifesto" of friendship between Russia and China. Joffe reiterated the protestations of the Karakhan statement. Today Sun's admirers, feeling that they must apologize for this move on his part, maintain stoutly that he was never sincere in his alliance with the Soviet; that he meant to use it to needle the Western nations into helping him. But the letter to Chiang proves that he was in earnest.

The Manifesto ushered in a period of triumph for Sun Yat-sen. For some time things had gone better for his cause in Canton in that they were going badly for Chen Chiung-ming. Now at last Chen was definitely driven out by a rival war lord, and the conqueror sent word to Sun that he could come back. During these pleasant occurrences Chiang was on sick leave in Fenghua, complaining that his eyes were giving him trouble. He was worried, too, about future plans for the Kuomintang. His correspondence with his friends was fidgety and querulous, even for him.

Was he in love? A novelist could make out a good case for the theory. Chingling's little sister Mayling, last of the Soong girls to return from America, had been home since 1917. In 1918 Charlie Soong died, but his reforming spirit lived on in his daughter. Mayling threw herself into public works with all the vigor of her father's clan, urged on by the shock her tidy soul received when she looked again on the China she had not seen since she was ten years old. Such dirt! Such squalor! Such suffering! She felt as if life would not be long enough to effect all the reforms that needed doing. Unlike Chingling, she did not interest herself in the theory of politics: she preferred immediate, practical measures of reform. She was a quick-moving, spirited girl; impatient, eager, intelligent, and, incidentally, pretty. This last quality was apt to be overlooked in her girlhood, not only by Soong associates (who preferred Chingling's fragile beauty) but by Mayling herself. The question of personal beauty was one of the things that made her impatient. Women's rights interested her more. She was a bluestocking and gloried in it. She joined the Child Labor Commission, and was a star member of the Y.W.C.A. She was an American dynamo. Eling and Chingling, departures themselves from the old-fashioned type, regarded her with indulgent amusement.

She must have frightened Chiang Kai-shek the first few times he encountered her in the Suns' house. He didn't know any other women like that. He knew his mother and his wife, and the pretty ladies who accepted his attentions when he was in the money, but he had never had much experience of foreign-educated girls sparkling with energy and ardent to improve the country, girls who argued with you and started all their replies with the phrase "Yes, but . . ."

Being a married man had never weighed very much on Chiang's conscience, though he accepted the status as a natural thing. In his world, everyone his age was married. His wedding was a dim, far-off, long-ago thing, impressed on him only by the presence of his little son Ching-kuo, and until now it had not interfered with such sentimental dalliance, or any other sort of dalliance, that came his way. In the years that followed Mayling's return he found himself contemplating a new idea for a Chinese of his upbringing; a marriage not of convenience but of choice, based on common interests. What was suitable for a village boy, he probably reflected, did not necessarily continue suiting a mature man whose outlook had widened.

In the Western fashion, he began a correspondence with Mayling.

Sun returned to Canton in February 1923, this time for good. It was roses, roses all the way. At the University of Hongkong he was carried from gate to auditorium by adoring students. In less than a year his reputation had soared from the depths. Chiang stopped complaining about his health and followed his Master, gloomily convinced that his services would soon be needed. He was not wrong. The war lord who had cleared a path for Sun's return regretted his act and tried to kick out the Nationalists once more, but lessons of the past had not been wasted. This time, Generalissimo Sun had a large and cohesive force of his own, and Chiang Kai-shek was chief of staff. Things quieted down under military control.

The friendship between Canton and Moscow developed apace, but up to the moment of commitment Sun was reluctant to turn his back on the West he had known so long. He had a last try at gaining the support of the powers, when Schurman, America's first Ambassador to China, came down to Canton on a visit and interviewed him. Sun suggested a period of five years' joint intervention by the powers in the form of military occupation by foreign troops of the chief Chinese cities, while the nation learned from Westerners how to govern themselves and native administrators were trained. At the end of this time, he was sure, the country would be ready for an election. But nothing came of his suggestion; Europe and America were not in a mood to invest men and money in a country which nothing, it seemed, could ever settle.

It was clear that China *must* turn to Russia, so Sun came out openly against the powers and blamed them for practically everything that was wrong in the country. Lawlessness and excessive militarism? They were due to the civil wars, and the civil wars were due to the short-sighted policy pursued by the powers themselves in shoring up Peking. "By their action, they have given Peking moral prestige," declared Sun. "Unconsciously, perhaps . . . they have intervened in China's internal affairs by practically imposing upon the country a government repudiated by it." He referred with bitterness to the fact that the increasing revenues of the Customs and the Salt Gabelle, both of which were managed by foreigners, were regularly handed over to Peking.

Sun's sense of grievance grew in direct proportion to the aid he received from Russia. With their advice and munitions and teachers, he was getting more and more material for speeches. China was a victim of foreign countries. "She is really in a worse condition than Korea or Formosa. They have one master; we have many. . . . If the foreign countries will let us alone, China will have her affairs in shape within six months. . . . The Peking government could not stand twenty-four hours without the backing it receives from foreign governments. . . . It can collect taxes in the provinces; it lives entirely upon foreign-collected money.

"We have lost hope of help from America, England, France or any other of the great powers," he said. "The only country that shows any signs of helping us in the South is the Soviet Government of Russia."

Then as an earnest of the new orientations of China's hope, Generalissimo Sun sent Chiang Kai-shek to Moscow to study military methods and political institutions.

Consistency is not one of the vices of public opinion. When Chiang Kai-shek came to the top he was attacked by his enemies on three counts; that he was too Chinese, that he was too Japanese, and that he was too Russian. Considering the shape of things which came, these complaints have not been heard recently, but in the late twenties the allegation against his Russian sympathies resounded through the banking streets of Shanghai. He was said to have a completely Kremlin outlook, for he had lived and worked in Russia and had doubtless picked up the contagion.

In fact, Chiang was in Russia for only a few months of 1923, and his brief visit was not highly important either to him or his hosts. To the Kremlin, China was merely one of a number of prospects, nor was Chiang the first pilgrim from his country. A large community of Chinese was there already; students from Peking with a scattering of others. Chiang and Canton, however, interested the Russians more than did the already converted.

The C.C.P. had grown big, but Moscow had still to be convinced of its worth. The leader Ch'ên Tu-hsiu had been in Russia just before Chiang's visit to attend the Comintern Fourth Congress. He was badly snubbed by Radek, who scolded him in open meeting, declaring that the Chinese comrades had failed to associate themselves with the masses. Instead they locked themselves up, said Radek, studying Marx and Lenin as they had once studied Confucius. Clearly, Canton was Moscow's favorite at the moment, and

the intellectual comrades must learn to collaborate with the Nationalists.

After considerable pressure, the C.C.P. announced meekly that
"due to the inroads of imperialism" China was still dominated by
feudal militarists and bureaucrats; that feudalism inhibited the
emergence of capitalism with its properly aggrieved proletariat; that
until such time as the proletariat was ready to seize power it must
unite with democratic groups against feudal militarism. In short,
Chinese Communists must join the Kuomintang.

The C.C.P. leaders were violently unhappy about all this. Union
with the Kuomintang, they protested, would confuse the class structure and curb their independence. On his side, Sun Yat-sen was
equally against the coalition; he had no desire to sell the Kuomintang down the river. He stipulated that any Communist who entered
the Kuomintang must submit completely to its rules and recognize
no party outside it. He seems never to have realized the true nature
of Communism. Or did he believe, perhaps, that in the last analysis
he could outguess Moscow? More likely he was simply guileless
and sentimental about these people who had offered to help him.
Always at his elbow was Chingling, who had dedicated her faith to
Communism.

Chiang went to Moscow without understanding the language—
he doesn't claim, today, to speak any Russian—and there he was
shepherded around by liaison officers and given as much practical
training as he could take in, in the time available.

"Few in Moscow probably noticed the youthful, thin-lipped
Chinese officer whose cold, beady black eyes probably noticed a
great deal," says Harold Isaacs, who, to understate the matter,
didn't like Chiang. But there were people who did notice him—
the other Chinese. They resented his position. After all, who was
he? A reactionary militarist; if not quite a running dog of the war
lords, still a low type from the Kuomintang. One day they assembled
to hear the man give a talk on Sun Yat-sen's work in the revolution,

and when he had finished they heckled him. They found fault with his knowledge of revolutionary theory. Hadn't Marx said . . . ? Didn't Russia's experience prove . . . ?

"I haven't been speaking about Russia," said Chiang sharply. "My talk was on China. You ought to learn more about your own country and your own great men's accomplishments before you are so glib on foreign theory."

"Nationalism! Arrant nationalism!" they said to each other, no doubt, and reflected that such abysmal ignorance and illiteracy could hardly be a danger to the cause. For the moment, however, the bitter fact was that nationalism was not considered a swear word in Moscow.

Chiang had only four months in Russia. He wasn't honored with an interview with Lenin, but Tchitcherin was nice to him and he met Trotzky. He saw the military and naval installations, and may have been awed—Isaacs thinks he ought to have been—but Russia's development in 1923 was not much ahead of what he had witnessed in Japan.

He was still away from China when the most important Russian yet seen in Canton made his appearance there in October. Michael Borodin had a complicated history. He was born in Russia and brought up in Latvia under his real name, Grusenberg. He returned to Russia and became a revolutionary, and got into trouble and went to America. In Chicago he changed his name to Berg and opened a business college. After the Russian Revolution he went back to Moscow, in 1918, and worked for the Party, and was sent out to serve in Mexico and then in Turkey as chief representative of the Third International. He had recently been imprisoned in Glasgow and then deported as an agitator.

Borodin came to Canton disguised as a newspaperman, representing the Rosta News Agency, but no one attempted to keep up that fiction. Nor did he come alone. By the time Chiang returned, the city was swarming with Russian advisers and Sun had written

off England and America completely. He now convinced himself
that the British supported Peking because they didn't like him
personally, and that America neglected him on Britain's account.

No mere sick fancy gave him this impression, but the very real
vexation of Canton Customs revenue. In the spring of 1923 he had
first raised the question of this money, which, as he pointed out,
though collected in his domain, was immediately handed over to
his enemies in Peking. Sun felt that the collectors in Canton should
turn Canton revenue over to himself. The collectors, however, took
the (legally correct) attitude that they were not empowered to
change the rules. Sun brooded about this, and finally came up with
a decision. He would seize the Canton Customs House itself.

The foreigners who were responsible for the service, with Britain
at their head, promptly took action. On the seventh of December,
1923, seventeen ships collected at Canton, a motley collection of
flags being flown—British, American, French, Italian, Portuguese,
and Japanese. It was an impressive sight, and it was intended to be.
Sun did no seizing of Customs after that, but his prestige among his
countrymen didn't suffer. Hundreds of people sent telegrams of
congratulation. In the end the British consented to a compromise
arrangement by which his government shared in the Customs surplus.

On the last day of the year, in an address given at the Canton
Y.M.C.A., Sun made the statement that has since been quoted,
over and over, by Communists:

"We no longer look to the Western powers. Our faces are turned
toward Russia."

Li Ta-chao, former employer and teacher of Mao Tse-tung, was
the first Chinese Communist to enter the Kuomintang. Many more
followed him. But Communists in the Kuomintang did not much
impress Kai-shek when he got back to Canton: he was more interested in the arrival of Blücher, or Galen as he called himself,

former army officer in Austria and one of Russia's most prized generals.

Chiang had met him in Russia and discussed with him the possibilities of a military academy at Whampoa where cadets could be intensively trained in Russian methods of warfare. At the beginning of 1924 Galen set to work on this project, and also advised the Kuomintang officers on the reorganization of the revolutionary army.

Advice was not the only commodity the Russians were free with. As they flooded in—at least thirty more military men arrived within the next six months—they brought funds, credit, and material. An officer who had been instructed by Joffe set to work on the workers and farmers, organizing labor unions and peasant movements. On all this activity Sun beamed approval. He was aging visibly; the secret disease that was to kill him was making itself felt, but it was poignant happiness to him that things were going his way at last.

Chiang, too, had reason to feel pleased with developments. The academy was quickly assembled, and by the middle of June opened its doors. Galen was chief of the Russian staff, Borodin hovered over it as Kuomintang adviser, and he himself, Chiang Kai-shek, led all the rest as President. He could have been so gratified by his position that his doubts were stilled, but he wasn't. The memory of certain impressions gathered in Russia remained with him.

"From my observation," he wrote to a friend a few months after his return, "the Russian Party is lacking in sincerity. Even when I told you . . . that only thirty per cent of what the Russians said was believable, it was said only because you . . . were so enthusiastic in believing the Russians that I had not the heart to disappoint you altogether. Regarding their respect for Mr. Sun personally, they are not Russian Communists but international partisans. As for those of our country who are in Russia, they have nothing except slander and suspicion for Mr. Sun.

"The sole aim of the Russian Party is to make the Chinese Communist Party its legitimate heir. They do not believe that our Party could cooperate with them . . . they want to make Manchuria, Mongolia, the Mohammedan Province and Tibet each a part of their Soviet, and even as to China Proper they are not without the wish to put their fingers in. . . .

"What they call 'Internationalism' and 'World Revolution' are nothing but Kaiser Imperialism. . . . Russians, as well as the English, French, Americans and Japanese, it seems to me, all have it in their minds to promote the interest of their own respective countries at the cost of other nations. One of them ridiculing the others about this is, as Mencius said, just like a man who had run only fifty paces ridiculing those who had run a hundred paces for having run at all. . . .

". . . some of our Chinese Communists who are in Russia always scold other people as slaves of America, of England and of Japan, never realizing that they themselves have already completely become slaves of Russia."

# 4 THE STRUGGLE FOR SUCCESSION
1923–26

They planned to start the academy with three hundred
cadets, but there were fifteen hundred applications and in
the end five hundred were chosen. Not all of these were green boys;
to start off with, Chiang collected soldiers from a disbanded northern army that had been driven out of its garrison in Chekiang. With
the new ones he went out of his way to discourage regionalism,
deliberately selecting boys from as many districts as possible, as
long as they were intelligent and had some education. He was determined to wipe out the old-fashioned prejudice against the military. In new China soldiers must be admired and envied.

Most of the teaching staff were Russian, which didn't make for a
very jolly faculty. The Russians disliked and suspected Chiang and
it goes without saying that he returned the compliment, but for the
good of the cause they all concealed their feelings—most of the
time. At any rate there were many Chinese names among those who
gave extracurricular lectures, and one of Chen Chi-mei's two
nephews, Chen Kuo-fu, was Chiang's assistant.

It was an exacting course, which Americans would have found
hard to take. Our students, conditioned to fifty-minute lectures,
can't concentrate for more than that without a brief recess, but
Chinese are used to lectures of two or three times that length. Their

teachers are capable of feats of filibuster that strike us with awe, and of all long-distance speakers Chiang is surely the champion. He addressed his academy at least once a week, administering hours at a stretch of improving discourse. He specialized in moral precept, recommending discipline and obedience; he urged the boys to think of the nation as an entity, to be loyal to China and Sun and the Kuomintang first of all, even before their commander or corps. They would be officers, he reminded them, with a duty to their men. They were also taught the fundamental political principles that Borodin thought they should know. And then, of course, there was the usual military routine and drill, under Galen's supervision. In four months' time the class graduated and dispersed to serve in the regular army near Canton, for practice, while the next group was indoctrinated.

The government itself was being shaken up and reorganized, but most of the big men remained as before. Minister of Finance was Chingling's brother Soong Tse-ven, or T. V. Soong. It is difficult to remember that T.V. was ever a colleague of Communists, he is such a perfect Chinese version of the typical American capitalist. But so it was; and he was a satisfactory colleague, at that. He knew what most of them did not, the Western methods of finance and industry. During his years in the States he had developed a strong regard for punctuality and efficiency. It is asking for trouble, perhaps, to add that he had learned to respect honesty in politics; the cynical reader might well ask, Where? But T.V. had learned it somewhere.

With Chingling married to Generalissimo Sun and T.V. a Cabinet Minister the Soongs were well represented in Canton, and Mayling often came down to visit her sister. Chiang had made up his mind. He could not bring himself to ask her personally for her hand, in spite of his determination to live up to the Western code, so he compromised with the old ways and spoke to Sun. Was Miss Soong likely to accept him? His first wife, as he assured the Doctor, was now divorced; perhaps it would be better to say detached. At any rate, she didn't count. Had he any chance with Mayling?

Sun seems to have favored the suggestion; at least he did not set himself against it, and he asked his wife's advice. But Chingling's reaction was violent. She didn't like Chiang at the beginning and she was never to like him, even in the few periods when their aims coincided. She flared up and reminded her husband that Chiang wasn't at all a moral man. All her Methodist background recurred to the Communist girl: Mayling must never marry such a roué! Why, even at that moment some woman was living with him!

Sun carried the message back to his academy president, advising him to wait until Madame Sun had cooled down and then try his luck again. Chiang was not discouraged: Miss Soong seemed not absolutely to dislike him, in spite of her sister's opinion, and in spite, too, of the pretty lady who was sharing his quarters at the time. He was a little puzzled by Chingling's attitude: in his world women didn't make a fuss over things like that.

There was an added complication in this complicated courtship. Borodin, too, was in love with Mayling. This doesn't fit in with Edgar Snow's description of the Communist character. According to Snow, Communists just don't indulge in sentimental weaknesses. They "talk only about committees, organizations, armies, resolutions, battles, tactics, 'measures' and so on, but seldom in terms of experience." (*Red Star over China,* p. 133.) But Borodin backslid. He couldn't very well pay open court to Mayling because he was married, but he couldn't put her out of his mind, either. One day a delighted servant brought to one of the Soongs a piece of paper filched from Borodin's bedroom, from his blotter, on which he had written, over and over, "Mayling darling. Darling Mayling." Her sisters teased Mayling: Sun laughed with them: in time, inevitably, the story came to Chiang's ears.

Probably this rivalry didn't have a decisive effect on his feelings about the Communists, but it couldn't have increased his affection.

Already he disliked them cordially. He had plenty of reason. He was jealously on guard where Sun was concerned, and he resented the way the Russians interfered with the Kuomintang. They persuaded Sun to expel from the Party all members who stood out against the Russian ways. Chiang disapproved of this, and there were many more evidences of the same superintending spirit. He had never swallowed Joffe's reassurances in that manifesto. The Russians were a great help, he realized, and they had a lot to teach the Chinese, and he was quite willing to learn it. But in the end, he knew, they would try to push him out, along with the rest of the faithful. World revolution? Chiang had no faith in the concept. It looked to him like a new technique for ordinary conquest by Russia.

As always, he quarreled with his colleagues. As always, Sun was distressed and tried to keep the peace. But Chiang was too busy now to concentrate on personal enmities. Resentful local merchants, who continued to view Sun's flourishing socialistic government with alarm, had collected a private army of their own, the Canton Volunteers, and with these forces, under a Cantonese war lord, they began a revolution.

Chiang promptly moved against the Volunteers with a picked party of academy cadets and put into practice the principles of modern, changed warfare that had been drummed into their heads. They attacked in small bands. They moved swiftly and with confidence, outguessing the enemy at every turn. They showed no mercy and much zeal. It was a bloody war and a destructive one, but at the end of it there was no denying that Sun and his Kuomintang— with the Russians behind him, more and more Russians all the time—were running Canton and the province. Chiang's reputation was enhanced as well.

The picture looks clear enough—Sun's party and the Russians, ostensibly allies, actually coming apart at the seams because of a fundamental difference between what the Kuomintang wanted and what Communism wanted. It is really a little more complicated than that. The Kuomintang left wing, the C.C.P., and the Russians made up a block against all the other Kuomintang members. But there was a dispute for power among these leftists, too. The Russians annoyed the Chinese Communists, just as they annoyed Chiang, with their cavalier behavior. In fact, they were nicer to the non-Red Chiang than to their own brothers in the faith. No Chinese Communist had any voice in the organization of the Whampoa Academy, and certainly no Chinese Communist had any say at all in top-level decisions. These were handled by Borodin and Sun Yat-sen exclusively. The C.C.P. no less than the Kuomintang had reason to complain of highhanded treatment from the Russians.

Early in 1924 Lenin died, and the faith and its future were thoroughly discussed at the Kuomintang's First National Congress in January. (Mao Tse-tung dropped in for the occasion; he was working in Shanghai.) If Chiang and the other Kuomintang leaders had not already been alert to danger, they soon had the evidence of it thrust upon them. In July of 1924 three zealous right-wingers brought out a "Proposal for the Impeachment of the Communist Party," which charged that the Reds were breaking their solemn promise to behave as "individuals" within the Kuomintang. They were taking orders from the C. P. Central Committee as a group; they were Communists first and Kuomintang members afterward; they were a party within a party.

Sun could not deny it. But he said that these infringements were the actions of inexperienced students, not the "experienced Soviet leaders." He begged the question; logically, he must have seen that there is no other way a Communist, either Russian or Chinese, can behave than to work primarily for the Party. But ill-health isn't conducive to logical thinking, and Sun was dying.

The North watched these various events, but in a rather desul-tory way. The leading war lord there, Wu Pei-fu, had got into a habit of ignoring Sun Yat-sen as a threat. He was busy unifying

his part of China, and the great part of his attention was focused
on his quarrel with Chang Tso-lin, the boss, or "Old Marshal," of
Manchuria, which at this time was complicated by Russian action.
To understand it, we must remember that Soviet Russia still dealt
with Peking on a diplomatic basis, as the rightful capital of China,
quite as if all this activity in Canton were not going on at all. It was
the Russian *Government* that dealt with Peking—promising among
other things, in a mutual agreement, not to engage in hostile propaganda against Peking—but it was the *Comintern* that aided Sun
Yat-sen, with hostile propaganda and everything else.

The Karakhan Manifesto of 1919 had made its effect on the
Chinese by voluntarily giving up all rights in China which had
been acquired by Czarist Russia. But now, in 1924, a rather odd
thing happened. Soviet Russia again wanted the control over the
Chinese Eastern Railway which had been handed back with such
fanfare in 1919. Other foreign powers naturally protested against
this breach of promise. Chang Tso-lin was particularly indignant,
for the railway ran through his domain. But Wu Pei-fu let Russia
have it on the old terms. He figured that he needed Russian friendship to keep out the Japanese in Manchuria, and he felt no obligation to listen to the Old Marshal's protests. On the contrary.

As things turned out, the treaty between Peking and Moscow was
to the Old Marshal's advantage. He made such a row about it that
to save trouble the Russians decided to make a special treaty with
him, similar to the one they had signed with Peking. This settled
his status, which had until then been hazy. He was definitely overlord of Manchuria, acknowledged as such by a foreign power.

The Old Marshal's attempt to take over Peking in 1922 had been
frustrated. He had been driven back to Mukden by Wu Pei-fu and
General Feng Yu-hsiang, a character who liked to refer to himself
as "the Christian general." Feng had a great flair for publicity and
was the darling of foreign newspapermen. A great fat man, he

always boasted of his peasant origin, wore fantastically shabby clothes, and played to the gallery; but he was a capable general, if you didn't insist on loyalty in your officers. He had contributed largely to the 1922 campaign against the Old Marshal, and when in 1924 Chang Tso-lin started again on the warpath, Wu naturally felt he could rely on Feng to defend Peking's cause. Himself, he took his troops to Shanhaikuan on the Great Wall and there prepared to hold the line; Feng he sent to Jehol, nearly a hundred and forty miles from Peking.

Feng Yu-hsiang started off as he had been commanded, but as soon as Wu Pei-fu was a safe distance away he sneaked back to Peking. There, with all Wu's troops gone, it was easy to take control of the government, according to the plan he had secretly worked out with Chang Tso-lin. Within a few hours Wu Pei-fu was out of power in Peking and his rivals were in. But Feng did not, after all, get the high position he had hoped for in the rearrangement that resulted. Chang Tso-lin, when they came to cut up the cake, put in another man instead of Feng as President. Feng's feelings were hurt by this betrayal, and he must have reflected sadly on the perfidy of human nature, but he did not break off relations with the new regime.

Now in the autumn of 1924 the busy plotters and counterplotters turned and looked southward, and what they saw worried them. Chiang Kai-shek's effective new academy training, the number of Soviet advisers swarming over Canton, the news of military equipment arriving in a steady stream, regular payments to the soldiers— most convincing evidence of Russia's friendship—all betokened something threatening. Nor was it a secret that Sun Yat-sen was planning another military expedition against them. They took counsel and wondered aloud: was this war necessary? Chang Tso-lin and Feng Yu-hsiang were neither of them sworn enemies of Sun Yat-sen. Chang had been allied with the Nationalists more than

once, making common cause against Peking, while Feng in his role
of hearty republican appeared, at least, to be in sympathy with
Sun's aims.

A second invitation went, therefore, from Peking to Canton, in
different language but conveying much the same message as the
first. Why should the North and the South continue apart? Let Sun
Yat-sen come up to Peking and talk it all over. Unification of China
was the aim of all of them; wouldn't it be better to achieve this
peacefully?

Sun had declined the first invitation primarily because of the
men in the saddle, Wu Pei-fu and Li Yuan-hung. This time he had
no such objections, and not so much reason to mistrust the men in
power. With Russia backing him, the northern generals should
hesitate to play monkey tricks. Besides, Borodin thought the meeting would be a good idea. Sun could well afford to leave Canton:
Chiang Kai-shek had the situation under control militarily, the non-
Kuomintang portion of the Nationalist Army was outside the
vicinity of Canton (this upon Borodin's advice), and Sun's old
friend Hu Han-min was perfectly capable of acting as his deputy
in civilian affairs. Accompanied by Wang Ching-wei and a number
of other men, Generalissimo Sun departed for Peking early in 1925.

No one knew how near the end was. Sun had barely arrived at
Tientsin when he collapsed and was taken to the Peking Union
Medical College Hospital for observation. It was cancer of the
liver, well advanced. He held bedside conferences and interviews
until he was operated on. He died on March 12. It is possible,
though not probable, that he himself wrote his famous will: the
generally accepted theory, however, is that Wang Ching-wei com-
posed it.

Had Sun died a few years earlier, before Soviet representatives
took over his party propaganda, things might have been very
different for his reputation. As it was, his name and fame were in
the hands of expert idol-makers, and Sun was given the full Lenin

treatment. He became half a god. His portrait still hangs in the place of honor in Chinese houses in Red China, Indonesia, America, England, wherever Chinese may be. As a piece of national property he is owned both by Communists and Nationalists, each party claiming exclusive rights to his philosophy. If Sun's Christianized Chinese soul ever backslides enough to come back to earth as an ancestral ghost, the father of his country must be puzzled as to whose hospitality, among all his heirs, he ought to accept. Let us hope he is spared the anguish of choice: his children are not.

The world, or that portion of it which was interested, watched eagerly to see who would succeed Sun. Because Wang was present at the deathbed and had been "entrusted" with the sainted will, most of the Canton contingent thought he was the logical candidate, yet a number of men had equal claims to the succession, and no doubt the Russians wondered which to back.

The strength of the new Communist influence showed up dramatically in Shanghai on May 30, 1925, at last justifying the fears of the bankers. For some time the organization of trade unions had flourished and here and there strikes and upheavals had taken place in industrial districts. During one of these small riots a number of Chinese workers charged a Japanese cotton mill, and in the fracas one of them was killed. The agitators fanned the flames; speeches were made against the wicked foreign imperialists, and on May 30 such a mood of violence prevailed in the International Settlement that the police stepped in and made a few arrests. Upon this the omnipresent students pushed into the Louza police station, where the prisoners had been taken, and there was a scuffle while they were shoved out. They stayed there in the street shouting defiance. More and more reinforcements arrived until there was a sizable mob. What happened next, or rather why it happened, depends upon who is telling the story. Sympathizers of the strikers say the British police inspector lost his head; others insist that he did the only thing possible. Anyway, he gave the order to fire into the mob. Four students were killed on the spot and many more were wounded: in the end there were at least thirteen deaths.

Had this incident taken place before the arrival of the Russians in Sun Yat-sen's life, it would have amounted to just that—the death of demonstrating students, no uncommon occurrence in the East. As it was, May 30 became the rallying cry of a crusade. After the fire and flame, Britain was the heaviest loser. More strikes followed rapidly, but the direst result was another shooting affray, the Shakee Massacre in Canton. The French and British at Shameen, in what they too insisted was a necessary act of self-defense, fired into a procession of demonstrators. This time the casualty list was much higher.

The Chinese united in furious indignation. It was only an aggravation to them when a diplomatic commission that sat on the May 30 incident decided that the shooting at Louza police station had been justified. Men of all parties joined together in showing their resentment. Chang Tso-lin was one sympathizer, Feng Yu-hsiang another, and Chiang Kai-shek for a while actually forgot his distrust of the Communists. They were in this together, facing a common enemy—Western imperialism. In such a mood Chiang sent his young son Ching-kuo to Moscow to study military science. Anywhere was better than the West.

The situation in Peking took on fresh interest for Sun's heirs, anxious to get started on the long-awaited expedition. Wu Pei-fu, dispossessed by treachery, had gathered about him a number of war lords south of the city, and another threat to Canton's success was a general, Sun Chuan-fang, formerly a subordinate to Chang Tso-lin, who had made himself lord of five provinces in the Southeast. The Nationalists would have to deal with three separate foes, or compound with three leaders, in order to unify China.

At the beginning of July 1925 Canton seemed peacefully busy, with all Sun's bright young men getting on like little birds in their nests. Hu Han-min was Foreign Minister. Wang Ching-wei was Chairman of the State Council of a new national government. On Borodin's advice, a model organization plan was drawn up for towns and provinces all over China. Most important of all, Kuomintang propagandists were busy preparing people in Kiangsu, Hunan, Shantung—all the provinces involved—for the great day when the Nationalists should arrive.

But schism was dividing the party, and a left-wing member Liao Chung-kai was its first victim. Openly Communist in his sympathies, his position became less and less popular as the right wing of the Kuomintang gained in strength. He was third in rank in the new Military Council, headed by Wang Ching-wei, but not for long. Six weeks after his appointment he was shot and killed, and among the instigators was the rightist Hu Han-min's brother. It was declared that they had been encouraged to do the job by "the British Imperialists in Hongkong," but everything was being blamed on the British that year, and there was never any proof of the allegations. There were plenty of Chinese who had reasons for wanting a pro-Russian out of the government.

In Liao, Chiang lost an old friend. Grief may have hastened his decision, though there was little time for grief: clearly he felt that the moment for dealing with plots and counterplots had arrived. The Central Executive Committee of the Kuomintang (the most important body of all) met with both State and Military councils and decided that the situation called for emergency measures. Wang Ching-wei, Hsu Chung-chih, who was Chiang's C-in-C, and Chiang himself were given unlimited powers.

Liao was assassinated on August 20. Four days later Chiang sent out a detachment of his Whampoa cadets in a search party. They broke into the houses and offices of all the government officials, and seized and examined documents. About a hundred men were arrested and imprisoned. Hu Han-min was taken under guard to

Whampoa, and later sent away on a "diplomatic mission" to Russia. That left, leading the government, Wang Ching-wei, Chiang himself, and Hsu Chung-chih.

Hsu had been on good terms with Chiang, or vice versa, a long time. But now Chiang quarreled with this friend. He was in no mood to knuckle down to anyone, and at that moment it must have galled him particularly that Hsu was nominally his superior. Hsu's judgment was not as good as his own: he was sure of it. In the hot-house temperature of Russian-dominated Canton, ambitions burst into bloom overnight like tropical flowers. Hsu and Chiang did not agree on the old vexed question of Chen Chiung-ming: Hsu had insisted upon letting that war lapse, and now it looked as if Chen were rising up to plague them again. Hsu's judgment was *not* good, according to Chiang. No one could accuse him of being a con-spirator, but some of his officers were mixed up in the affair. Alto-gether, it would be better for Hsu, too, to retire. . . . Before the end of September, Hsu Chung-chih was taking refuge in Shanghai, and Wang Ching-wei and Chiang Kai-shek now shared the responsi-bility for the government.

The Central Executive Committee awarded Chiang full military powers, and he marched against Chen Chiung-ming and his allies in full strength, determined to put down these local disturbances for good and all, before he set out for the North. On this campaign, which was called the East River Expedition, the Chinese proved to the world what a transformation had been wrought by reorganiza-tion. The first encounter with the enemy took place at Tamshui; the war lords were beaten off and the Nationalists marched on to Waichow. Waichow, a walled city surrounded by a moat, had been captured only once before in all of China's history, and that was a thousand years ago. Chiang stormed the town himself, leading a contingent across the moat and fighting with reckless courage. Several officers who later became famous in their own right bore testimony to his bravery.

"It is now only a month since we started . . . but we have captured from the enemy over six thousand rifles, seven field guns,
more than thirty machine guns and over six thousand prisoners.
. . . Today we are in Swatow," he said in a telegram to Canton on
November 6. He added that propaganda had wrought a tremendous
change in the public. "The common people from all four directions
have come out in crowds to see us and welcome us with food and
drink."

Everything should have been set now for the final great adventure, the march to Peking. The troops had been tested and passed
the test brilliantly. But politically Canton was still not strong, the
Communist question having stirred up so much trouble that it was
bound to break out here and there in spite of Wang Ching-wei's
skillful handling of both extremes. While Chiang was still marching
toward Waichow, anti-Communists held a secret meeting near
Peking, at Sun Yat-sen's tomb in the Western Hills, and passed a
number of resolutions—that all Communists be expelled from the
Kuomintang, that Borodin and the other Russians be sent back
to Moscow, and others of the same sort. Chiang was in sympathy
with the spirit of these proposals, but in his position he couldn't
afford to admit his sentiments.

When the news came out Borodin offered to resign and go away,
but the Kuomintang wouldn't hear of it. They repeated the old protests of friendship for Russia, and Chiang even made fun of the
Western Hills Conference for demanding the expulsion of Communists from the C.E.C.: "There are 24 members in the . . . Committee, and only four of them belong to the Communist Party. That
shows a ratio of six to one. If we still fear that the Communists will
slowly gobble us up, we indeed have no self-respect and no confidence in ourselves." As an added assurance to Borodin of the love
they bore him, the Party made a public presentation to him of a
silver souvenir, inscribed with the words "Co-operative Struggle."

So it was a letdown when Canton heard that Borodin had sud-

denly gone North to confer with Feng Yu-hsiang. The gossips got
busy with a story that Chiang had broken with the Russians after
all and was going to attempt the Northern Expedition alone and
independent of Moscow. What had happened? Had Wang Ching-
wei given in to him? If so, thought many foreigners abroad, China
was in the grip of a new dictator, Chiang Kai-shek.

Now, in 1925, American papers began to take notice of his
name, and their general attitude toward it was disapproving. They
interpreted Chiang as an opportunist, working his way to the top,
heedless of his people's good. Americans, not unnaturally, couldn't
unravel the complexities of the Chinese scene, but they could see
that the Canton government was splitting into two factions. It
looked as if the leftist faction was for the People, and so of course
the rightists, because they were opposed to the leftists, must be
oppressors of the People. By their own traditions Americans felt
themselves committed to be on the side of the leftists, again because
of the People. . . . Of course this wasn't consistent with American
distrust of Soviet Russia, but most of them weren't aware that
Soviet Russia was deeply involved in the business, or, if they were
aware, they felt that Russia, no matter how objectionable she might
be at close quarters, was all right for China.

Happenings early in the next year added to the sinister element
in Chiang's reputation. While Borodin was in Peking, two other
Russians took his place as advisers in Canton. They hadn't Borodin's brilliant tact, and Chiang didn't like them. Not being an
American, not being far from the scene or full of innocence and
ideals, he could see only that they represented a rival power and
treated him as something to be used. They insulted his intelligence.
Chiang had his own, or anyway Sun's, notions of what was needed
for the country. He may have been mistaken; it is hard nowadays
to decide that, but he was not unreasonable in wishing to avoid
being taken over by Soviet Russia. Chiang had no illusions about
their intentions.

"I offer them sincerity," he wrote in his diary. "They return deceit. It is impossible to work together with them."

The disputes were especially rancorous on the subject of the Northern Expedition. Chiang kept pressing to get it moving, and the advisers continued to put him off, for what minor strategical reason it is impossible now to say. There was another difficult point; Chiang could not pin down the war lords who controlled Kwangsi and Hunan. He had to assure himself of their support because he needed their troops, but they held off, objecting to Russian influence in the high command. And the Hunan war lord was especially important for another reason; he must ensure a peaceful, swift passage for the expedition across his territory, as everything depended on speed in the early stages. Chiang decided to reduce the Russians' participation in his affairs. As a first step he arrested a divisional commander suspected of working for them under cover. The chief Russian adviser promptly protested, and Chiang was plunged into a long argument with Wang Ching-wei.

A few weeks passed tensely. He complained to his diary that he could not sleep. His mind was made up, but he had to wait for the right moment. He couldn't go to the C.E.C. and put the matter through proper channels because that would tip off the Russians. "My Master and the martyrs of the Party in heaven have pity on me and protect me," he wrote.

On March 20 he moved as suddenly as he had done in the raid of the government offices. The police under his orders arrested a number of officials. They disarmed a regiment suspected of wholehearted allegiance to Communism rather than the Kuomintang. They surrounded the headquarters of the Canton Strikers' Committee, a concentration of Communist adherents. But their most startling arrests were of several Russians, including those who had so annoyed Chiang; these men were told they must get out of China.

It was all highly unconstitutional, and Wang Ching-wei did not pretend to be pleased. Chiang stopped short of declaring himself dictator, but he didn't deign to give more than partial explanations of his actions. (It was rumored, however, that he had moved quickly to nip in the bud a kidnaping plot against himself.) He went through the formality of trying to make peace with the Council Chairman: Wang himself, he declared, had lately given him a warning and suggested that he leave Canton. Surely it was only natural to defend himself? What else had Wang expected him to do?

Apparently, Wang had expected him to take fright and follow his suggestion, and get out of the city. As Chiang had not done so, Wang himself found it more prudent to retire, which he did, disappearing only five days after the incident. From his hideaway he wrote to Chang Ching-kiang that he was henceforth eschewing all political activity. A few months later he went to France. Chiang was left triumphant, the only survivor of the original three.

Now, having made his point, he behaved in a more conciliatory manner. It had never been his intention, he said, to break off completely with Moscow. Sun Yat-sen had believed in co-operating with Russia, and so did he. His behavior didn't belie the statement when Borodin came back from the domain of Feng Yu-hsiang in May. (At the same time, Hu Han-min returned from Moscow and was treated as one who had expiated his crime. But he soon moved on to Shanghai. He seemed to consider Canton crowded.) Chiang and the Russian had an interview from which they emerged calm and friendly. Immediately thereafter Chiang piously criticized the extreme anti-Communists of the Party and went through some elaborate play-acting regarding the Chief of Police, who had carried out his directions in March. The Chief was punished by a prison sentence, but he took it philosophically; it was all part of the show.

For several weeks Chiang might as well have been Wang Ching-wei. He trod the middle path and earnestly scolded everybody who deviated from it. Then, abruptly, he came out again squarely pro-Right. Something must be done, he said, to curb the power of the Communists in the Kuomintang, and thereupon he called an emergency meeting of the Central Executive Committee and made a fiery speech. Henceforth, he said, the Reds must refrain from attacking Sun Yat-sen and his Three Principles. It was a safe enough suggestion as no Red would ever have admitted doing such a thing in any case: the Committee docilely accepted the command. Chiang continued with a resolution that no Communist should hold high office in the Kuomintang; this, too, was passed. But the Committee voted down his next suggestion, that all Communists should be expelled from the Kuomintang—the same resolution that Chiang himself had opposed when it came from the Western Hills Conference—though they agreed that relations between the parties must be revised, and that the Reds must supply a list of their members to the Kuomintang. Various other rules were formulated, all aimed at curtailing Communist powers. Throughout the meeting, Borodin listened and said never a word in disagreement. The two men had evidently promised each other to get along until the Northern Expedition should be successfully carried through.

In June, in preparation for the now imminent expedition, Chiang was named commander-in-chief of the Army. He was Chairman of the C.E.C. and of the Military Council as well. Every Communist who held too high a post in the Army was removed. Every Communist, even in civilian life, who seemed to be getting too big for his boots was shifted. One of those was Mao Tse-tung, head of the Propaganda Department. By the middle of June, Mao was looking for another job.

# 5 SUCCESS, AND A BREAK WITH MOSCOW
1926–27

Chiang was ready to begin marching as soon as the Canton air cleared. On July 9, '26, the C.E.C. gave him unlimited powers over the military. Careful plans had long been laid for the two-thousand-mile trek. Feng Yu-hsiang, sounded out by Borodin, seemed amenable to suggestion; he was to withdraw from the vicinity of Peking into the Northwest. The friendly war lords of Kweichow and Szechuan would stand by and protect the Nationalist Army on the southern side from an unfriendly general who was running Yunnan. Sun Chuan-fang of the five provinces of the lower Yangtze was willing to remain neutral—at least he said so, though later he changed his mind. The war lord of Hunan had finally promised to permit a quick passage through his domain and would join the Nationalists as soon as he was assured they would win, which guaranteed a swift take-off. Chiang's chief enemies were Old Marshal Chang—who would very probably be supported unofficially by Japan—and Wu Pei-fu, now hovering about in Central China.

Chiang had eight corps, each under a general to whom, in the old-fashioned way, the men owed their allegiance. As he had never collected a personal army for himself, this might have put him at a disadvantage, but the concentrated training given at the

Whampoa Academy had changed all that. Junior officers in all the corps were Whampoa men. The combined troops numbered fifty thousand, only half the size of Wu Pei-fu's army.

At Hengchow, in Hunan, Chiang met his men on August 10. There had not been the slightest opposition to their entry into the province, and when the main army moved on to Changsha, the capital, there was little resistance, though Wu's forces were supposed to hold the city. The propagandists had been hard at work in Hunan, and the Nationalists moved forward to cheers and shouted slogans from the populace.

Two subsidiary Nationalist armies made their own way, going in the general direction of the main branch; one through Kiangsi toward Nanking and the other through Fukien. All this activity was not a secret to the North, but Wu Pei-fu was slow getting started and his forward troops were a second-string lot. The Nationalists were well along by the time he got to Hankow, approaching Hankow's sister city, Wuchang, and they arrived in its environs at the beginning of September.

Here, for the first time, they encountered soldiers of good caliber and a garrison commander who refused to turn coat. Wuchang was a walled city and it held out against several attacks led by Chiang. Tired of losing men and gaining nothing, the Nationalists turned their attention instead to the third of the cities, Hanyang, whose garrison was willing to listen to reason. Hanyang was occupied on September 6, and Wu fled from Hankow, and the Nationalists moved in on the eighth. In another month Wuchang too had fallen.

Next item on the list was Kiangsi, where Sun Chuan-fang of the lower-Yangtze provinces had massed his troops against them after all. Chiang had good reason to feel cocky. So far, he was ahead of his timetable. The generals of the North, already quarrelsome among themselves, became less and less cohesive as their enemy approached. Now, however, as was inevitable, the initial

Nationalist push slowed down. At the Hunan-Kiangsi border there was a battle which neither side won. On September 19 the Nationalists, aided by sympathizers within, captured Chiang's goal, Kiangsi's capital city of Nanchang, but a couple of days later they were driven out again, and for two months thereafter the struggle stalled in the Nanchang area, with Chiang vainly trying to recapture the city. All his army was committed to this task, so he sent General Ho Ying-chin, commander-in-chief of the Eastern Route Army, to carry on in Fukien meanwhile. When, in November, Nanchang did fall, Sun Chuan-fang retreated to Nanking and enlisted under Chang Tso-lin's banner.

Fukien fell to the Nationalists early in December; Chekiang was to be next. The northern war lords belatedly realized that their personal troubles must be shelved while they dealt with the threat, and they redistributed their power in a new pattern in the common cause. But old habits die hard, and at least two northern generals had soon double-crossed their companions. While they wrangled, their cause went wrong in Chekiang.

During these maneuvers, the places already occupied by Chiang's army were living in uneasy imitation of normality, with temporary military governors in charge of a people who had been stirred by Communist-type propaganda to anticipation of a bright new world. The public were in volatile mood; a lot of excitement was floating around, and in January the bubble burst in Hankow. A mob of locals listened to a fiery speech against foreign imperialists, made, it is said, by some anonymous attaché of the conquering army, and then rushed to the British Concession and stormed it. The Concession was guarded by British marines, who were forewarned, being under standing orders not to fire. Protecting all foreigners as well as they could, they ushered their charges straight to the foreign ships riding at anchor in the Yangtze, while the Chinese mob, exultant, had its own way with British property and houses in the Concession. In older days the incident would have been followed by apologies from the Chinese authorities and some sort of restitution, but nothing of the sort now happened. The mob remained in the Concession and the British stayed away. This unorthodox arrangement was made official in the Chen-O'Malley agreement, when Eugene Chen, the Kuomintang Foreign Minister, signed a treaty with the British representative whereby the concessions of both Hankow and Kiukiang were returned to the Chinese as their rightful territory. Every Chinese, regardless of his politics, was wildly happy at this symptom of growing independence. Foreign imperialism was at last on the wane! (But Chiang Kai-shek, in the midst of triumph, looked thoughtfully toward Moscow.)

Meanwhile the Chekiang campaign, so important to Chikow's native son, was flourishing. Under the command of Pai Chung-hsi, the Moslem lord of Kwangsi, Hangchow was occupied by the southerners in February 1927, and soon the whole province was in their hands. Central China was practically theirs, and nearly half the long trek to Peking was over.

The northerners now hastened to occupy Nanking, but they did not stay there long. The Nationalists were on their way to nearby Shanghai, and entered it on March 22. Inhabitants of the foreign concessions were in wild alarm. Troops of European and American countries stood at the ready while their warships waited all along the Bund for the sack of the city. However, the soldiers didn't interfere with foreigners or their belongings. After a day or so the denizens of the Concession calmed down and began congratulating each other, and Chiang Kai-shek, for the control he maintained over his men.

But congratulations swiftly veered back again to panic at the news from Nanking, occupied by the Nationalists two days after they took Shanghai. Why what happened did happen is still a point of argument. Looting and lynching in the town began on the twenty-fourth, as soon as the Nationalists arrived: mobs attacked foreign buildings regardless of their nature—missions, consulates, and all—and handled the people roughly before the men aboard the British and American gunboats on the river realized what was going on. Then a bombardment from the boats quieted the male-factors, but not until six foreigners were dead, several of the women raped, and a number of people wounded.

Chiang was on his way downriver by boat from Kiukiang while this was happening. He didn't arrive until several days afterward, when all the foreigners had been evacuated to Shanghai. He was terribly angry. His office claimed that the mischief had been done by the fleeing northern troops, but the foreigners would not accept this explanation: among their excited voices were those of mis-sionaries who insisted they had recognized the Cantonese dialect. For a little while Chiang hesitated. He could come out publicly with a possible defense that Communists among his troops were re-sponsible for the incitement but that would mean a definite break with the Reds, and he had not expected to bring things to such a point quite yet. On the other hand the foreign governments were clamoring for satisfaction; Shanghai milled with terror and rage. He could hardly permit the accusation to be carried by default.

At last he apologized all round and sent word to the foreigners involved in the incident that he would investigate carefully, punish everyone who had taken part, and hold himself personally respon-sible thereafter for the safety of the whites. A rough inquiry promptly followed. Chiang continued being conciliatory to the na-tionals concerned, but other Kuomintang officials' reactions were not thus calculated to soothe ruffled feelings. Eugene Chen made wild claims: he declared that more than a hundred Chinese had been killed or wounded for every foreign casualty. Chiang brusquely denied these figures: seven Chinese lives had been lost in all, he said, and fifteen Chinese were wounded. He made a good impres-sion on the intermediaries who were managing the matter, and in Shanghai the strain relaxed. In Hankow things were different.

"He is rather clever," said a Russian just returned to Moscow from China, reporting on Chiang. "He understands pretty well political questions, not only of a local Chinese but of a world-wide nature. . . . He uses us and the Chinese Communists, but only as long as we assist him and are useful to him."

Since this one Russian, at least, understood Chiang as well as Chiang understood the Russians, it is all the more strange that the others should have underrated him so fantastically. He had resolved to get on with the Communists, come what might, until the Northern Expedition should be successfully concluded. He and Borodin had a gentlemen's agreement to maintain an armistice until then. But later events made it clear that the Reds had no intention of permitting him to come out winner in Peking. When the Wuhan cities were captured in October, while Chiang was with his troops in Nanchang, Borodin moved the government to Hankow and immediately called a meeting of the Central Executive Committee. They elected a new standing committee, voted Chiang out of office as Chairman and Generalissimo, and announced that Wang Ching-wei, who was still abroad, was to be his successor in the civil post. It is extraordinary that they should have expected Chiang to let this attack pass unchallenged. Stalin's plan, as Robert North says, was "brutally clear; to use the Wuhan government for building Communist strength and then to take it away from those to whom it belonged."

The Communists evidently thought that repeated public statements would reassure Chiang, even when they had already voted him out of his posts. Wang Ching-wei came back from Europe in April and published a joint declaration with a Communist leader contradicting rumors that the Reds intended to overthrow the Kuomintang and opposite rumors that the Kuomintang intended to make war on the C.C.P. In Moscow, Stalin replied to criticisms and demand for immediate action from the Comintern Executive Committee with reassuring words:

"Why drive away the Right when we have the majority and when the Right listens to us? The peasant needs an old worn-out jade as long as she is necessary. He does not drive her away. So it is with us. When the Right is of no more use to us, we will drive it away. At present we need the Right. It has capable people who will direct the Army and lead it against the imperialists. Chiang Kai-shek has perhaps no sympathy for the revolution, but he is leading the Army and cannot do otherwise than lead it against the imperialists. Besides this, the people of the Right have relations with the generals of Chang Tso-lin and understand very well how to demoralize them and to induce them to pass over to the side of the revolution, bag and baggage, without striking a blow. Also, they have connections with the rich merchants and can raise money from them. So they have to be utilized to the end, squeezed out like a lemon, and then thrown away."

Naturally, Chiang decided to jump the gun. He went to Shanghai on the pretense of tracking down rioters escaped from Nanking after the looting incident, and there he had an interview with Chang Ching-kiang and the leading businessmen of the town. The Shanghai men agreed to back him in his coming action and to give him, immediately, three million Shanghai dollars to make up for the Russian support which would be sacrificed.

Some Communists must certainly have expected the blow, yet the Comintern continued to order inaction. "The bulk of their weapons lay carefully buried. On March 26 Chiang arrived aboard a gunboat unannounced and walked ashore without opposition from anyone." (North, *Moscow and Chinese Communists,* p. 95.) Two more weeks elapsed, and still the Reds did nothing. Then on April 12 Chiang acted.

— In the subsequent outcry, Communist sympathizers claimed that Chiang's attitude and behavior were those of a wicked bully. Their writing is full of clichés—"running dog of Western imperialism," and so on—and from those days there is left in most

American minds a residue, a conviction that he didn't behave nicely. Even non-Communists feel that Chiang used honest companions in his campaign, climbing on them as on a ladder, and then, as soon as he saw his chance and felt himself strong enough, kicked the ladder down and away. Without going into the fundamental question of the rights and wrongs of military force, it seems pretty difficult to figure out what else he could have done with the Reds. Quite simply, they wanted to get rid of him and take control of China. To talk of his "betrayal" seems a strange sort of logic.

Still, his diary shows that he didn't arrive at his decision without a good deal of soul-searching and sleeplessness, for it was no light matter to reverse the trend set by Sun Yat-sen. Already he was at outs with his revered Master's widow, and with a good many of his old companions who were either in the Red conspiracy up to their necks or hopeful that unity might yet be preserved. Most troubling was the personal question of his son, young Ching-kuo, now in Russia as a student. What would happen to Ching-kuo?

On the "white massacre" that began April 12 Communists are eloquent. Chiang did not wait to be betrayed; he committed the unforgivable sin; he outguessed Stalin and struck first. "Chiang's long-sword detachments marched through the streets, executing workers on the spot; some of the strikers in the Railway Department were thrown into the furnaces of the locomotives. Communist Party, Trades Union movement, all workers' organisations, were smashed to pieces and driven into illegality. The Chinese counter-revolution, backed by imperialism, reigned triumphant in Shanghai. . . ." (James, *World Revolution*.)

It is a fair description of what happened. Chiang did not use many soldiers for the coup: to be effective the stroke had to be administered in a lot of places at once, and he was reluctant to draw troops from the expeditionary front line. Instead he employed the strong-arm men of two of those secret societies that have flourished in China for centuries. Much capital has been made of the fact that he had connection with secret societies. Westerners have been told over and over that it proves what a sinister figure he really is, whose friends are gangsters and gang leaders. But though secret societies and gangs are not socially acceptable in New York or London, in China they are a part of ordinary life. Had he not been intimately acquainted with such characters, especially after his years in the Army, Chiang Kai-shek would have been a freak.

The killings were only a part of the action: the trade unions were closed, and all units organized by the Reds among peasants and workers were disbanded. But the executions were the most horrible and sensational of the proceedings. Thousands of people died, not only in the first flush of the attack but for days thereafter. Trials were summary, where there were trials at all. As in other upheavals in Chinese history, beheadings often took place on the spot of apprehension, in the street or the house. On the whole, however, the character of the action was not markedly Chinese; a new influence was apparent. "Oddly enough," writes Mr. Berkov, perhaps not as ingenuous as he sounds, "the purge was organized on principles similar to the early institutions of the Soviet Union."

The ruthlessness of the coup is undeniable: the "treachery" depends on your point of view.

Sharply criticized by Moscow for Moscow's own stupidity, the Hankow government was unhappy. And now the Generalissimo added to their troubles by sending them directions which they keenly resented. All Communist propaganda must cease forthwith; Nationalist soldiers must thenceforth be controlled only by their regular officers; political agents traveling with the Army were to be stripped of all authority. Indignantly, Hankow rejected the demands and once more voted Chiang out, this time out of everything—command, government posts, and the Kuomintang. A large reward was offered for "the counterrevolutionary," dead or alive.

Chiang ignored all this and set up in Nanking the rival government he had promised to his banker friends. Once again the West scratched its head and sighed over these confusing Chinese. People had barely got used to having two capitals in the country, north and south, and here was a third one. The situation was a worry, too, for the foreign businessmen in the treaty ports. Who were they to deal with? Who was boss? They hoped fervently that Hankow would not win out.

Waiting in Honan, Feng Yu-hsiang grew increasingly thoughtful as the expedition fought and marched toward his domain. He knew he must soon make a decision. North or south? And, if south—which seemed the obvious choice, because they were winning—Hankow or Nanking? A difficult question, even for so supple a general. Both governments were now carrying on with the expedition, in separate movements, and it was the Hankow army that pushed into Honan. Feng finally moved against Chang Tso-lin, and he made gains, but for which government he fought he himself didn't know.

Six or seven weeks passed: the Nationalist Army still had two heads. The Wuhan government was in the throes of internal disagreement. A new Communist had recently arrived from Moscow, the Indian M. N. Roy, and he disagreed with Borodin on questions of strategy. Borodin and the Kuomintang leftists of the government wanted the Army to continue toward Peking, and also against Nanking: Borodin felt they could not rely too much on their position in Wuhan. Roy said they should drop the expedition for the time being and concentrate on strengthening themselves by capturing the South, Kiangsi and Kwantung; consolidating their position there. Later they could cut off the Nanking forces by marching in from the south to Shanghai.

To resolve the dispute, Roy referred it to the Comintern in Moscow, but when he got the reply everyone was worse off than ever, Moscow simply saying to go ahead with both plans at once. It could not be done. The potential split between what the Kuomintang wanted and what the Communists wanted was beginning to show up. Of course the Kuomintang leaders, being landowners for the most part, didn't want to see the agrarian revolution put into action; it would mean losing their land. But the peasants were beginning to demand it: they had been organized to this end, and it was getting difficult to hold them back. There was the notorious Autumn Crop Uprising at Changsha, when twenty thousand peasants marched on the city and would have attacked it, without doubt successfully—there were only seventeen hundred Kuomintang soldiers there—if orders had not come from the C.C.P. leader in Hunan to wait for directions from the C.E.C. at Wuhan. The C.E.C. decided against the attack: they were afraid of upsetting wealthy Kuomintang members. So the peasants had to turn around and go home, and many were killed by the Nanking soldiers who occupied the city. It was a grievance that has never been forgotten or forgiven by people who later rebelled against Stalin and his works.

In Moscow, Stalin argued stubbornly that things had not yet reached the point where the Communist Party could defy the Kuomintang. The agrarian movement must be curbed, he said. To fight with the Kuomintang meant certain defeat. But other members of the Executive Committee said that the agrarian revolt could no longer be curbed, the peasants were already seizing the land. They insisted that if a break were to take place, most of the people would go to the Communist side.

Stalin finally gave in and sent a telegram to Roy and Borodin with the famous directive. The agrarian revolution was to be allowed to go forward; those old leaders of the Kuomintang C.E.C., who were "vacillating and compromising," must be discarded or stiffened by the recruitment of new peasant and working-class leaders. Unreliable generals must be liquidated. Twenty thousand

Communists, and fifty thousand revolutionary workers and peasants should be mobilized. A revolutionary tribunal was to be set
up to punish officers who maintained contact with Chiang Kai-shek.
Possessions of Kuomintang officers and men should be spared in
the general sharing.

Either Stalin expected all this reorganization to be done under
cover or he was singularly lacking in imagination as to the reactions
of the non-Communist Chinese. Borodin was not stupid; he said
nothing about the telegram to the Chinese. But the Indian, Roy,
thought it would be safe to confide in Wang Ching-wei. Wang had
been in Moscow, stopping there on his way from France, and it
was Roy's impression, as the Indian later said, that he had already
discussed the agrarian reforms and agreed to them, in return for
the assurance that he would be leader of the reorganized nation.
Perhaps the Comintern-disciplined Roy simply thought that the
telegram was as good as a *fait accompli,* and that Wang would
never dare fight against Fate.

But Wang was shocked and scandalized by the message, and
promptly said it was no use, that the Kuomintang would not hear of
such action. Sun Fo was on his side, and agreed that the Reds
must be got rid of. Eugene Chen, though at first he professed as
much horror as Wang had done, objected to making a break with
Moscow, and Madame Sun was of his mind. They could not do
without Russian help, said Chen and Chingling; they could not
resist Chiang without it.

Having stirred up the wasp's nest, Roy wanted to go on and carry
out Stalin's orders to the best of his ability. But Borodin and the
others had been frightened by the Kuomintang stand, and they
backed water and said the directive should be washed out. It was no
use; already the Kuomintang was thoroughly up in arms. Roy quarreled with Borodin, and was the first to leave. Borodin soon followed, sent packing to Russia by the Kuomintang Madame Sun

and Eugene Chen also left Hankow, voluntarily and in a hurry, in case they too might be asked to go.

Chingling went to Shanghai for a little, while she thought it over; then she too moved on to Moscow. On leaving, she declared that this was what her husband would have wished. In any case, she said, she was not safe in China. Her decision was hastened by the news that Mayling had finally decided to marry Chiang Kai-shek. It was very depressing. Sun was being forgotten, superseded, outshone. Where did that leave Sun's widow?

And her *younger* sister, too!

# 6 MARRIAGE 1927

Chiang's blow at the C.C.P. had repercussions in the North,
land of its birth. Chang Tso-lin didn't love either the Reds
or the Kuomintang; in fact, he classed them together. Soon after
the Shanghai uproar, his police, alerted to dig out sympathizers of
both bodies in Peking, reported that they found thousands of
Kuomintang members and at least a thousand Communists in the
universities. The Old Marshal pounced. Arrests were made; twenty
Communists, including Li Ta-chao, were hanged; and Li duly became a sainted martyr in the hearts of people who would certainly
have pilloried him, ultimately, if he had survived.

In Hunan his former assistant, Mao Tse-tung, was organizing
peasants and coming to the conclusions that would one day save
the Chinese Party. He had just published an article holding the
seeds of his new idea, "Report on an Investigation of the Agrarian
Movement in Hunan," a departure from the accepted revolutionary
formula. Marx laid it down as a fundamental rule that the urban
workers, or "proletariat," of a country should be the dynamic force.
His theory was based on his own experience of highly industrialized
European countries; he had never envisaged the predominantly
agricultural civilization of China. But Mao, who knew nothing else,
believed that the revolutionary strength of China must depend
primarily on her peasants.

His writing rose to poetic heights. "The force of the peasantry is like that of the raging winds and driving rain. It is rapidly increasing in violence. No force can stand in its way. The peasantry will tear apart all nets which bind it and hasten along the road to liberalism. They will bury beneath them all forces of imperialism, militarism, corrupt officialdom, village bosses and evil gentry. . . . The democratic forces in the village have arisen to overthrow the feudal forces in the village. The overthrow of feudal forces is, after all, the aim of the national revolution."

A few weeks later the C.C.P. was plunged into chaos by Chiang's attack. There was no time to argue the point of strategy with Mao's masters, but he did have a stormy encounter before he got permission to continue organizing in Hunan. The abortive Autumn Crop Uprising was the result, and Mao was left with the sore conviction that he could have proved the worth of his peasants amply if only the effort hadn't been sabotaged by Hankow. He himself was taken prisoner, but managed to make his escape from the soldiery, and was severely rebuked by the C.E.C. for his pains.

Other survivors of the purge, pro-Communist generals, broke away with their troops and made a successful attempt to capture, and an unsuccessful effort to hold, Nanchang. After being driven from the city they dispersed in Kiangsi, but later they found each other again and formed the first guerrilla bands that operated in the Red region. Some forces under Tang Sheng-chih advanced straight toward Nanking. As far as they were concerned, the drive for Peking could wait. They were the Eastern Expedition, intent on defeating Chiang.

The way should now have been clear for the reconciliation of Nanking and the Hankow Kuomintang rump Parliament, but there was too much bitterness floating about to be forgotten so easily. Chiang returned to the expeditionary front, and in his absence from Hankow enemies worked busily against him. Military reverses gave them fresh cause to complain. The Nationalists, continuing to make good time, marched into Shantung. Peking was not far away, and Chang Tso-lin was beginning to think seriously of suggesting a compromise and making peace when two new troubles halted the Army. One was the defection of Feng Yu-hsiang, who was based on Chenchow: the unreliable Christian general welshed on his earlier promise to create a diversion by attacking Chang Tso-lin. The other setback was unexpected.

There were Japanese troops stationed at Tsingtao, near Tsinan, who had been moved in there when Japan took over the former German territory of China. As Chiang approached Tsinan a large number of these soldiers were suddenly sent to garrison the capital. Apparently Japan didn't want to see China united.

Chiang could not possibly afford to embroil himself in another war at this juncture, and he realized that the Japanese were more than willing to force the issue. He had no choice; he had to submit to the loss of face entailed by his action and withdraw to Hsuchow.

Upon this, Feng Yu-hsiang, of all people, approached him in the unfitting role of peace dove and suggested that Chiang meet the Wuhan group and talk things over. By this time nobody was quite sure whom to fight or what to fight about, but Feng could not drum up any eagerness on the part of the disputants to make friends. Wuhan wanted Chiang out, that was the heart of the matter, and at last they had their way.

Chiang would have continued to hang on politically, but another military push from the north dislodged him from Hsuchow and he had to fall back to the Yangtze, almost as far as Nanking itself. This was no light affair, and his stock hit rock bottom. Now, even his hitherto loyal generals, Li Tsung-jen, Pai Chung-hsi, and Li Chen-sen, were in favor of easing him out. On August 12 the Military Council held a meeting in Nanking which Chiang attended. Somebody opened proceedings by stating that it was all-important to reunite the Nationalists. This being agreed, somebody else

pointed out that unity could not be achieved as long as Chiang
Kai-shek was commander-in-chief. This too was agreed, and when
it was suggested that Chiang voluntarily submit to demotion, he
promptly resigned altogether. He turned and walked out of the
meeting, and the Military Council immediately appointed a Cantonese general in his place.

Afterward there was outcry enough to bring considerable comfort to his angry heart. Hardly had he left for Shanghai for the inevitable consultation with Chang Ching-kiang than Hu Han-min,
too, resigned, as did a majority of the Nanking Kuomintang officials,
with Chang Ching-kiang himself included. There were indignant
mass meetings and telegrams of protest. Chiang announced his
resignation and made a declaration on the subject in the press the
day after the meeting: the declaration was long, like all his utter-
ances, but pithy nonetheless.

"For several years I have been credited with advocating the
policy of seeking Russia's friendship and co-operating with the
Communists. When I returned from a tour of inspection through
Russia, I had very clear-cut views as to the essential differences
between the two policies. This was known to both Liao Chung-kai
and Wang Ching-wei.

"I was unable to convert the learned Doctor [Sun Yat-sen] to my
views, but I learned his. He said, 'China has no room for the co-
existence of Communism and the Kuomintang. We must admit the
Communists and convert them, and the Three People's Principles
will serve as a melting pot.'

"This is more than enough to indicate that in admitting the Communists into the Kuomintang's fold, Dr. Sun had no intention of
doing so at the expense of the Party."

Chiang always goes back to the mountains, preferably his own
mountains, when he wants to get away from everything, and this
time was no exception. There was a difference, however, between
this return to Fenghua and the last one, when he had spent his time

alternately mourning for his mother and popping out to extricate Sun Yat-sen from difficulties. Then he had been a bright young hopeful, one general among many. Now he came as a leader—a leader resigned if not deposed, but nevertheless a strong man with a past and a future. He brought his two hundred-strong bodyguard with him, and though he took up quarters in a Buddhist monastery on a high mountain he did not, after all, get away from everything, or indeed from anything at all. The world followed him. Friends, advisers, reporters, telegrams . . .

Speaking of telegrams, five pro-Chiang men took the greatest pleasure in sending an elaborate one to the elusive Feng Yu-hsiang, now himself eluded and left with the bottom dropped out of his proposed press conference.

"To Commander-in-Chief Feng, Chengchow:

"When we received your telegram dated August 11, asking us to meet in Anking, we agreed gladly. When we sent you the reply on the evening of the twelfth, our elder brother Kai-shek was getting into his train for Shanghai. We showed him the draft of the reply and he smiled and signed his name at once. Who would have thought that the news of our elder brother Kai-shek's resignation would be announced on the morning of the thirteenth? We went to Shanghai to get him back; but when we reached there, he had gone to Ningpo. In the spring of last year Li Shih-tsang and Wu Chih-hui went to the North to get you back and you had left for Mongolia. They missed you only by a few hours. The sun moves exactly as fast as it always does. In a moment it has disappeared. We are unhappy now, exactly as we were last year. . . ."

"The Chinese people turned from the conservative friendship of America and accepted offers from Russia," said Chiang Kai-shek, in an interview with some gentlemen of the press who climbed up the mountain to see him ensconced in his temple. "There were reasons, of course, which you all know. But Russia has now betrayed us, and we must look to America as our only real friend among the nations."

It must have reminded the journalists of Sun Yat-sen's statement in Canton not many years before.

Chiang stayed in his mountain eyrie only a month; late in September he went to Japan. He had various vague plans to call on old acquaintances in Tokyo and refresh his contacts, but they were secondary; a more important errand filled his mind. The Soongs too were in Japan, and Mayling was reputed to have said for publication, in a version the accuracy of which this writer takes liberty to doubt, "I sincerely love the great general."

Her mother must now be persuaded and placated. For a long time Mrs. Soong had opposed the idea of this match. Chiang had corresponded with Mayling five years. The fact that Chingling had never liked him did not matter very much, for Eling Kung, the eldest of Charles Soong's children, was on his side, and her word counted most with her mother. No one was crass enough to admit it, but the result of the interview was practically settled in advance; otherwise Chiang would never have been exposed to the ordeal of asking for his lady's hand. He would not have got to see Mrs. Soong at all.

As it was, he had some difficulty in cornering her. The Soongs had taken a house in Kobe, but when Mrs. Soong heard that General Chiang was on his way, she fled. With Eling Kung and Mayling she went all the way to Kamakura on the other side of the island. There at last Eling persuaded her to receive him and let him state his case.

It was not mere mother-in-law skittishness that sent her on this impetuous journey; Mrs. Soong was not a skittish person. She was simply afraid of not liking Chiang after all. Mrs. Soong, for all her modern ideas and her Christianity, was no longer young. In her day people hadn't approved of the soldierly caste. There was also the fact that Chiang was older than Mayling by a dozen years. There was his boyhood marriage. What had he done about that? There was—perhaps—his reputation as a womanizer, but it is doubtful if Mrs. Soong listened to such gossip. Her gravest doubts had to do with his religion.

When the General succeeded in getting his interview, they discussed two of these matters. The others it was no use discussing. After all, if he was a soldier, that was that; times had changed. The same could be said of the discrepancy in age; it was not so very important. But what of the earlier marriage and his state of grace?

Forewarned, Chiang had brought with him a paper proving that his first wife and he were as divorced as they could possibly be according to Chinese custom. Chinese divorces are beautifully easy to get. A printed announcement in a newspaper that the couple agree to call it off will serve, but he had provided himself with a legal document in order that the Soongs could make quite sure.

There now remained one thing—the matter of religion. Mrs. Soong said that she understood Chiang was not a Christian; was he willing to become one? At that point the aspiring son-in-law won her heart. Instead of protesting hastily that of course he would be a Christian, or anything else that pleased her, he replied slowly that he would look into the matter. He would read the Bible and see what there was in it. He was perfectly willing to have a try.

Chiang's mother had been a very pious Buddhist, but she herself would probably have made a similar reply, for Chinese of the old school were completely free from religious intolerance. This cheerful catholicity has often been the bane of earnest missionaries from the West, who cannot see eye to eye with a convert who reconciles Confucianism and Christianity without the slightest difficulty, nor sees why he must give up one merely because he accepts the other. After all, Confucianism is not so much a religion as a code of ethics, and Buddhism and Christianity are not incompatible.

Mrs. Soong was impressed by the General's honesty. She gave her consent with more warmth than she had intended to do, and the engagement was official. Chiang announced it as soon as he stepped off the boat at Shanghai in November.

There were other matters involving him—the Northern Expedition was not going well, and things were getting messed up in Canton and Nanking—but the newspapermen who crowded around the General at the pier were more interested for the moment in his private life. At least some of them were surprised by the news, for though Chiang's long courtship of Miss Soong was well known among his intimates, foreigners had not been informed. Journalists acquainted with the gossip of Canton had heard other stories, however; they knew of the pretty singsong girl who had until recently called herself Chiang's wife; they were titillated by the current tale that the General had given her a magnificent farewell dinner and then shipped her off to the States for a nice long trip.

Another point was the matter of Chiang's genuine wife, the mother of his child. They asked him about her outright, for American newspapermen, as Chiang already knew, are strange creatures with no courtesy. You wouldn't find a Chinese so unmannerly. Still, he replied politely. He and his wife, he said, had long been divorced. As for the other lady, she too was now detached. . . . Foreigners didn't understand Chinese customs, he added. And though there was ribald comment among the boys on this remark, I am bound to say that in my opinion Chiang was in the right of it. In 1927 he wasn't even pretending to live up to an alien moral code.

"I am at present married to no one," he said firmly, "and am free to marry in accordance with the most monogamist practices. Miss Soong would not consent to marriage under any other circumstances and I should not dare to ask a lady of her character to marry me in any other circumstances."

One story is that the bride wanted to be married in the Allen Memorial Church, but that the pastor, an old friend of the family, refused to marry the couple because he was not satisfied about

Chiang's divorce. This hardly seems likely. Had the General's first marriage been a Christian one there might be some point in demanding a foreign-style divorce, but what has not been tied, as it were, cannot be untied: surely the reverend gentleman was not so unreasonable. Instead, a new sort of marriage was worked out, not so much a compromise between foreign and Chinese ceremonies as a combination of the two. On the first of December, 1927, Miss Soong and General Chiang were married in a private religious ceremony in the Soong house in Seymour Road, Dr. David Yui (general secretary of the Y.M.C.A.) officiating. Afterward they moved on to the public part of the double event, a Chinese-style wedding in the ballroom of the Majestic Hotel in Bubbling Well Road.

This was the show occasion, to which thirteen hundred guests had been invited. Another thousand people crowded the streets outside, craning their necks for a glimpse of the proceedings. The bride was given away by her brother T.V.; the best man was Chiang's chief secretary, Liu Chi-wen. Except for a few foreign trimmings—the playing of "Here Comes the Bride" by the orchestra, and so on—the wedding was like all Chinese weddings, a civil ceremony consisting for the most part of bows. Tsai Yuan-pei, Minister of Education, presided. Bride and groom bowed three times to Sun Yat-sen's portrait, which hung over the platform in the center of the room, draped with national and Kuomintang flags. The marriage certificate was read aloud and then sealed. Bride and bridegroom bowed to each other once, once to the official witnesses, and once to the guests. A lavish tea party followed.

They made an attractive couple: both were good-looking people. Kai-shek has regular, refined features and the posture of a soldier, and though he may have been ill at ease in the unfamiliar trappings of tail coat and stiff collar, he showed no sign of discomfort. Mayling, too, had eschewed the national bridal costume, which is always red or pink, in favor of conventional foreign-style white satin, lace, and an immense bouquet. After the wedding party they went on their honeymoon to Chiang's beloved Chekiang—Hangchow and Mokanshan.

No wedding of such political interest in China would have been complete without a published statement from the groom, and Chiang did not disappoint his public. However, he said nothing particularly definite. He expressed the proper emotions about his and his bride's determination to further the people's welfare and work for the cause of the revolution, but there was no specific reference to plans for the future. One would almost have thought he had none in mind, but that did not matter: as the world already knew, the Kuomintang had plenty of plans for him. The most determined of his enemies in the Party admitted that Nationalist affairs had not gone well since his resignation.

On the expeditionary front the retreat for which he had been blamed by his generals continued at the same pace without him, until the foremost part of the Army found itself in Pukow. At this critical point, however, two other portions, or "armies"—each general had his own in the amalgamation—headed by Ho Ying-chin and Li Tsung-jen, diverted the attention of the northerners, gave them stiff battle, and drove them well back. That particular danger to Nanking was hardly over when in Hankow the leftist General Tang Sheng-chih, whose Eastern Expedition against the city had been one of the chief reasons Chiang was forced to resign, gave trouble of a different sort. He quarreled with another general on his own side. Nanking backed the other man and Tang had to give up and run for his life while the Nanking forces occupied Hankow. But Tang Sheng-chih, when he wasn't making war on his own superiors, had been an able and valuable general, and his loss was felt. All this may not make sense from our point of view, but it is the way things went in China during the war-lord era. In political life around the Yangtze, few men felt they could afford to cherish grudges or attach themselves too fondly to consistency.

Without Chiang's insistence on the final aim—his pigheadedness, as many of his colleagues considered it—the entire project of the revolution began to come unstuck. While he drank tea with the Soongs in Kamakura the situation at home became acutely dangerous. The remnants of the Communist army that had been dispersed in Kiangsi pulled themselves together and marched on Canton. They occupied a couple of towns and fought the Kuomintang troops sporadically. While Chiang and his wife enjoyed the magnificent scenery at Mokanshan, hitherto dormant war lords of the South woke up and saw their chance to raise a little hell in the good old way and joyfully seized it. Deterioration of the expedition not only set in, it galloped along. One hesitates to talk too glibly about "the people" and their opinions because most of "the people" didn't yet know enough about the situation to have opinions, but those who did know began to ask for a strong leader again. Under Chiang's command, things had not reached this pitch of disorder. Why was he out?

The Central Executive Committee itself began to ask questions, to which it was all too easy to find the answers. They already knew why Chiang was out: they knew he was in Shanghai, living as a private individual. They knew what they had to do. It was time, again, for them to forget old grudges, but was Chiang willing to be equally forgetful? Wang Ching-wei went to Shanghai to find out and had several interviews with his old friend and enemy. The errand must have been deeply distasteful, but it had been proved that he himself was not big enough for the job. It was settled that Chiang would return, given certain agreements as to future procedure in the C.E.C. General meetings were held, Wang Ching-wei duly resigned from his post as Chairman, and Chiang resumed the office. A few weeks later Wang sailed for France.

Chiang promptly announced that diplomatic relations between China and Russia no longer existed. Soviet consulates were closed down and all Russians who still remained in China were expelled. In Canton, where there was a large concentration of Communists

who had gone there from Hankow and Hunan, the news stimulated
the people to rise up and create a riot, now known to the C.C.P. as
"the Canton Commune." For four days, from eleventh to the
fourteenth, the troubled and troublesome city was given over to
arson and terror, until Nationalist troops arrived and put down the
Commune, with all the customary bloody accompaniments of a
purge, including public executions.

The end of the sans-Chiang interim was marked by a telegram
sent to the General on January 2, 1928, formally requesting him to
return to Nanking and resume both his offices, that of Chairman
of the C.E.C. and commander-in-chief of the Northern Punitive
Expedition. On January 4 the reinstated Generalissimo answered
the call. Twice on the journey up there were frustrated attempts to
wreck his train, but his welcome to Nanking was an ovation.

One of the things that Chiang and Wang had agreed on was a
meeting of the Central Executive and Supervisory Committee of the
Kuomintang during the Fourth Plenary Session, which was to be
held as soon as possible after his reinstatement. This conference
now took place, and an important detail, hitherto neglected, was
attended to. Though the Communists had been first resisted and
then purged, many of them were still official members of the
Kuomintang. Now all the acknowledged Reds were expelled, and
Chiang turned to the matter of the expedition.

Until August of the same year, 1928, he was to have dictatorial
powers, it being presumed that the expedition would have achieved
its goal by that time. Among other statements of his intentions, the
Generalissimo announced that as soon as it was over he hoped to
call a National People's Convention. He recapitulated the program
as Sun Yat-sen had outlined it—the stage of military supervision,
the stage of political tutelage, and the final, long-awaited stage of
constitutional government.

The meeting closed on February 7. Two days later Chiang went up to inspect his army at its most advanced point, which at the moment was Hsuchow. The Generalissimo reorganized his command, naming himself leader of the First Army Group. Immediately under him were General Feng Yu-hsiang heading the Second Army (Yes, Feng. I repeat, the Chinese system is adaptable.), Yen Hsi-shan, able and popular war lord of Shansi, as head of the Third, and Li Tsung-jen commanding the Fourth, to be held in reserve.

In March, Chiang returned to Shanghai to inspect the Lunghua garrison and gave them a sharp warning to behave themselves and maintain good terms with the foreigners beyond the concession border. "The environment of Shanghai is so bad," he said, "that almost any army stationed here for three months, or at most for half a year, becomes demoralized and practically useless." Then he went back to Nanking and arrested a few more men accused of having contributed to the 1927 disorder. Finally, he sent a message to the powers that during the approaching campaign there would be no repetition of that outrage; foreign residents, who had been growing apprehensive at his preparations, were glad to hear it. In return the Generalissimo requested the foreign authorities to prevent their nationals selling arms to his northern enemies, or otherwise aiding them. The question of armaments was an old grievance, and we cannot claim truthfully that Chiang's polite request got any more attention this time than similar ones had on other occasions.

Yet another Western importation occupied some of Chiang's busy moments. He had not forgotten his promise to Mrs. Soong in Kamakura. Under his wife's eager surveillance he took time out every day to read the Bible. Apparently Madame was a little too eager for him. One day she telegraphed from Nanking to the Reverend Kiang in Shanghai, another old family friend in the Church, asking him to come up immediately. When he arrived she explained that she thought her husband was just about ready to become a Christian; she wanted the pastor to talk to him about it and, if possible, baptize him then and there. Chiang, however, would not be free until that afternoon at four—"and even then there were so many distractions that Madame suggested we might go out for a ride as we talked." This was done; a solemn little cavalcade of three cars set out, with bodyguards riding ahead and more bodyguards behind. Kiang sat between the Chiangs, and they talked about Christianity. Madame urged her husband to be baptized, reminding him that the pastor was soon going to America for a journey of some months. The Generalissimo, however, would not be rushed into anything ahead of himself.

"I have just finished reading the New Testament for the second time," he said, "and am now going to begin to read the Old Testament. I want to learn more about this Christian faith before I publicly accept Jesus Christ as my Savior."

# 7 JAPAN MOVES IN 1927–32

The Northern Punitive Expedition started its second phase on April 7, 1928. The new plan of attack called for three main prongs of the Nationalist Army, approaching from different directions. Feng Yu-hsiang led his troops from Honan, where he was based: Yen Hsi-shan closed in from his province of Shansi, while Chiang brought the main army along the Tientsin-Pukow Railway. Within little more than a week Chiang's command was again in Shantung, and another ten days brought them to Tsinan, the turning point of his earlier attempt. Here the Generalissimo expected to run into more trouble, and he was not disappointed.

Tsinan was full of alert Japanese troops. Chiang ordered his men not to even attempt to enter the city, but to by-pass it along the railroad. The Japanese, however, were straddling the railway and had no intention of permitting a detour. According to one of the stories, a Nationalist officer ignored the orders, or didn't get them, and deliberately tried to get into the city. In any case the result could scarcely have been avoided because the Japanese were definitely looking for a fight. Suddenly it flared up. There was firing from heavy Jap artillery. During the next few days the Chinese of the city suffered: seventeen civilians were tortured and murdered by Japanese.

Chiang was facing a problem that was to haunt his life for years. Was a struggle with outside forces of more immediate importance than the taming of dissidents within the nation? He decided it was not. There could be no question at that moment of taking on Japan. He was not ready: it simply could not be done. While the troops waited, stranded in the road to Peking, the higher-ups of both sides talked and haggled.

Already the Old Marshal had sent a circular telegram offering to withdraw into Manchuria. This setback for the Nationalists persuaded him to reconsider, but as the other two armies drew closer and closer he was bound to think yet again and then retreat. He soon did so, all the faster because the Japanese abruptly changed their tactics and advised him to go. His alliance with them was showing signs of strain. A fretful point at issue had to do with the two north-of-the-Wall railways, Chinese Eastern and South Manchurian. That these roads, though running across Chinese territory, were controlled by Russia and Japan had long irritated Chang Tso-lin. He had lately set in motion a conspiracy to shake loose all foreign control of the railways, and the Japanese were aware of the plot.

Yet, though the Old Marshal was retreating and Peking would soon be free of his men, Chiang Kai-shek's army was still kept stranded at Tsinan. Finally Chiang accepted the fact that his could not be the personal glory of entering Peking at the head of the expedition. He wasn't a glutton for personal glory anyway. He named Yen Hsi-shan as his deputy. Yen accordingly made ready for the last triumphant sprint when exciting news arrived: Chang Tso-lin had been assassinated.

The Old Marshal was beating his retreat on a branch line of the South Manchurian Railway: his train, passing under a bridge near Mukden, was blown up by a mine, and he died almost immediately. It couldn't be proved that the Japanese were responsible, but among the Old Marshal's friends there has never been any doubt on the question. Not long afterward Chang Tso-lin's son Chang Hsueh-liang, the Young Marshal, caused the chief suspect to be killed.

The Young Marshal stepped into his father's shoes with a rapidity that astonished the Japanese and postponed their plans. His sudden accession to power was of great importance to Chiang Kai-shek. It seemed to this youth (he was not yet thirty) that China ought to be united, and he had no objections to Chiang as the leader of the nation. In fact his admiration of the Generalissimo was high. Within the month after Chang Tso-lin's death the Young Marshal declared his intention of withdrawing his army to Manchuria, following his father's program, and he urged the other, minor, Manchurian war lords to do likewise. His zone of influence henceforth, he said, would be limited to Manchuria and Jehol.

For the Nationalists it was now merely a matter of getting there as fast as they—or at least some of them—could march. On July 5, 1928, Yen Hsi-shan entered the northern capital with his men. Chiang Kai-shek came afterward, alone: he had left his stranded troops, doubled on his tracks, and come in by way of Yen's trail.

The timetable had served; the expedition was over before the first of August, as he had said it would be. Now, according to the agreement, he tendered his resignation. With due regard for decorum the Party refused to accept it. Instead the Generalissimo was "commanded" to visit the tomb of Sun Yat-sen in the Western Hills, in company with his generals, and render an account of his accomplishments to the dead Master. It was a simple, impressive ceremony. Chiang wept as he stood before the shrine.

Peking was a symbol of the Manchu past, and the revolutionaries hated it for that reason. Besides, the position was not central; it was suitable only for a government of North China. They decided that the national capital should be moved to Nanking. Nanking too had an ancient history as a Chinese capital, more ancient, actually, than Peking's, but there was a good deal of opposition to the change. The scholars didn't want it, the northerners didn't want it, and members of the foreign legations howled miserably. They loved the northern city with its shops and restaurants and traditions, and they pointed out that Nanking couldn't compare with Peking in beauty. But the beauty that appeals to Europeans is not always to Chinese taste. The Nationalists assured themselves that they would build a better capital in Nanking than had ever been seen before. Western persistence in looking upon them as charming fossils irritated the modern-minded. They changed the name of Peking to Peiping, "Northern Peace." (However, to simplify things through the ensuing seesaw of events I shall continue to call it Peking.)

There were other pressing problems. First of all came demobilization of the very costly armies, which the Kuomintang couldn't seem to get under way. Other governments have run into difficulties on that score, but Chiang's troubles were peculiar to China. His was no simple homogeneous collection of men, drafted from their homes to serve in the fighting and happy to be released: it was a combination of professional armies, made up of men who had never been anything but soldiers and had no desire to assume the responsibilities of civilian life. Even if one disregarded their preferences— and in those days one usually did—their leaders had to be taken into account. Like the mercenaries they commanded, the generals intended to carry on as generals. It was all the career they knew. More than two million men were on the military pay roll in June 1928. T. V. Soong, the Minister of Finance, believed in keeping the books straight, and he protested that this expense was wildly disproportionate. Obediently the Committee passed resolutions and made sensible plans: the standing army, they said, must certainly be cut to 715,000. But when it came to deciding whose men should be disbanded the Committee ran into trouble, and there they stayed for months to come.

Then there was another vexing question, that of the mechanics of government. In the first days of peace Chiang Kai-shek proved himself a good manager of men. The quarrelsome youth who was always flouncing off from Sun Yat-sen's neighborhood had grown up into a quieter man. He had Hu Han-min at his side, and their relations were cordial. Authority brought balance, and in those early days Chiang's popularity seemed assured. But very soon that authority was suspected, questioned, and at length attacked.

The first bitter quarrel occurred when Chiang attempted to do away with the political subcouncils in Canton and Hankow. He argued that a united China didn't need more than one central federal government office. These small councils were hang-overs from prewar days, but since then the respective governors of the two provinces, Pai Chung-hsi and Li Tsung-jen, had become attached to their status, and they resented Chiang's attempt to take away their power. They said he was getting too big for his boots; they used the word "dictator," a term which was rapidly becoming a coin of ordinary verbal currency in the world.

One of the fundamental hopes Sun Yat-sen had imparted to his disciples was that of a national constitution. For nearly two decades this hope had waned, flared, and waned again. Sun's own suggested constitution, what with being cobbled and rewritten and finally flung out of Peking, was out of the question; anyway the Chinese had become wiser, and they could see it wasn't simply a matter of writing down laws. Once again, therefore, while a new constitution was being drafted, they resolved on a period of readjustment and education for the people. Five years—1930 to 1935—of "political tutelage" were to transform China into a genuine voting republic. In the meantime the country was to be controlled by a government of five "yuans" or committees: Executive, Legislative, Control, Judicial, and Examination. High officials of these yuans were to be members of the State Council, or Cabinet, headed by its President. Chiang Kai-shek himself was the first President, and he was careful to see that the Council should include Yen Hsi-shan as Minister of the Interior, and Feng Yu-hsiang as Minister of War. He knew that the secret of handling war lords is to keep them happy if possible but, above all, to keep them in view.

Nanking hummed with activity that might have been contented if it hadn't been for disgruntled souls pointing out that it wasn't the right kind of activity. No strides in demobilization were made, though the months went by. Still pepped up with revolutionary spirit, people didn't realize how long it takes to do these things tactfully, and tact was of the essence when it came to dealing with generals.

However, such disadvantages were temporarily offset by the charming behavior of the Young Marshal of Manchuria, who was determined to stand by his decision and support the Generalissimo and the new unified China. He had considerable resources and his aid was enormously valuable. He came to Nanking in time for the important celebrations of October 10, the Double Tenth: he too was appointed to the State Council. Soon the Kuomintang flag fluttered cheerfully in the breeze over Mukden, and the fashion spread throughout Manchuria.

It was a happy, creative time for Chiang Kai-shek. Carpers might point out with justice that unity hadn't really been achieved: the government was full of potential traitors, and great tracts of the land weren't assimilated—the inhabitants of these provinces, indeed, had never heard of most of the goings on in Nanking. But it was the nearest thing to unity that anyone within some centuries had seen in all his great country, and Chiang had reason to feel proud. He was full of energy, and though he was overworked it was work that he loved. There was time now for a widening of interests. There was this matter of Nanking, the capital, which he had promised himself must be rebuilt in a fitting style, the most beautiful, inspiring, modern yet dignified capital city in the world. He had been rather offended by the scorn exhibited by foreigners when his government insisted upon leaving Peking; he was determined to show them that China was something better than a museum, and could build new glories as well as molder away among walls erected by the people's ancestors. Like a lot of other Chinese, Chiang resented the implication that their living world was necessarily a comedown from the past.

A magnificent tomb was planned on the slope of Purple Mountain, above the ruins of a Ming temple, ready to receive Sun Yatsen's sacred remains. Later in the year the body was installed with great ceremony. (Chingling wouldn't play. She sent rude messages and stayed away from Nanking, but everyone pretended not to notice.) Then the remodeling of the city began. Old, narrow, stinking streets were cleared out and rebuilt. The town had possessed the beauty of antiquity, and there were many people to cry out and protest against vandalism when the destruction began, but no one could argue that a large part of Nanking was not overdue for reform. Besides, Chiang and his wife had no desire to emulate the raucous modernity of Tokyo. They visualized a compromise; a Chinese style of architecture in which characteristic sloping roofs, brilliantly painted ceilings, tiles, and courtyards need not disappear, but could be combined with clean, cool interiors and electric appliances. An American architect was called in and between them they worked out a style that blended well. It was Chiang's first experience with building on such a scale—after all, not many people ever get such a chance—and he was fascinated by the whole business. When the Ministry of Foreign Affairs was going up he went over to the site every day with his wife; his spare figure in its familiar cape was to be seen contentedly strolling through the workings, arm in arm with Mayling, checking up with bright-eyed interest, or pointing out something he had just been reading about.

There were other advisers; the Generalissimo studied lists of foreign experts as farmers' wives study the pages of Sears Roebuck's catalogue, ordering this one from a university, turning down that proffered name because of the expense, and ending up with a list of

German military advisers, American educational advisers, medical advisers, highway advisers—it was a golden time, a hopeful time.

The climax to all this was that the Nanking government was officially recognized by the powers. The British Minister presented his credentials, not without a backward, regretful look at beautiful Peking, and other important diplomats followed suit. Interviews with these diplomats began to take up a portion of the working day; that is to say, of other people's working days. As far as the Chiangs were concerned, they almost never stopped working, day or night. The Generalissimo was up at dawn and at his work table shortly afterward. He carried on all day, with breaks only for lunch and dinner, and one hour after lunch for relaxation. Mayling kept pace with him, for she was his secretary and it was her task to translate important messages, act as his interpreter in all interviews when English was necessary, and make a digest of foreign news.

For a little while there was a notion in the family circle that Chiang ought to learn English and become less dependent on his wife's help. During their lighter moments at home, when the Kung children were there and Eling and her sister joked and teased Chiang—a process he enjoyed, in a reserved way—the theory seemed sensible enough, and Mayling set about teaching him. He might have made good headway if it hadn't been for a small accident. One day he attempted to try out his English on the British Minister. He got his signals mixed—it could happen to anybody— and instead of saying, "Good morning, Lampson," he said, "Kiss me, Lampson." He hasn't tried to talk English with foreigners since then.

All things considered, it was fortunate that Mayling never had children. There wasn't time in her life for them. Theoretically, she adopted Chiang's second boy, Wei-kuo, but he was unco-operative and resentful of the relationship, and they didn't actually have much to do with each other. He was growing up to be a vigorous boy, inclined to wildness; perhaps he needed a regular family life that of necessity he had always missed. A conventional Buddhist family circle, or a conventional Christian one, would have filled the bill, but the Generalissimo's son was between two worlds. As for Ching-kuo, nobody really knew. When last heard from he had been a student at the Chinese Institute in Moscow, the Sun Yat-sen University, and for all Chiang knew the boy was developing into an arrogant young Red like the ones who had attacked him that memorable day in Moscow. There wasn't any word from him at all. Rumor said he had been killed in revenge on Chiang for the purge.

In May, Nanking had its first taste of responsibility for the new acquisition, Manchuria, in an incident that might well have been disastrous. For some time the Young Marshal's lieutenants had been aware that the Russians attached to the Chinese Eastern Railway, which they virtually controlled, were conspiring against the government. Emboldened, no doubt, by Chiang's action in splitting with the Reds, Manchurian police suddenly raided the Harbin Soviet consulate and found ample proof of their suspicions. Arrests of the chief consular officials followed, and the C.E.R. was swept completely clear of all the Russians on the management staff, who were sent back to Russia and replaced by Chinese.

The Young Marshal must have expected to get away with this drastic action, but he didn't. Moscow's reply was prompt. An ultimatum arrived on July 13: unless the Manchurians restored the railway to its former status within three days, further action would be taken. Chang Hsueh-liang thereupon forwarded the whole quarrel to Nanking to negotiate for him. It could not have been a welcome present to Chiang's Foreign Office, but the Foreign Minister did the best he could, stalling and counterdemanding. In vain: Moscow withdrew all consular officials from China, stopped her end of the railway, and sent a concentration of troops to the Manchurian border. The Young Marshal dispatched an equal number of troops, as heavily armed as possible, to meet the threat, but before they had got very far the Russians attacked, crossing the eastern border with bombers and the western with infantry led by China's old friend, General Galen. Soon they had occupied a large part of Manchuria, and by the end of November the Young Marshal was forced to give in and accept the original Soviet demands. The railway went back to Russian management, conspirators continued to conspire, and Chang Hsueh-liang was left smoldering, with Russian encroachment as well as Japanese to worry about.

Though Wang Ching-wei prudently remained in France, he was still the acknowledged leader of the Kuomintang Left. Now his coterie was being edged into a position of very minor importance, and Chiang was holding hands with Hu Han-min. The exiled man could not bear it. In March 1929 he raised his voice in protest and sent out a manifesto accusing Chiang of illegality and one-sidedness. His followers took up the cry and announced that they were quitting altogether. And quit they did, taking with them when they left the capital a veritable prize, Feng Yu-hsiang. Feng had a grievance. The Japanese had just departed a year after they had occupied Tsinan, but the Generalissimo wouldn't let him move in and take over Shantung. Therefore the Christian general left Nanking and retired to the country, where he did have power, in the Northwest, and there waited balefully for events.

This was the opening move in a civil war that was to last until the end of 1930, the fiercest yet fought in China. Thousands of men were to die, and thousands of civilians to be driven from their homes. Traditional war, in comparison with this nightmare of planes and bombs and armed transport, seemed a gay, harmless affair of banners and drums and generally operatic sound and fury. Unfortunately, its day was over.

The first phase was that of the Kwangsi revolt. The Kwangsi faction, headed by Pai Chung-hsi and Li Tsung-jen, had won their point in the subcouncil argument and still held control of the

Hankow zone of influence, which comprised Kwangsi and Hupei but not Hunan. The generals felt they should have Hunan too—and Hunan's revenues—because this province lay between the other two. But the governor of Hunan insisted that the taxes he collected were the property of Nanking. Pai and Li thereupon drove him out of Hunan, and relations between Hankow and Nanking, as the newspapers put it, rapidly deteriorated. Chiang sent troops to the Hupei border.

Pai Chung-hsi happened to be away from his home base when all this took place, in the North. He chose the discreet way out and went to Japan, later making his way by roundabout route to South China. But his colleague Li Tsung-jen continued talking back to the Generalissimo. By the end of March the Nationalists were across the border, led by Chiang himself. Frightened by his planes, the rebels evacuated Hankow and the Nationalists entered the city on April 4. So far, it had been easy.

The rush of events of the past five years had changed Chiang Kai-shek but left him no leisure to examine the change. Here at the rising of the curtain, the start of one of China's bloodiest dramas, we might stop for an arbitrary breathing space—a purely imaginary one: actually there was no surcease—and look at the man who was beginning to make an impression on the Western world.

He had been, and still was, self-confident in a way that would strike us as youthful. He looked like a young man, though he was forty-two. It was not only that his frame was strong and spare as a youth's; there was something direct about his expression, a look of simplicity. The tortuous self-questionings of the intellectual had not marked his face. He looked guarded but peaceful, if one can use that word about a man whose business was war—and I don't really see why one can't.

The quietude of his face was not, of course, a purely natural phenomenon. Chiang practiced restraint in his emotions, and he finally succeeded in achieving the outward manifestation of it. Even in involuntary anger, he didn't allow his features to distort themselves. Voluntary anger—that which he felt he should display for purposes of oratory or to evoke an answering enthusiasm—was a different thing: even he could not always give the impression of being completely frozen. But he usually looked calm, as Confucius's gentleman is supposed to do.

It was this expression that stirred the imaginations of the foreign newspapermen who interviewed him, or watched him addressing public meetings or celebrating new buildings. They found it strange, even repellent, that a rather slightly built man who looked like that, so quiet and nongiving, should be the inflexible Generalissimo who had led the purge against the Communists and outguessed Feng Yu-hsiang and continued to defeat Wang Ching-wei. Westerners do not trust a poker face: they like to know what goes on behind the brow, and when they don't, they suspect the worst. Chiang Kai-shek personally wasn't good copy. He had none of the engaging warmth, for example, of the Christian general. (And then, too, it was vaguely bad of him not to speak English.) If it hadn't been for Madame with her sparkle, her petite dignity, and her pretty speech, Chiang would have had a worse press than he got. Not that a Confucian gentleman cared what sort of press the world outside might read.

Actually, behind the smooth face he was emotional enough. In 1929 Chiang Kai-shek was beginning to feel his oats. His rise had been too rapid for conceit to have overtaken him before, but now the thought must have begun to stay with him as a certainty, instead of in the occasional flashes felt by every soldier, that he was something important in history. Did he reflect sometimes as he looked at himself in the glass, in full panoply, that Fate must surely be on the side of this fine fellow with his brilliant wife? If so, it was only for a moment. His austere past, the austere religion he was studying, all the austerities of a war-obsessed existence were enough to smother pagan exaltation. What remained was a heightening of assurance, that quiet cockiness that made him accept, as a foundation of philosophy itself, the rightness of his aim and the wrongness of his enemies.

In Hankow the Generalissimo took charge and put reforms into practice: Pai Chung-hsi and his boys had had a heavy hand with the taxes, and the change was welcomed by the local businessmen. It was from an atmosphere of relief and good feeling that Chiang went back to Nanking six weeks later. Peace was what he wanted, he declared, peace and unity for China. As soon as he could be assured that these were safe, he would resign his posts and go abroad for a holiday. He was always saying that: it was the conventional thing to say.

But the unrest had simply been shifted to other regions. In the always turbulent South were Pai Chung-hsi and his allies; in the Northwest was Feng Yu-hsiang, who had helped to stir up the trouble; scattered here and there, biding their time and building their strength, were the Communists. Chiang could not really have expected to make that trip abroad for a long time to come.

The Kwangsi clique could not bring themselves to settle down in their home province. They started one or two campaigns against Canton, but Nationalist soldiers chased their troops back across the border. It was the first time such severe action had ever been taken against the war lords. They were surprised and offended; they were also defeated.

. But Nanking had neither time nor cause for jubilation. Almost before he had achieved the victory Chiang was summoned to a new outbreak in the North, where Feng Yu-hsiang was acting up. The Christian general now began making overtures to Yen Hsi-shan, Governor of Shansi, and was not repulsed. An alliance, or at any rate an understanding, was quickly attained. The two generals were a formidable combination, because each in his own way was a strong man, firmly entrenched in the affections, or loyalty, or feudal respect—call it what you like—of his followers. Feng with his theatrical affectation of rustic simplicity, Yen with his record of benevolent dictatorship, were types their soldiers felt they understood and could depend on. The name of their combined forces was "the People's Army."

Yen Hsi-shan, called "the Model Governor," was a sincere and capable man. But in this adventure he and Feng had similar aims, two Chinese war lords with a power drive. "Militarist!" they said scornfully of Chiang Kai-shek; considering the source it seems an unreasonable accusation. Between themselves, the pair lacked the political fervor to raise their struggle above its original level. Wang Ching-wei now joined them, hopeful that they might dethrone Chiang: he supplied them with loftier motives and a more stylish vocabulary. He declared that Chiang Kai-shek had departed from the original spirit of the revolution and betrayed it; that he was that scourge of democracy, a military man who had pre-empted the powers of civil government. Wang, who had no army of his own, expounded the evils of military power to the war lords and they piously echoed his words. The Generalissimo must be overthrown.

There followed a period of telegram bombardments between Nanking and the North; long, leisurely, and doubtless costly messages. While the authors at both ends droned on about duty and republicanism, the People's Army started on their march toward Nanking.

The weeks dragged on. Now the Young Marshal in Mukden joined the telegraph-wire conference and urged the northern generals to think better of the whole matter. But a few days later Yen Hsi-shan's army moved into the government offices in Peking. Kuomintang troops were disarmed. Two weeks after that, on

April 1, 1930, Yen assumed command of the "National Forces," and the Christian general was appointed deputy commander.

With stronger backing, Chiang would have gone to war against them long before this, but he was reluctant to do so. The terrain was the difficulty; he would have to fight in Shantung, where local sympathy was likely to be strongly pro-Feng. Instead, he continued to battle with words and diplomatic action as long as he could. But the issue was at last joined in Shantung and Honan and the war was on.

The ins and outs of the struggle are too confusing to attempt to recount them in detail. In August the deadlock was broken. The rebels evacuated Shantung in a sudden rush.

The scale of these operations had ravaged old China, and she was never to be the same again. The nation was now clearly divided into a few big blocks: the Nationalists in Central China, the Feng-Yen sphere of North and Northwest, and the occasional insurgents of the South. The Communists had no fixed territory and they blurred the outlines of the struggle: their activity was obscured by the greater war. Yet they had actually captured Changsha at the end of July and held it for a few days, burning the city as they retreated.

The part of the map that did catch the eye, Chiang's as well as the outside world's, was Manchuria. Save for his ineffective telegram in March, the Young Marshal had not made a move in either direction with his enormous army. Where did his sympathies lie? Everyone waited to see. As long as Chiang offered the only strong leadership it had been logical to approve of him and support the government. Chances seemed remote that the young man should grow ambitious himself for more power. If he had been a chip off the old block it might have been different, but he was no Chang Tso-lin. Hsueh-liang was a thinker, an idealist, and—which is perhaps most important—a morphine addict. Morphine makes philosophers, not men of violent action: the Young Marshal sought his

ideal outside himself. It looked as if he had found it in Chiang
Kai-shek when he pledged himself to Nanking's future constitution.
But here was Wang Ching-wei, a rival of respectable proportions,
promising a better constitution in Peking. Would Chang Hsueh-
liang prefer this new look?

Nanking didn't wait to find out, but hastily announced that the
Young Marshal had been appointed deputy commander-in-chief
of the National forces. Feng and Yen followed this up with their
bid, a place for him on the Peking State Council, then in the process
of formation. Still the Young Marshal held his hand until the
middle of September. Chiang now had the enemy on the run to
such an extent that Yen Hsi-shan was thinking of pulling out of
his alliance.

He was still thinking when, on September 18, came the long-
awaited word from Mukden: the Young Marshal wanted to arbitrate. First he suggested a relaxation of the Kuomintang monopoly
in government. The Generalissimo readily agreed, though this same
proposal from his foes in the Northwest had been indignantly
turned down just a short time before. His march toward dictatorship, if that is what it was, had been deflected.

Chang Hsueh-liang then sent out a circular telegram to the
generals, calling for a cease-fire. Problems should be settled peace-
ably, he declared, by the Central Government in Nanking. To
bolster up his plea the Young Marshal sent troops to Peking from
Shanhaikwan. By the time they got there, not a trace remained
of the Wang Ching-wei government.

With Tientsin and Peking safely occupied by Mukden soldiers,
Chiang's forces found it easy to wind up hostilities in their own
terrain, Honan. The war was over, but it had taken its toll—
hundreds of thousands of casualties.

The war was over: so too was Kai-shek's self-imposed period
of tutelage in Christianity. As soon as he returned to Nanking he

told Pastor Kiang that he had decided he was ready for the Church. For one thing, he said, Christian officers seemed to fight better than others: he had been impressed by the old scalawag Feng. Moreover, Chiang had undergone a crisis during a crucial battle near Kaifeng when he found himself in danger of being cut off from his troops.

"In this desperate situation, he prayed to God for deliverance, pledging that he would publicly acknowledge Jesus Christ as his Lord after the Lord had delivered him," the pastor reported. "God did answer his prayer by sending a very heavy snowstorm, which was unusual at this time of year, so that his enemies could not advance any nearer. In the meantime his reinforcements came from Nanking by rail, thereby not only sparing his own life, but turning a certain defeat into a victory."

One side of the bargain having been fulfilled, Chiang in the approved Old Testament manner kept his word too, and Pastor Kiang duly baptized him.

Whatever one may think of this conception of God as military strategist, it is hard to conceive of any branch of the Christian religion better fitted to Chiang's starkly uncompromising character than the Methodist.

The Communists could not have gone so far as to capture Changsha without having gained immensely in strength and technique since the days of 1927 and the Canton Commune. While Chiang Kai-shek was polishing off the Northern Expedition and dealing with the Kwangsi revolt and fighting the Yen-Feng combine and trying to watch the Japanese, the wanderers in the wilderness of Kiangsi and Honan found their feet. They carried on as guerrillas, fighting when necessary, teaching and enlisting where possible, and setting up soviets wherever they halted. Mao Tse-tung and Chu Teh soon established themselves as the leaders of the Army. "Our main tasks, as we saw them," said Mao, "were two: to divide the land and to establish soviets." In this they were first opposed by the Central Committee, which "had grandiose ideas of rapid expansion," but they carried their point.

The Comintern Sixth Congress, held in Moscow in 1928, had drawn up plans for the C.C.P.'s future and delegated over-all power to Li Li-san and Chou En-lai, the man who founded the Paris branch of the C.C.P. In general outline the program was much the same as before—organizing peasants, fomenting strikes, and educational preparation of soviets—and it continued to place emphasis on "the working class," that proletariat upon which European revolution so much depended. In Moscow, where Stalin had got rid of Trotzky and was now in complete control, it was decided, again and again, that the time was ripe for revolution in China. Chiang's troubles in 1929 and 1930 gave plenty of opportunity, it was felt, to enroll the workers of the cities in the cause, so that the blow was imminent. But in actual fact, what the war afforded was opportunity for Mao and Chu to bring over more and more peasants to the cause, the dissatisfied, dispossessed, and hungry of the countryside. The urban workers remained apathetic. Rigid Marxism was not equipped to exploit this unorthodox situation, and Li Li-san could not explain satisfactorily, in the only language it was permitted to use, why he did not follow the directives. For months Moscow waited in vain for "the great upsurge of the masses." Li Li-san didn't hold with the surge idea; he was in favor of picking off cities and provinces one by one in local floods rather than with one all-over tide.

Told that the moment had come, Mao and his army obediently set forth to conquer the cities. Their peasants and soldiers would encircle these headlands of reaction and engulf them, just as Moscow directed: there would be an answering upsurge within the city walls, and thus the proletariat would fulfill its function.

But at Nanchang, the scene of their first attempt, the magic formula did not work, and they made another attempt on Changsha.

Here, as I have said, they actually captured the city on July 28, and there was rejoicing throughout the Party. Yet somehow the great upsurge of the masses was either missing completely or did not suffice. The brunt of the battle was borne by the Army; the proletariat of Changsha lacked enthusiasm, and it was only five days before the Reds, wary of the approaching Nationalists, had to leave the city again, after experiencing the first air raid many of them had ever encountered. The disappointment called forth a burst of angry scolding from headquarters in Moscow, and soon afterward Li Li-san was removed from his high position and sent to Russia for "more schooling."

There was bitterness in China about this injustice, but Chinese Communists were to learn it was no use arguing with Moscow. Li Li-san was subjected to an inquisition and quickly reduced to the babbling, breast-beating, apologetic figure that has since become so familiar a part of Communist trials.

To take his place the Comintern sent into China a number of specially trained young Chinese who had attended Sun Yat-sen University in Moscow, those same students who had once heckled Chiang Kai-shek. They were the elect, and from now on they were to be the only trusted political leaders of the Party until Mao managed to assert himself. Russia herself moved in with these missionaries. The C.C.P. was now a genuinely satellite group.

Jubilantly the Nationalist Army came back to Nanking in time for the Double Tenth celebration, and the Generalissimo took the occasion to announce that the People's Congress would definitely be held on May 5, 1931. He had already proposed an amnesty for Wang Ching-wei and all other political offenders. The irrepressible Christian general was soon back in Nanking's circle of acquaintance on the old terms of cautious cordiality.

A few weeks later there was a Plenary Session of the C.E.C., and Chiang outlined his plans for the near future. He came out in

favor of an autonomy system for districts and provinces, which had
been one of the bones of contention before the northern war, when
he was on the other side of the argument. He also declared that it
was his intention to eradicate "Communism and banditry"; this
task, he figured, could be accomplished within the following six
months. Already the campaign was under way, for Chiang had sent
three divisions from Honan to fight the Reds in Kiangsi and Hunan,
as soon as the Young Marshal began to support him in the northwest war.

Unfortunately for the timetable, Chiang's soldiers weren't used
to dealing with guerrilla warfare. When they went into Kiangsi they
were entering strange territory and were greeted as the traditional
enemies of the countryfolk. The Reds, on the other hand, were at
home among the villages. For years they had lived among the
people and befriended them; it was an important part of Communist strategy to make friends. Whenever Chiang's men got un-
comfortably close, the guerrillas simply merged with the population.
They formed their soviets, proselyted at their leisure, and melted
away when troops approached. They were a quicksilver army.

The Chinese public after a time grew not so much worried about
the continued existence of the Red Army as tired of the subject.
Those who didn't live in Communist-infiltrated country couldn't
see the urgency of this perpetual grinding conflict, and they began
to wonder if it wasn't costing more than it was worth. Very little
news was published about it, and that little was the conventional
government handout; this battle was won by the Nationalists, that
had ended in splendid victory for the Nationalists; the Kuomintang
troops now had the Reds definitely on the run. . . . A few days
later there would be another dispatch from the same front posts
saying it all over again, as if the first battles hadn't been fought
at all. The frontier never seemed to move very much.

The alliance between Chiang and Hu Han-min had never been
easy. There was too much jealousy inherent in their common his-

tory, and in February 1931 they came to another parting of the ways. At a Kuomintang conference, Hu disputed the provisionary constitution sponsored by Chiang on the ground that it was laying down the law prematurely on a lot of points concerning the functions of government departments. He said Chiang was arrogating too much power to himself. Chiang retorted that Hu was only worrying, really, about party authority.

It was quite like the old days in Canton, when the young men had squabbled over theory in Sun Yat-sen's shadow, but now they had more power behind their words and the squabbles didn't end in mere argument. Hu's temper carried him off his feet and he resigned from the presidency of the Legislative Yuan, a post which in those days was a powerful one. Chiang, similarly stirred, had him placed under house arrest, or as the Chinese more prettily called it, "in soft detainment." The fact was not at first announced; Hu simply disappeared.

This was going pretty far for a man who spoke well of democratic procedure, and Chiang was besieged with questions by curious Europeans. What had happened? Where was Hu? Why had the harmless, negative Lin Sen been put into the presidency of the Legislative Yuan?

For a long time the Generalissimo was silent, but at last he reluctantly uttered. Hu was all right, he said, quite all right; it was merely that his personal liberty was for the moment being restrained. It was all for his own good and that of the Kuomintang. Without this restraint, the misguided man might well flee to Shanghai, and that would only stir up dissident elements and incite disorder. He was *quite* all right.

The affair was added as yet another item to the rapidly lengthening catalogue of what his opponents claimed were Chiang's misdemeanors. He was turning into a dictator. Just to keep his army mobilized he was wasting the country's wealth chasing Communists who didn't matter, who in fact would probably be very good citizens if only they were left alone. He was building up a corps of young bullies, said the rumors, like the strong-arm men in Italy —the "Blue Shirts." And what about the sinister Chen brothers? Moreover, they said, Chiang was in close touch with Gangleader Tu Yueh-sen in Shanghai, and was pocketing vast sums from the opium trade by means of this connection. (Chiang had indeed recently announced that opium was thenceforth to be a government monopoly, like that maintained by the British in Hongkong. He needed the revenue.) And now, this! Everywhere, especially among the students, the Generalissimo was criticized.

April came and went, and the Hu Han-min flurry subsided into sullen mutters, for the People's Congress was close at hand and arguments about the provisional constitution could then be aired freely. But by May 5 people had other things than the constitution to worry about. The South was kicking up a fuss again, with Wang Ching-wei to lead them. Eugene Chen was in on it too.

It started with the usual manifesto, or circular telegram, signed by Wang Ching-wei and the Kwangsi generals: they "impeached" Chiang for his sins. Another telegram followed from the war lord who governed Canton, accusing the Generalissimo of having assumed dictatorship. Chiang called a hasty conference of Kuomintang leaders and said that the charges must be openly discussed and investigated.

He should have been able to depend on the Party's support in such a crisis, but the times were extraordinary because of Hu Han-min's detention. Some of his own camp took the opportunity to turn on him. Sun Fo and Wang Chung-hui withdrew to Shanghai, and later went to Canton. Then the Canton war lord announced that Kwangsi and Kwangtung were friends, shoulder to shoulder in the fight. On May 25 the southerners sent an ultimatum: Chiang must retire within forty-eight hours or bear the consequences. A few days later they proclaimed a new national government in Canton.

The foreigners in the treaty ports were in a turmoil. It was war again, they were sure. Really, these Chinese!

Chiang announced that he must suppress the rebels, but he didn't rush into the task. There were talks, and then more talks, in the neutral surroundings of Shanghai. Through June and most of July the discussions dragged on, with Chiang hoping to avert the clash the country could so ill afford. The southerners pressed on with their demands. The fact that they applied to Japan for support was remembered against them for a long time to come.

Their eagerness carried the day, and on July 21 it was announced in Canton that the punitive expedition was on its way. By the middle of August, Pai Chung-hsi's army was marching through Hunan on the old road to Nanking. Chiang got ready. The capital bristled. And in the North, when nobody was looking, Japan suddenly moved into Mukden.

Later the Young Marshal claimed that the invasion was not a surprise to him and should not have surprised the rest of China, either. But in fact he too was taken unawares, with most of his army garrisoned south of the Great Wall. Japan had indeed been behaving in a bullying manner for some months, but the country had got used to living with the danger. After all, for years Japan had been just as provocative. That month Chang Hsueh-liang had attended the People's Congress in Nanking, as befitted the deputy commander. On his way back to Mukden he was smitten with typhoid, which is a long, tedious illness, and took to his bed in a Peking hospital. September 18, exactly a year after he signed up with Chiang, he got out of bed for the first time. That was the day the Japanese came into Mukden. There was little he could do about it, now that they were there; they were well armed and far more modernly equipped than the Manchurian army. Helplessly, the Young Marshal watched from Peking as the invaders moved at will through the countryside and took over and settled in.

In the South the generals and their colleagues stayed their hand and waited, expecting war to be declared at any minute. But Chiang and his advisers knew that he was even less capable than the Young Marshal of initiating an offensive war against a strong foreign country. There was the League of Nations, formed presumably for just such crises as this; there was also the Kellogg Pact. Chiang referred the question to the League. His prospects of satisfaction weren't bright: America, who might otherwise have been interested, was wrapped up in the depression at home, and Britain was indifferent.

The hotheads of China felt that this was not enough, and the dissidents of the South clamored for something better. But it was the students who were angriest. On September 28 hundreds of these youngsters in Shanghai decided to take a hand in the matter. They went down to the railway station, took command forcibly of a train, and rode to Nanking. There they teamed up with colleagues from the capital's university and marched in a shouting body, five thousand strong, to the Ministry for Foreign Affairs. They pushed past the guards and stormed the Minister's office, and pulled him out of doors and beat him up. The Minister, when he got out of hospital, retired. The students then staged a sit-down strike and announced they would remain in Nanking until they got action instead of mere diplomacy. Nobody knew what to do about them and there were more important matters claiming government attention.

It was obvious that the South and Nanking must make up their differences. The public demanded this. And so although impolite noises kept resounding from Canton, where Eugene Chen was virtuously condemning Chiang Kai-shek for being weak in his diplomacy, Nanking offered to come to terms. In October, Chiang released Hu Han-min from his soft detainment, none the worse, apparently, for the involuntary holiday. Together with three others they went to Shanghai for a peace conference with the southern leaders. Hu Han-min urged the southerners to be reasonable and stop shouting for Chiang's resignation. Chiang added, "Whatever may have been the right or wrong, the whole blame may, if desired, be placed entirely at my door."

But this edifying spectacle didn't last long. As the Canton contingent continued to demand Chiang's resignation, Hu suddenly about-faced and improved on the suggestion. Chiang should not only resign, he said, he should be banished from China altogether. The conference closed in disorder.

Other suggestions were made and abandoned. The South was adamant; Chiang must go.

The sit-strike students, tired of merely sitting, began stirring up more trouble. Their numbers had been growing steadily since the first demonstration; boys hurried into Nanking from far afield, until at the end of November there were twelve thousand of them. Again they marched to the new government buildings, and this time they shouted for Chiang himself to come out and argue. "War on Japan!" they cried.

Chiang let them wait in the cold winter weather a full twenty-four hours before he appeared. Then he scolded them severely and told them to go back to school, and the meeting dispersed in a chastened calm.

On December 15, Chiang gave in to popular demand and resigned. The rest of the officials threw in their hands as well, but none of their resignations was accepted save T. V. Soong's and one other. Lin Sen was appointed Acting Chairman of the government. He was always the one man who could be guaranteed harmless. The new government could hardly be called rash: they stationed a crack Cantonese unit, the Nineteenth Route Army, along the railway line from Nanking to Shanghai. One never knows when protected retreat might be advisable.

The change-over was celebrated in a manner the government could have dispensed with. After the snub administered to the students by Chiang Kai-shek they began building up to a bigger, better effort. More and more young men flooded into the town until seventy thousand of them crowded into the dormitory buildings and the surrounding houses of Central University. Just after Chiang's resignation they sallied out to see what they could do. They swarmed into the Foreign Affairs building again and destroyed it. They attacked the Central Kuomintang Headquarters and beat up an old man there. He was rescued by the guard, who fired over the heads of the crowd and scared them off. Then some of the boys, still light-hearted, attacked and pulled down the building that housed the party paper, the *Central Daily News,* and completely smashed its printing press. Next morning, bright and early, the Army took over, rounding the students up and escorting them out of Nanking.

Once Chiang had given way, his opponents relented a little. They elected him to the C.E.C. standing committee of three, with Hu Han-min and Wang Ching-wei the other two, but he refused the honor. (So did Hu and Wang.) Other offers were likewise turned down by the Generalissimo. As always, he went home to the mountains.

The excuse offered by Japan for her actions was that Chinese soldiers had sabotaged the South Manchurian Railway. In the presence of the flood of trumped-up accusations issuing from the Japanese Foreign Office, dealing with first one imaginary "incident" and then another, or alleging that China and Russia were in league against her, only an imbecile could have doubted that Japan was not yet satisfied with her conquest and that Fate was closing in on Nanking. Sitting uneasily in his presidential chair, Sun Fo looked around for veteran statesmen who could help him with expert advice. He found none. Hu Han-min had cannily gone to Hongkong before the dust settled. Wang Ching-wei, who was morally responsible for the whole shake-up, had retired to a Shanghai hospital. Wang was really ill; he was a diabetic.

Chiang Kai-shek represented the good will of the moneyed classes. With his resignation the bankers abruptly lost interest in

Nanking and went back to their Shanghai occupations. The government coffers were soon empty. How was the government to pay the Army? Nobody knew, but every war lord in Nanking was well aware of what happens when you don't pay your generals; they had been there before. Already there were rumors of unrest. . . .

Chiang and Mayling, in the chilly wind-swept hills of Chekiang, had only begun to dig in for the winter when the summons came. Once again Achilles was implored to come out of his tent. Chiang held off until he was assured that Wang Ching-wei would also go back. The two rivals agreed to return together, on condition Hu Han-min would come into it as well. Together they went to the capital, and there was a general meeting on the twenty-third of January.

Immediately they quarreled with the new Minister for Foreign Affairs, Eugene Chen. He wanted to break off diplomatic relations with Japan, but neither Chiang nor Wang Ching-wei saw it his way. Eugene went to Shanghai and resigned from there, and told his grievances to the press. Sun Fo followed, and likewise resigned. Wang was appointed to his post in his place. Thus on the eve of the Shanghai trouble Wang Ching-wei held the presidency of the Executive Yuan, or premiership of China, than which he could hardly have wanted anything better, whereas Chiang still held only his honorary post on the C.E.C. special committee. He was not yet back in the saddle as Generalissimo, and the situation was to have its effect in the near future.

Japan had discovered a new incident at Lunghua, close to Shanghai. A Japanese seaman was coshed and murdered there, and the Japanese vowed it was part of a deliberate political attack. On January 28, a week after the Chiangs went back to Nanking, the Japanese attacked Shanghai in force. Two days later the Nanking government moved inland to Loyang, in Honan. The Nineteenth Route Army, still stationed back of the city as a bodyguard de luxe for the short-lived southern government, found themselves bearing the brunt of a very different kind of war than they had expected.

The story of their brave month-long resistance against great odds is well known, far better known than a vast number of even more stirring stories about China's other soldiers. The reason is easy to understand; they were fighting around Shanghai, defending not only their own territory but a number of treaty-port foreigners.

In the post-mortem that inevitably followed the engagement, Chiang was assailed on all sides for having failed to send any support to the Cantonese army. He was accused of holding back his own men. Foreigners as well as Chinese were furious with him, but the criticism was unfair. Chiang had no authority to send a single soldier into battle. He was now only a civilian member of the C.E.C. He offered to help, but he wasn't allowed to do so; the officers were jealous. What Chiang could do, he did; kept in touch with the commanders of the Nineteenth Route Army by telegraph.

Eyewitnesses of the fighting agreed that Japanese military talent had until then been vastly overrated. Everyone was surprised. The invaders were well equipped, but their command was inept. But the Chinese too had their faults. Chiang warned the Nineteenth Route General to guard Liuho, a village across the Yangtze behind the Chinese, for if the Japanese should land there they would be able to cut off the enemy. General Tsai neglected to keep a guard on duty. When the Japanese at last made the landing, the game was up, and the Nineteenth Route Army quietly moved out. The siege had lasted forty days.

Afterward the affair was sorted out by the powers, who were interested in it because of Shanghai. The Japanese kept control of a part of the city, and limits of influence were agreed on. In time the government was to come back to Nanking. But, more than ever, the Chinese people angrily looked forward to revenge. All their minds were fixed on the Japanese encroachment. It was a sentiment Soviet Russia approved, for good reasons; the Russians didn't like the Japanese advance into what they meant to be their territory, but it did distract Nanking's attention from what the Chinese Reds were doing.

But even Shanghai's plight could not forever mask the fact that the Communists continued to consolidate their positions and were now menacing Hankow. Chiang resolved to put a spoke in their wheel, and his preparations were bitterly criticized. "There he goes again," said the patriots, "making war on his own people instead of attending to the real threat, Japan."

"It is useless for China to talk of resisting Japan," said Chiang, "when it has not yet stamped out the enemy in its midst. If China ventures to fight the Japanese, the Communists will attack from the rear and chaos will quickly overtake the whole country."

The critics were not convinced.

Authority after exile, and the setbacks of the past year, stimulated the Generalissimo and gave him new ideas. It had taken him a long time to outgrow his tendency to personal resentments. He was forty-five, and that is late in the day to relinquish prima-donna behavior, but for Chiang with his background, among his companions, it is remarkable that he should ever have achieved a more adult attitude. Many other big men in China have never done so. The passionate young officer who caused Sun Yat-sen so many hours of uneasiness, of writing and writing to soothe his feelings, had developed into a good moderator on his own account.

Official life in China is a tempestuous affair. The grave young secretaries on guard at the Generalissimo's office doors, the quiet, dignified gentlemen with their brief cases and their high-buttoned Kuomintang uniforms going in and out, the military officers standing at attention when he made his public appearances seemed calm and inscrutable to foreign onlookers, but the reality was very different. Within those cold, high-ceilinged, dingy rooms there were rage and confession, self-betrayals, reconciliations, promises, often tears. It was life as it is lived in China, and Chiang was learning how to surmount it. He became better at managing men than Sun had ever been because he was harder, and thus hardened the men who worked for him. But he still lacked the streak of humanity, however facile and pseudo, that was Feng's chief stock in trade.

To some extent Madame made up for this deficiency. She was hard too, in her way, like all efficient social-service workers, but she was beautiful and vivid, and she had the knack of letting go with people. The wives who met her on committees and who slaved away over officers' orphanages or comforts-supply clubs would come home dazzled by her warm energy. For a little while they could even forget their distrust of a woman who had no children. But her real appeal was to the poor women who weren't familiar with great ladies. Mayling provided them with a short cut to a vast number of new ideas: that child labor was not the inevitable way of life was the most surprising.

For all that, the Chiangs observed, the Communists made better headway wherever they had the chance to dig in and work on the people. Military conquest alone would never be enough. However, conquest must be the start of it, and so, driven by impatience with his commanding officer and with the poor results that showed up again and again in this endless war, Chiang himself took over the command of the anti-Red forces. In the confusing manner of all dealings that have to do with Moscow, preparations for a reconciliation between China and Russia—on the diplomatic level—got under way at the same time.

Chiang's onset was marked by a new vigor and organization, and he made progress. The Reds were driven back, first from the Hankow area and then from surrounding provinces. But there was still a long way for the Chinese forces to go, and Chiang, of course, was distracted by political considerations.

He had begun to feel a genuine fondness for the Young Marshal, coupled with a sense of responsibility for this boy who had come to his rescue at a bad time and then lost everything of his own. Chang Hsueh-liang had been appointed deputy commander of the Kuomintang forces in North China, partly because he was at loose ends but also because it was his native terrain and he was really useful there. Within a few months of the appointment, however, Wang Ching-wei found fault with it. Wang was predisposed to resist Japan; the period of patient preparation advocated by Chiang was not to his mind. As early as June he made a trip of his own to see how things were going in Peking, and what he saw alarmed him. At least he said it alarmed him. The Japanese had consolidated their position in Manchuria and were now making threatening gestures at China itself.

Wang stormed back to Loyang and reported that Chang Hsueh-liang was not putting up any sort of defense, and that before they knew it, North China would be lost by default. They must have a stronger character as commander up there. The Young Marshal retorted that he couldn't do any better than he was doing without more backing. He had no up-to-date equipment and it was hard to pay the soldiers. The quarrel mounted in warmth until in August, Wang Ching-wei sent out one of those circular telegrams and resigned as President of the Executive Yuan. This was disturbing. Chiang knew what power Wang wielded over a large part of the Kuomintang. He hurried to Loyang from the front and tried to persuade his difficult Premier to stay in office.

But the Young Marshal was also aroused. Three days after Wang's telegram had made the rounds, the Kuomintang had another one to read: Chang Hsueh-liang, too, had resigned. Agitated conferences followed, and the day after the second telegram, on August 9, the whole government resigned. Poor Chiang did the best he could. He accepted the Young Marshal's resignation and gave him the same job over again, under another name. He would not

release Wang permanently, but he did let him go abroad for three
months on his favorite gambit of sick leave.

December 1932 was a busy month. For one thing, the government moved back to Nanking, and for another, the arrangements
for resumed diplomatic recognition between Russia and China were
completed. Without mentioning the incongruity of these proceedings, Chiang at the same time made his report to the nation on
the anti-Communist campaign. To a sulky, bored assembly he said
that it had been definitely successful. Not only had the Army been
driven out of the central provinces, but the Nationalists had got to
work rehabilitating the formerly occupied territory. They had reformed the local governments, instituted schools, started counter-
propaganda. . . . His audience did not listen. All eyes were turned
northward, toward the Great Wall and the Japanese crowded behind it.

# 8 CONSOLIDATION 1932–36

Few Chinese had entertained hopes of satisfaction from the League of Nations decision on Japan in Manchuria. They were disgusted and impatient when the Generalissimo referred the matter to Geneva, and the ultimate outcome of this reference was as futile as they had feared. The League passed a resolution "condemning" Japan, and the angry Japanese delegates walked out of the meeting; later, the country itself retired from the League. But it was all words, said the angry Chinese. What good were mere resolutions? There the Japanese were, rooted in Manchuria and all around Shanghai; all the fine talk in Geneva didn't change that. Once more students gathered together and tried to stage a mass demonstration in Nanking. That the government was ready for them and dispersed them in their thousands at the city limits did nothing to calm public resentment.

Chiang found little sympathy. Many of his best men agreed with the public and talked as wildly as the students. A majority were in favor of forgetting the Communist campaign altogether and turning concentrated attention on Japan. As a sign of the national feelings, they said, the government should at least sponsor a boycott against Japanese goods, which would certainly have been an effective way of registering protest, for Japan's economics depended on her healthy trade with China. But the Generalissimo opposed the idea. A boycott would hasten the inevitable, and what he wanted was more time, not less.

His colleagues could not, or would not, see his point of view. He was a coward, they cried bitterly: worse, he was pro-Japanese. He must have made a secret treaty with the enemy. In a country where Feng Yu-hsiang's caperings and intrigues did not seem particularly outrageous, the accusation was believed by large numbers of people. Without government sponsorship the aggrieved patriots went ahead with their boycott and organized a number of associations to spread the gospel. As Chiang had feared, it was all too successful. On New Year's Day, 1933, the Japanese stationed just across the Wall in Jehol Province started off new hostilities with an air raid. The implied truth—that Chiang had no treaty with them, after all—was forgotten in this disaster. The Japanese claimed that the Chinese garrison had fired first, but this was a mere routine comment and fooled no one. By January 3, in spite of a spirited defense, the Chinese garrison was overpowered and the Japanese occupied the city.

Jehol lies between Manchuria and China, geographically speaking, a buffer state except for one corner of the border where the other two meet. The Japanese, to fulfill their program, were bound to occupy it sooner or later, and now they made short work of the campaign, bombing all the chief towns and cities regardless of military objectives. There would not have been much of a defense anyway; the useless General Tang Yu-lin ran away as soon as he realized what was happening, and so did all his officers. Jehol fell.

The turbulent South rallied as usual, yapping at Nanking's heels; they sent the customary denunciation by wireless, saying that the Generalissimo had betrayed them; they grew specific and accused him point-blank of selling out to Japan. Wang Ching-wei's followers in Nanking, though not so outspoken, rebuked Chiang. This, they said, was what came of having ignored Wang's warnings. If the Young Marshal had been on his toes, or better, had been replaced by somebody more capable . . . It was useless to argue that no one could have kept the Japanese from attacking unless he had been far better armed for war than was Chang Hsueh-liang. China simply couldn't fight back. She didn't have the material and she wasn't ready in any case, but the Kuomintang would not take Chiang's word for that.

When the miserable affair was finished and Japan had moved into Jehol with her customary smooth efficiency, the Generalissimo went up North and talked it over with the Young Marshal. The younger man, reasonable as always, agreed for the good of all concerned that he had better go away. It seems surprising that any of Chiang's stable of egocentrics was capable of such disinterested judgment, and we must give the credit for it to the Australian, William Henry Donald.

Donald had been in China or its vicinity, drifting about in close contact with Chinese, for nearly three decades. From Hongkong to Canton, where he worked as a newspaperman, he moved north by degrees: he knew, and was not much impressed by, Sun Yat-sen, and he had long been acquainted with the Soong family and Chiang Kai-shek, and most other Nationalist officials. For a while he was stationed at Peking; during those days he got acquainted with the Young Marshal and slipped little by little into the very special job of adviser to him. Donald had faith in Chang Hsueh-liang, and a fondness for him. Notional, cross-grained, sternly honest, bossy —there have not been many advisers in the adviser-ridden East of Donald's caliber. He was no superman; he had his vanities. He knew he was a character and he lived up to the part, boasting that he had never taken a drink, had never learned to speak a word of Chinese, and detested Chinese food. Yet he was seldom out of reach of his Chinese acquaintances, though this was necessarily confined to English speakers. China was his life.

He observed with much displeasure a friendship that sprang up

among the legations, between his "young fellow," as he called
Chang, and the Cianos. Count Ciano was head of the Italian legation. Peking society was notoriously gay, and Edda Ciano was
the gayest and maddest of its leaders. The political implications of
her interest in Chang Hsueh-liang (Italy was eager to trade with
China) and his in her (he had an intense admiration for Mussolini
and the Fascist idea) didn't worry Donald. What he didn't trust
was social life, not for his Young Marshal. He himself never went
to parties but he knew what happened at such affairs. Drink! And
the young fellow already had more vice than was good for him.
Donald glowered at the Countess Ciano and heaved a sigh of relief
when the Italians sailed home on leave. He sighed too soon. When
Chiang Kai-shek suggested the customary nice long trip abroad for
Hsueh-liang and the Young Marshal enthusiastically agreed, the
crusty newspaperman groaned aloud. He knew what was going on
in that smooth head—Edda had made her admirer promise to look
her up if ever he came over to Europe.

"Italy!" said the young fellow. "We'll go to Italy."

There was no dissuading him, but at least Donald had his own
way about another matter before they sailed. He dragged his apprehensive charge to Dr. Miller of Shanghai. Miller had a long
record in China, and plenty of experience with narcotic addiction.
He put the Young Marshal to bed, withdrew the drug, kept him
otherwise doped during the first agonizing days, and with the
help of Donald's alternate bellowings and coaxings, actually succeeded in disintoxicating the patient. It was a shaky but recon-
stituted Young Marshal who sailed at last for Italy, and he was
lively enough on the Continent to give his adviser a considerable
chase. Once he slipped the leash and went A.W.O.L. for two
anxious weeks.

The outgoing holiday party passed an ingoing one en route: for
a few uneasy days, both Chang Hsueh-liang and Wang Ching-wei

were in Shanghai. But there was no conflict: Wang had his mind on a fresh battle. He was back at his post in April, just in time for another circular telegram from the South, carrying the usual compliments of the season to Chiang and the Nanking government—a denunciation. The primary cause of this one was a well-founded rumor that Chiang intended to come to some sort of agreement with the Japanese, accepting their recent inroads. They had grabbed control of several passes on the Wall and were advancing on Luanchow, but they hinted that they would be willing to retreat if the Chinese would promise to maintain a neutral area south of the border. Chiang agreed. He was canny enough not to publish the news, but word got around anyway. Once again students went on the warpath.

The old merry-go-round promptly started up. Feng Yu-hsiang, now self-styled commander-in-chief of the People's Anti-Japanese Army in Chahar, called on all patriots of China to help combat the Japanese menace and forswear Nanking's pusillanimous attitude. He got a certain amount of response; Canton joyously threw itself into the chorus. But nothing more came of it. Some of the southerners were beginning to grow up a little bit, and the more balanced of their leaders saw Japan as a genuine menace, not merely a stick to beat Chiang with. The hotheads, baffled by moderate Pai Chung-hsi, finally removed themselves to Fukien Province and operated from there.

The Tangku truce was signed at the end of May, and the news leaked out almost immediately. There was to be a demilitarized zone just under the Wall, in which Chinese troops must not make war on anyone. The Japanese could keep an eye on it by reconnaissance plane whenever they thought it necessary to make sure the Chinese were not indulging in "provocative acts." Yet Chinese police must be responsible for keeping the rules.

Busily the dissident southerners set about their plans to join forces with Feng Yu-hsiang, intending to stop off at Nanking on the way and deal with the government there. They were not dissuaded by the fact that Chen Chi-tang, the big boss of Canton, had counted himself out of the project like Pai Chung-hsi. They mobilized a number of comparatively petty generals under the one big name they could count as theirs, Tsai Ting-kai of the Nineteenth Route Army, and so the "Anti-Japanese Relief Army for Marshal Feng Yu-hsiang" started out on the old, old road that leads through Hunan. History does not often repeat itself; it didn't this time. The Governor of Hunan, by prearrangement with Chiang, sent forces to block the road at the border. The expedition called it a day, dispersed, and went home.

Chiang didn't wait in the capital to deal with each crisis that developed. Handling difficult southern generals had become a familiar task. Through the months his real attention was riveted on the Communist campaign, and he spent much time on that front. But by the middle of November it became clear that something stronger than usual was needed to quiet the insurgents at Foochow. Chiang had used soft words and soft soap; he had even sent President Lin Sen in person to Fukien to talk things over, hoping that this sign of taking them seriously might flatter them into a reasonable state of mind. Nothing worked. On November 20 the Foochow crowd announced their government. Hu Han-min wasn't in it; he had thought better of it at the last minute. But Eugene Chen was Minister of Foreign Affairs. He always loved being Minister of Foreign Affairs.

The announcement sputtered and went out like a wet firecracker. Eugene Chen was amazed: he had been confident of a great upsurge of anti-Chiang feeling, certain that the Communists, above all, would rally to his banner. But his venture came at a time when Moscow was changing policy and wondering if Chiang Kai-shek might not be just what the Reds wanted at that point to hold off Japanese attempts against their own territory. A quiet directive went out: Eugene's effort was boycotted. Even Madame Sun, zealously obedient, published a disclaimer of any interest in the Fukien movement. It was a bitter blow to her erstwhile comrade.

The Canton crowd too, of whom Eugene had never quite given up hope, had no sympathy with him. The Cantonese already possessed a certain amount of autonomy, and though they would never hesitate to attack Chiang from their home base, they didn't want to give any rope to the rival party of independents. The Southwest Political Council, like Madame Sun, hurried to send a disclaimer. So did Chen Chi-tang, who never pretended to have connections with the legal government of Canton, though everyone knew he ran it.

Hu Han-min added his remarks of disapproval. Even Feng Yu-hsiang went on record; he did not support Foochow.

But just to keep Chiang from getting delusions of grandeur, the Southwest Political Council followed up their gesture against Foochow with another message of defiance to Nanking, imploring Chiang to resign. The signatures included that of Wang Ching-wei, and Chiang must have been stung by a sudden impatience with the dreary old round. At any rate he brought in a change. He eschewed resignations, noble renunciatory speeches, and long telegrams. Instead, he stuck out his jaw and waded in and opened hostilities against Fukien.

It may not have been worth his wrath, but he had other reasons than wrath. Orderly administration was what he wanted. He unloosed the full strength of his army, complete with the modern equipment he had been keeping under cover all this time. Among other things he unwrapped was the new air force. Until now, December 1933, the only time Chinese bombers had been used to any effect was when a few planes had flown over Changsha to rout the Communists. Now there were more planes, quite a respectable number, flown by men who knew how to handle them. These machines had been imported in small numbers at a time, and the pilots had been trained in the States.

It was the modern world against the old, Western methods against outdated Oriental; the Fukien rebels didn't stand a chance. Even the Nineteenth Route Army, in spite of its Shanghai record, broke ranks and fled. In a few weeks nothing was left of the revolt, and by the end of 1933 all that remained for the Nationalists to do was reorganize the beaten army. Chiang incorporated the Fukien government's men in the Nanking forces, as he had already done with Chang Hsueh-liang's dispossessed troops. One way and another, Nanking was collecting an impressive force.

Then the Generalissimo turned to Canton, which had hatched out so many of his headaches, and said it was time to stop fooling. He promised to subsidize Canton's military expenses, and even to permit their autonomous Political and Military councils, but Chen Chi-tang must in turn support him in his anti-Red drive. No more distracting clamor about resisting Japan, he said sternly: Communists first!

Chen Chi-tang promised, and the war lords of the other Red-infested provinces followed his lead.

The Central Soviet Government of the Chinese Communists was located at Juichin in Kiangsi. In spite of Nanking's most vigorous attacks it remained deeply rooted. Mao Tse-tung and his next in command, Chu Teh, were slowly gaining control against the strong competition of the Returned Students clique which had supplanted Li Li-san. Little by little Mao proved his point about agrarian reform as a major strategy. There were still discussions in Moscow, and contradictory orders and an occasional reprimand, but Mao continued to gain ground. In the autumn of 1932 he scored in an important move when he persuaded Moscow, in spite of opposition from the Returned Students, to shift all party activity from its underground position in Shanghai and concentrate it in Juichin.

Japanese aggression favored the Reds in an immediate way by

distracting Chiang's attention. To force the Generalissimo into a
change of emphasis the Communists continued to condemn the
island empire in loud tones. If they were running China, they declared, Japan would not be permitted to carry on like this. Yet
they did nothing themselves against the Japanese. They tried to
maintain a nice balance in their attitude: the time might come
when they would need something to hold the Japanese off Russia
herself. It suited them to keep the Generalissimo suspended between two threats. Solidly sitting in Kiangsi, acquiring an aspect of
permanency, the C.C.P. evolved away from its original form of a
guerrilla army. The more regular their life, the more rapidly they
could spread teaching and land reform among villagers and farmers. They recruited the dispossessed who were wandering about,
the victims of local wars; they fed these people and educated them
and sent them out to carry the word. Kiangsi and the other provinces where they worked were in a hinterland that had never been
more than nominally a part of Chiang's domain. All their lives the
people there had been at the mercy of war-lord rule, with its ac-
companiment of rapacious landlords, officials, and usurers. They
were pathetically easy to convert.

In 1934, for the first time in years, Chiang looked around him
in Nanking and realized that he had the leisure to start a thorough
program of Red eradication. Like the villagers, he had learned
something from their methods. Force alone would never suffice
to stamp out their influence, but force was the first thing necessary,
and its application would be costly and slow. He was sure of his
ground in that part of the campaign. But the Communists, even if
driven out, would leave their doctrine and disciples, and unless
the vacuum created by their absence could be filled, their spirit
would still reign. The country needed political and moral reconstruction.

Chiang marshaled his knowledge of both Confucian ethics and
Methodism. He talked it over with his wife, with some of the

high-ranking Kuomintang, and with Donald, safely back with his
young fellow from the pitfalls of Rome. The conferences discussed
matters that had never before interested the China-bred Generalissimo; Western standards of cleanliness and probity in public life.
It was a sore point, for example, that Westerners said China was
dirty. The Chinese had always resented this statement, but defensively laughed it off and maintained that they *liked* to be dirty,
and, anyway, Westerners were much dirtier. Who cared what the
outer barbarians might say? But the Generalissimo was married
to a woman who agreed with the foreigners. Mayling's ideas
were passionate and fierce; she had been in a state about China's
hygiene ever since she came back from her American schooling.
She was miserable about the filth of city streets, the happy-go-lucky
dirtiness of Chinese kitchens, the communal feeding bowl into
which everyone stuck his sucked chopsticks. She carried clean
sheets about with her to put down on chairs or floors, and in her
own house she invented a system of serving the food with special
chopsticks, and of using individual helpings. But even she had been
able to do nothing about the hawking and spitting that were a
familiar part of the Chinese scene.

The more Chiang thought about it, the more he liked the idea of
teaching cleanliness, as well as austerity, to his troops. It was
in tune with his philosophy of regular exercise, careful eating, and
all the rest of it. The New Life Movement got under way.

Madame decided that Donald would be a useful friend to keep
around. His management of the Young Marshal had stirred her
admiration; she had a proper missionary horror of opium. Moreover, she had heard him speak up and harangue Chiang about
everything he considered wrong in the government: corruption,
opium-dealing, nepotism, inefficiency, all the things an old-style
Chinese administrator pretended not to notice and old-style officials were too polite to mention. Of course he couldn't say this in
Chinese, but Madame interpreted it all with relish. The friend-

ship was to continue, by correspondence, after the Young Marshal and Donald went to Hankow, where Chang Hsueh-liang had been given a new post commanding the "Bandit Suppression" troops. In the meantime Donald sat in on some of the discussions of the New Life Movement.

So did Chen Li-fu, one of the two Chen brothers, in his capacity of expert on young China. Chen had been associated with the Whampoa cadets in the early days before the break with the Russians. He still kept his fingers on the pulse of military youth; he was in charge of the mysterious "Blue Shirt" organization, a pallid imitation of Europe's rainbow-shirted brigades of Fascists. There was a lot of resentful whispering about these Blue Shirts. Their methods never approached the bullying terrorism of German and Italian organizations of the same sort, but the public had no assurance that they wouldn't. The label of Fascism, as a matter of fact, was not damning in itself: the Chinese weren't particular whose ideology they borrowed from. Their committee system was Russian and their Blue Shirts Fascist. But the New Life Movement was peculiarly Chinese.

In conference, the Generalissimo expounded his plan—more stringent rules for neatness and hygiene, the popularizing of the toothbrush in the Army and among civilians as well; reminders of the usual rules of courtesy. Chen thought it an excellent idea as far as it went, but he argued that the concept merely of cleanliness and austerity was too limited. Leaders must give their people something inspirational, he said. People wanted ideals; they *liked* ideals. One must go back to the good old Chinese virtues and give the whole thing uplift. So in deference to this theory, four solid, ancient—and, to a Westerner, confusingly vague—virtues were added to the list of those to which good Chinese should aspire: *li, yi, lien,* and *chih. Li* means etiquette, or rather propriety, or even things as they should be. *Yi* means justice. *Lien* is integrity. *Chih* is conscientiousness, which is not the same thing as integrity because it applies more to one's private, personal life. (Any Chinese scholar is at liberty to differ with these interpretations; a number, doubtless, will. No two of these dissidents, however, will agree with each other, so we may as well let them stand.)

Nonmissionary Westerners and many Western-educated Chinese greeted the New Life Movement with impatient skepticism. It was muddled and sanctimonious and do-goody, they complained, and full of platitudes. What was wrong with dancing, anyway? Why should you need all that fanfare to tell people to clean their teeth and keep their collars buttoned? Some of the admonitions were resounding emptiness, said the critics. Scornfully they cited, "Observe rules, have faith, honesty and humility." Or, "Act on your promises. Better, act without promising."

But pious precepts are in the nature of Chinese things. Their education consists in a series of such commandments, and some of the new precepts embodied ideas which, however platitudinous they sound to us, were new to the people. Many persons had actually never been told before that improved eating habits would make them healthier or that streets should be kept clean and swept. Furthermore, when Chiang exhorted the public to be frugal, he was saying something that needed saying. Thrifty though the Chinese were, there were points on which tradition forced them to be lavish to a reckless degree. The New Life Movement discouraged expensive funerals, deprecated "showing-off" dinners where the host served thirty or forty dishes that no one could possibly finish, and introduced the custom of "mass weddings," in which all young couples in the town who wanted to marry were polished off in one day during the season, with one ceremony and one feast. Frugality became fashionable.

So did hygiene. At schools and colleges girls threw themselves into the New Life Movement and did exercises and sports. Willowy pallor went out of style; Amazonian beauty came in. Shrilly the women protested that though they were doing their best, the men were lagging. Girls wrote to the newspapers complaining that their Chinese boy friends were sickly, weedy-looking specimens; they threatened to look for sturdier beaux elsewhere. This was all new to a race that had hitherto deprecated rude good health as being unaesthetic.

The whole thing was formally inaugurated in March, at Nanchang, with one of Chiang's marathon speeches. Within a few months, though the intellectuals sneered and jeered, there were placards everywhere urging the people to be neat and clean. Arrests were made of anti-social characters who spat recklessly on the sidewalks or in railway stations. Enthusiasts deprecated smoking in public. Opium was denounced. Dancing was frowned on. The old happy-go-lucky men's fashion of wearing the collar open—no small relief on a summer day, when a Chinese collar can be torture—went out. It was a laugh-worthy mixture of values from our point of view, but it worked. Through it, the Chinese were steamed up for the great all-out anti-Red drive.

Chiang spoke of another plan, to be put into effect as soon as he won the victory he was so confident of. Once free of the Communists, he said, the land would be made over according to the "People's Economic Reconstruction." No longer would the Reds hold the monopoly for reform, education, and exploitation of natural resources. He had reason to speak in more detail about the reconstruction during a meeting he called in June to address the generals and governors of the provinces involved; Kiangsi, Fukien, and Kwangsi. If these men would co-operate with Nanking to the best of their ability, said Chiang, and with all the troops at their disposal, he would include them in the national reconstruction, and subsidize improvements in their domains afterward. Though these men had no love for the Generalissimo—Pai Chunghsi definitely hated him—they had even less affection for the Reds. They promised. They sat in on military meetings with Chiang's

considerable corps of German advisers, and with exclusive knowledge of the terrain helped to evolve the over-all strategy.

Already the campaign had begun, with advance guards of soldiers
making roads and building blockhouses. The whole sovietized
area was marked out and encircled with these little forts and an
efficient network of communications. Slowly tightening the circle
the Nanking army of about four hundred thousand men set up a
blockade, preventing supplies of any sort going in or any exports
coming out. The people inside the circle, unfortunate civilians who
were caught on their home ground, soon felt the pinch. They began
to desert the Communists, for when things got tight even the amiable Reds took their food from them by force. The Communists ran
out of ammunition, and they needed salt. All the while the Nanking
soldiers with their allies moved inward, coolly and methodically
tightening the belt.

As activities continued and peripheral towns were evacuated by
fleeing Reds, Chiang's secret police moved in. This "Special
Movement Force" was organized much on the lines of a similar
body of Soviet youths, a fact which did not prevent the Communists making capital, in their propaganda later on, of the
iniquity of such proceedings. It appears that there was nothing
especially sinister or terroristic about the Special Movement Force,
though that doesn't make it more palatable. The Westerner dis-
likes any sort of secret police however restrained. In all there
were about twenty thousand of them—"a combination of the intelligence section and of the military police, such as are to be found
in all modern armies," says Tong defensively—but their duties
smacked more of the Y.M.C.A. than is usual in modern armies.
They wore plain clothes and were supposed to round up deserters
or stray Communists, enforce the blockade, search travelers, see
that the troops didn't molest the farmers and other civilians, organize and train the masses, shepherd the troops and billet them,
"elevate popular morale," re-establish schools, train volunteers—

everything, in fact, except put out the cat at night. "All of them were educated men, some of them graduates of higher primary or middle schools, while others were graduates or former pupils of the Whampoa Military Academy. . . . The members were required to take a special oath to act justly and to deal fairly in and with all things." (Tong, *Chiang Kai-shek.*)

We would not like it at home—all those stern, important young prigs in power bustling about—but the Generalissimo liked it. Something in him has always responded to the voice and spirit of Lord Baden-Powell. One of the confusing aspects about this far from simple story of Red eradication is that although the Communists had long been claiming to have wiped out gambling and prostitution from all their occupied territory in Kiangsi and Hunan, the lads of the Special Movement Force claimed that *they* put down gambling and prostitution, which they found in a flourishing state at the take-over. We can therefore conclude that, at any rate, whoever chased out vice, it must have been well and truly eradicated by the time both armies finished with it.

But this is a comparatively minor point. A more important one is that when the conquering troops marched in they found a cruel state of starvation among the people, and the Special Movement Force was efficient in carrying relief to them.

Chiang Kai-shek grew confident, then cheerful, then exultant. The new tactics were working like a charm. Reds evacuated town after town, retreating further and further, from Hunan and Fukien and Hupei, until they had been pushed at last into an unhappy huddle in Kiangsi and Juichin itself was threatened. Nanking left them no chance to play at the old game of luring vanguards into mountain ambushes. The Reds abandoned their guerrilla technique and adopted positional warfare, and continued to lose ground at an even swifter rate. Mao Tse-tung, struggling for mastery over his fleeing troops, blamed his rivals the Returned Students for this shift in the old pattern, but it was probably inevitable.

By October, Chiang's forces had chased one large contingent of Reds, who broke out of the circle, into Fukien. In Kiangsi they captured two thousand prisoners in one battle. A month later they were preparing to close in for the kill. They were outside Juichin, the last stronghold, and expected to find the main part of the Red Army there. But the Communists outwitted them.

The southwest part of the cordon was at its weakest point, where Hunan and Kwangtung troops were stationed. Ninety thousand Communists—men, women, and children, carrying whatever they could of arms and machinery and supplies—had secretly replaced their army lines with local partisans, and themselves slipped to the south of Kiangsi. On the fifteenth of October they suddenly attacked the belt that had held them in its grip for so long, and the surprise and ferocity of the onslaught carried them through, bursting into freedom out of Kiangsi. Then they set out on the famous "Long March" that was to lead them, after a year of wandering over at least six thousand miles, to the Northwest. They did not march as one band of brothers, however. There was a lot of bickering, and many were the angry messages telegraphed to Moscow. Accusations and self-defense crowded the air, but within four months, at the beginning of 1935 at a party conference en route, Mao won out.

There was no more competition in the Chinese Communist ranks, at least none that counted. Mao was the acknowledged leader of his band, for what leadership was worth at that low ebb of their history. The conference disbanded; the Communists continued the Long March; and in Kiangsi, Chiang Kai-shek set to work on the next phase of his program, reconstruction.

In 1934 several governmental crises swelled up and broke. The earliest of these was a hang-over from the year before—dissension not only within the government, but in the Soong family itself. In this, T. V. Soong, the white-haired boy of treaty-port banking circles, was a victim of his Western education.

He had a tidy mind to begin with, and Harvard had made it tidier. When T.V. came back to China and took up in turn the various appointments culminating in his ministership of Finance, the most outspoken critics of the "Soong Dynasty" among foreigners could find no fault with this choice. They had their grievances against the other Soongs, especially Mayling herself; people do hold grievances against other people in power. But T.V., they told each other, knew his stuff. You could deal with T.V., he talked your language, the language of American banks. You could depend on him. T.V. was always on time for an appointment, and this in a country where two hours one way or the other made no difference to most natives was noteworthy indeed.

But the qualities that made him popular among Americans and British brought trouble upon his head. He was so American that Chinese methods of finance, or what they fondly considered methods, drove him as crazy as they drove native Americans. He started out full of energy and determination to put China on the map as a sensible, solvent country. Almost before he knew it he was running into that great stone wall, his brother-in-law Chiang Kai-shek. Chaing had no use for facts and figures. When he meant to spend money on army equipment, he didn't want his Finance Minister coming in and making a scene and telling him it couldn't be done. When he planned to start government schools in the hinterland or construct roads for the Army or build up his air arm, it irritated him to be told the nation couldn't afford it. T.V.'s alternative plans for money didn't interest Chiang.

The friction between Mayling's husband and her brother could ordinarily have been smoothed over, for family spirit was strong in the Soongs. But it so happened that the old clan cohesiveness was under a strain about that time. It grew out of the fact that T.V. was quite a man for the ladies. He was tall and broad and good-looking, the most eligible of all the government crowd; naturally he was much in demand. New Life Movement or no New Life Movement, the moneyed young ladies of Nanking and Shanghai had begun to indulge in the joys of independent life. T.V. was said to have got mixed up with a girl. Madame Kung was a friend of this girl: she tried to interfere and put a stop to what she considered a disastrous relationship. T.V. resented the interference. He said there was nothing to interfere with anyway. There was a quarrel. He who quarrels with Madame Kung quarrels with Madame Chiang, and so the next time T.V. was at outs with the Generalissimo, no devoted little sister stood ready to pour oil on the waves. When next Chiang demanded extra money for the anti-Red campaign T.V. resigned, and his resignation was accepted. He went abroad, and H. H. Kung took his place in the Ministry.

So it was more than a routine upheaval, and it was also part of a long history of trouble among the Soongs on the subject of political beliefs. In the purge of 1927, T.V. had havered between sisters; Mayling and Eling on the Right, Chingling on the Left. Because they nearly got him the Communists have always looked upon him with a certain proprietary fondness. There, they feel, with just a little more push, goes a man who could be saved. His American briskness, his Babbitt-like exterior, never put the Reds off. During all their propaganda campaigns for foreign consumption they condemned Kung and built him up in their cartoons as a great fat devil, but T.V., whose weight at that time was at about the same figure and whose background is even more damningly Wall Street, has always been left a loophole. There were many times when in a burst of anger against Mayling and Eling and their husbands he nearly made up his mind to step across the line and join hands with his other sister. He never quite did.

While he tightened the bonds of co-operation between southern war lords, Chiang tidied up a few other matters, as, for instance, what face China should now show the world in foreign affairs. The nation was becoming a respectable entity and he thought she held enough rank now to support embassies rather than mere legations. Hitherto most of the foreign powers had not agreed with this estimation. Only Russia maintained an embassy, and that was a dubious compliment at best. Now the attitude was changing; Mussolini's Italy was especially keen to take her place in world trade, and that meant grabbing some of China's custom from the other foreigners. Already Shanghai was thronged with Italian munitions salesmen: in March 1934 it was announced that thenceforth Italy's legation would be an embassy. Japan promptly followed suit, jealous for her enormous market. Rather more majestically, Great Britain and America followed, and then Germany. There was an exciting reshuffle in various foreign offices, and social life among the foreigners in Nanking received a jolt in the arm, though this made small difference to Chiang and his immediate circle.

At the same time that Japan was exchanging such diplomatic compliments with her neighbor, unfriendly goings on were clearly visible north of the Wall. A Japanese adventurer, Major General Kenji Doihara, had finally carried out the old plan formulated in Tokyo, years before, and "restored" Pu-yi, the former child Emperor of China, to a throne in Manchuria, which country the Japanese had by this time renamed "Manchukuo." The enthronement made the Chinese boil with rage, and Chiang was just in time to keep the Southwest Political Council from sending a "manifesto" off to Japan and Manchuria on its own bat. No, no, said the Generalissimo, the autonomy of Canton was all very well but it didn't go as far as that. Nanking, and only Nanking, was empowered to deal with foreign countries in that way. Wonder of wonders, the Cantonese submitted. The manifesto was signed by Nanking. This was a negligible matter, as diplomatic exchanges so often are, but it was also a triumph of a new sort. The lords of Kwangtung and Kwangsi were actually beginning to be reasonable.

Chiang followed up his victory with a suggestion that the whole lot of them—Chen Chi-tang, Hu Han-min, Pai Chung-hsi, Li

Tsung-jen, and all—get together and talk things over at a Fifth
Plenary Session of the Central Executive Committee. Hu Han-min
still held out, muttering about dictatorships and Blue Shirts. Pai
Chung-hsi was dubious. But there seemed no harm in mere discussion, and the plenary session was held in December and plans
laid for a Party Congress on November 12, 1935. At the same time
it was agreed that Nanking should thenceforth be the central point
for all economic control. It was a long step toward unification.

Donald and Madame had long been cherishing an idea to jog the
Generalissimo loose from his grim routine of conference-cum-war;
to make him travel far and wide, to see for himself and be seen.
They got their chance at a moment when they were able to join
forces. In October the Chiangs stopped at the Young Marshal's
headquarters in Hankow and whisked him off—with Donald, of
course—to accompany them on a voyage of inspection to a new
military academy at Loyang. There, instead of going back to
Hankow, Donald persuaded the Generalissimo to take his train in
the other direction, to Sian in far-off Shensi. After all, he had never
seen this ancient place, Donald reminded him, and it was one of a
ruler's fundamental duties to know his own country.

Chiang didn't need much urging; he liked sudden action, change,
and swooping down to get information fresh and hot. They arrived
in Sian, then, with little advance notice. In China people make
speeches at the drop of a hat, and that is what happened; everybody
made speeches—the Chiangs, their hosts, and the missionaries who
eagerly rushed forward to meet Madame. There were so many
speeches that the Chiangs stayed in Sian three days. It was agreed
that first on the list of abuses to be reformed was the suppression
of opium raising, selling, and smoking. The missionaries could not
have been more enchanted: a captious lot after all the years of war
and mismanagement, they felt that here at last was the reward. And
to think that Mayling was one of their own girls! Her manifest
popularity with these foreigners pleased Chiang, though he was a

little overwhelmed. He decided that foreigners, after all, were not so bad.

From Sian it was easy to coax the truant farther. They flew everywhere to save time and get in as much as they could—to Lanchow and Ninghsia and Peking and Kalgan: they stopped in on Yen Hsi-shan at Taiyuanfu; it was a packed and busy time, forty days in all.

Madame suffered grievously from airsickness. It was suggested that she carry an oxygen tank with her on long high journeys. Fortunately there was no crystal-gazer to tell the poor lady how many, many miles she was going to have to fly in the course of her subsequent life.

At last Chiang had seen for himself the mysterious Northwest. Having viewed Yen Hsi-shan at home in his fastness and inspected the famous cave dwellings of the loess mountains, he was never again to be narrow or unimaginative about other people's ambitions. He developed a new pride in the country, and a new confidence in himself. In Lanchow and Kalgan he had felt safe. The fleets of cars, the dozens of bodyguards, could be forgotten when he traveled. Only one incident marred that sensation of escape; between Chahar and Suiyuan a bomb was thrown into the train. Were the throwers pro-Japanese? Pro-Red? Nobody admitted they knew, and the news was suppressed, but two arrests were made.

All in all, it was decided, these trips were better made by air, and after that the air age arrived for good in China. Crowds gathered on the airfield whenever the Chiangs appeared. The difference Chiang's personal appearances made is incalculable. Through the centuries the Chinese peasants and workers had been ruled by some mysterious far-off figure away in the capital, and it never occurred to them that they would ever be close to one of their great men. As a result they did very little thinking about such great men. Law and order, or oppression, as the case might be, was bound up

for them in the local mandarin or taxgatherer. With actual vision of
the Generalissimo, actual hearing of his voice and his words, came
a stimulated interest in being Chinese. Realization of nationality
brought pride. Chiang Kai-shek was the first man the Chinese
could be proud of; not a village hero, but one of their own people
in a bigger way.

The Japanese liked to start their operations early in a new year,
and 1935 brought no change to the old routine. Chahar, adjoining
Jehol, was next on their list. They had left the situation there alone
since the Tangku truce; now in January they suddenly presented
a complaint against Sung Cheh-yuan, the Governor of the province,
demanding that he withdraw his troops from the districts near the
border because they had been trespassing on Jehol ground in the
Tatan district. Nanking retorted (a) that they hadn't, and (b) that
the area in question wasn't in Jehol anyway, but in Chahar. The
Japanese promptly did the usual and attacked across the Great
Wall, after observing the formality they never omitted, of accusing
the Chinese of firing first. A battle took place on January 23, the
Japanese moved in, and after that nothing was heard from the
Chinese defenders for a week. At the end of that time it was an-
nounced by the Japanese that a treaty had been signed between
Sung and themselves. There was nothing Chiang could do unless he
wanted a showdown.

Worse followed. It was not always completely imagination on the
Jap side that "incidents" occurred. The Chinese could not refrain
from a stray shot now and then; a large number of these soldiers
near the Wall were Chang Hsueh-liang's dispossessed Manchurians.
Hopei, the danger area, was staffed with these Manchurians, taken
over by Nanking when the Young Marshal joined forces with
Chiang, but still resentfully, staunchly loyal to their home country.
Every bit of news they got from "Manchukuo" stimulated their
anger, against the Japanese first, but also, secondarily, against that

stubborn man in Nanking who wouldn't let their Young Marshal lead them back. Chang Hsueh-liang had been shifted to Sian. He was in touch again with his men; there was a strong feudal bond between them, and he was just as homesick as any of the others. He was becoming less starry-eyed about Chiang Kai-shek and his promise to co-operate, and he had lost Donald. Madame Chiang had taken the Australian away. He now lived in the Chiangs' house and worked as her secretary, and gave his pungent advice to the Generalissimo whether or not he was asked for it. The Young Marshal felt the loss of his mentor.

The anti-Red campaign was over, the new publicity drive was started, various gestures had been made toward reconstruction projects, and all would have been smooth sailing if it hadn't been for Japan. But Japan was there, crowding ever closer. She had Jehol, she had some of Chahar, and now it looked as if she meant to move in on North China altogether—Chahar, Hopei, Shantung, Shansi, and Suiyuan. If you were a Japanese looking at the map, it would seem obvious where the country should next expand. The chief militarists who were running Japanese foreign policy, however, could not quite bring their home government to take such a big bite openly. However, if the provinces themselves could be induced to demand "autonomy" like that enjoyed by Manchukuo, there would be no awkward moments explaining things away. Doihara set to work persuading the Chinese that they wanted independence.

From one province to another he made the rounds, talking, promising, explaining, and threatening in turn, and wherever he went, whatever he said, Chiang Kai-shek got to hear of it. That Japanese activity had branched out in this direction instead of taking its usual form of thinly veiled aggression, the Generalissimo figured, was significant; evidently they weren't quite sure of their backing in Tokyo. If he was very careful and gave them no shadow of a chance to pick an open quarrel, it might postpone the day of reckoning, and Doihara's plans, indefinitely.

He set to work padding all the places where friction could generate sparks. Ruthlessly he muzzled the noisy students in Peking. The turbulent Manchurians were sent to garrison towns in Kansu. He disbanded the Peking branches of the National Military Council and the National Political Council, and sternly put down all the demonstration processions organized by Doihara, with their signs demanding autonomy. He persuaded the northern provincial governors to defy Doihara when the conspirator tried to force them to demand independence. He called the Japanese Government's bluff by reporting Doihara's doings to their Foreign Office. He asked in hurt tones if it was on their orders that the major general was acting in this matter, or was it merely a private enterprise? The Japanese hastily assured him that they knew nothing of Doihara's activity in Peking, and soon afterward it ceased abruptly.

The final outcome was satisfactory in a negative way, for North China heard no more of autonomy, but the Japanese were still determined to get in sooner or later. They managed to occupy Peking by peaceful methods. Unofficially they were all over North China. Chiang hadn't even scotched the snake, and he had made crippling concessions.

On the credit side of the ledger was the Kweichow affair. There were still some Communists there, enough to kick up a fuss in 1935, and the Generalissimo found the circumstance advantageous rather than otherwise. His journey to the Northwest had given him an appetite for personal appearances, and Kweichow offered an excellent excuse to see more of the way the other half lives. Chiang went west in person to deal with the revolt, and when he got there he put the place through the same treatment he had given Sian and Kalgan. He traveled from one town to another making speeches, getting acquainted with the local officials, and telling everybody to be good and work hard. It was timely advice, for the province was backward and there was much oppression and overtaxation, as there always was in these semi-autonomous outlying districts—a hard life for the peasants, and a heaven-sent chance for the Communists to dig in.

Szechuan, far to the west, was next on the list, for the Reds were there too, and found an even richer field for conversion. In Szechuan the staple industry and chief occupation was opium. The turbaned populace was yellow-complexioned, anemic and languid from underfeeding and oversmoking. The war lords of Szechuan were accustomed to absolute power: no Manchu Emperor in Peking had ever taken an interest in their far-off country. There actually were genuine bandits, lawbreakers who were not Communists, living among the Szechuan and Yunnan hills and plundering the villagers whenever they needed food or cash, but whether the villagers feared them more than they did the tax collectors is a moot point: it was not an easy life in either case. The Communists who split off from the Long March and settled in these Szechuanese hills found disciples by the hundred ready to their hand.

Chiang Kai-shek brought his forces in and operated from the few cities of the province, in a long drawn out, rather easygoing campaign. The Reds were not as well entrenched as they had been in Central China; they had had less time to take root. More important than his few encounters with guerrilla bands were the acquaintances Chiang made among the ruling families. He sniffed out a few facts about the deplorable administration and applied his angriest energy to the job of reform. He assailed the Governor for the corruption and extortion that made the province the most notorious in the nation. Then he did a courageous thing that endeared him to hundreds of missionaries; again he tackled the question of opium. Little by little, he said firmly, it must be abolished.

This was a task most people declared impossible. It meant stamping on the only really flourishing industry of the province; it meant recasting the economy of Szechuan. There were rich men there whose entire fortunes depended on the opium crop; there were peasants of whose poor living the same could be said. Yet more formidable was the proposal to cure the great number of Szechuan addicts. There has been a lot of nonsense talked about opium since its use was first observed, and in those days people were convinced that an addict simply could not give up his addiction without losing his life. It could be done, said Chiang, and it must be. Laws were passed, time limits set, clinics founded for the treatment of addicts, and a deadline set after which there was to be no more opium grown, extracted, or smoked in Szechuan. The missionaries admired Chiang immensely for this, but he made a lot of enemies, too.

In the early summer of 1935 a Chinese magazine, published in Shanghai, brought out an insulting article, or an article deemed insulting by the Japanese, about their Emperor. They made angry representations to Nanking, and the results of these should have gratified them. Chiang could not, it seemed, do enough to humiliate his own country and placate the bullies, and his people were furious about it. The editor, author, and publisher were thrown into prison, and press censorship was tightened up. Again the students boiled and bubbled. Everyone was angry—angrier with Chiang, probably, even than with the Japanese Emperor.

In Shanghai, where the concentration of foreigners was large and the city's nearness to Nanking made people feel proprietary about the capital, Chiang Kai-shek was becoming a kind of legend. Since he had taken to traveling through the far provinces by plane, a paradoxical situation had been created: the treaty port where he had got his first chance in the Army and made his first fortune, by way of the stock exchange, now saw almost nothing of him. He rarely made personal appearances even in Nanking. Yet the people of Szechuan and Shansi could claim to have heard and seen their leader pretty lavishly.

The paradox was not Madame's creation, or Donald's. They tried to spread the publicity a bit more evenly, but they weren't successful. It has never been easy to push the Generalissimo when he doesn't want to do something, and he didn't like publicity at home, or near home; he preferred privacy. His days were too full to give up to official banquets or unnecessary interviews. As for Shanghai —well, he didn't like Shanghai; it represented a lot of things about China's position in the world that he didn't approve of. Chiang was not thoroughly anti-foreign. He had begun to see a good deal, comparatively, of the missionary friends Mayling brought home. But his ambition was to place China on a new footing with the Western world, and he felt the resentment most Chinese nationalists did for Europeans. He wasn't fond of extraterritoriality, or of the placidly smug businessmen from the other side of the world, who lived in Shanghai as if Nanking simply did not exist.

Some of the businessmen who knew that Nanking *was* there, especially bankers and brokers, realized his attitude and resented it. Chiang had two sets of opponents who were diametrically opposed to each other as well: the business element, including some important Japanese members of the international colony, who didn't want to see him or his nation become too strong, and the Communist sympathizers who had the same idea. These groups coincided in their criticisms of the Generalissimo, and their complaints swelled in unison until the outside world heard them.

One of their grievances was the old charge that Chiang was aiming at dictatorship. The pious accusation sounded strange coming from people like Chen Chi-tang or Feng Yu-hsiang. It carried weight, however, when Hu Han-min said it, and he often did. Chiang's advisers urged him to ignore the attacks and take on more trappings of power. He did not do quite all they asked; he still hesitated to assume the presidency of the government. But there is no doubt that power *was* being centralized by the Kuomintang, taken away little by little from the provinces. This in itself, he could have argued, was not necessarily a sign of sinister intention, but Hu pointed out angrily that truly democratic leaders don't use secret police.

The only reply Chiang could have made to that—and if he made it, he knew better than to do so publicly—was that conditions outside and inside China simply rendered democracy impossible. Premature self-government would have meant undermining by some war lord or other, most probably Chen Chi-tang, followed by an all-out attack by Japan and inevitable collapse. However, such things could not be said in the open. So the complaints continued, most durable on the pettiest plane, as complaints usually are.

You never get to see him alone, frustrated people would say angrily after unsatisfactory interviews. That woman was always there. Mayling was blamed for all the Generalissimo's unpopular decisions, and when Mayling alone did not seem a reasonable scapegoat for quite everything that went wrong for the petitioners, they enlarged the blame. It was the family, they said, the whole Soong family. The old joke "The Soong Dynasty" did not now seem quite so funny.

The public demand for resistance to Japan grew louder and louder; no amount of press censorship could contain it. One of the by-products of this sentiment was a comitragedy, and Wang Ching-wei, of all people, who had more than once taken advantage of just this sort of clamor to embarrass Chiang and pull him out of office, was its victim. Somehow word got round that he was pro-Japanese —there is never any reasonableness when a nation gets into a hysterical state—and he was nearly assassinated while coming out of a C.E.C. meeting one November afternoon. The assassin had hidden a revolver in a tripod camera; it was the easiest thing in the world to shoot the Premier at close quarters, and only a very nervous man could have failed to kill. He did fail, though. Wang was badly hurt, and carried the bullet near his spine for the rest of his life, but he survived.

He had to give up his post and go abroad, and Chiang Kai-shek was appointed Premier in his place. To allay the inevitable wrath of Hu Han-min at this considerable accession of power, Chiang saw to it that Hu was appointed chairman of the C.E.C. standing committee at the same time, but Hu was too angry to be appeased by this. He stayed in Europe and wouldn't accept the job. Other criticisms, from the usual quarters, were forestalled: Chiang had invited Feng Yu-hsiang to come to Nanking and see for himself how very, very democratically everything was being run. Feng seemed convinced, and Chiang told him to carry the good word to Canton.

"We will fight the Japanese when they go too far," the Generalissimo insisted. This was becoming a platitude; every time he said it, extremists and middle-roaders grew angrier. Just when was Chiang going to admit that so far was too far? Japan was pressing harder and harder for what she called "co-operation" with Manchukuo; in other words, recognition of that stolen country. Toward the end of the year she moved again in her gradual taking over of North China, inciting the wild Mongols of the North to overrun that part of Chahar that adjoins Jehol. The Chinese garrison was forbidden by the terms of the Tatan treaty to prevent the Mongols' occupying this district; everyone had foreseen what would happen, but that didn't make it any pleasanter when it actually came to pass. In January 1936 the Mongols expanded their area and seized Kalgan, straddling the Peking-Suiyuan Railway. In their arrogant footsteps came the little Japanese, quietly jubilant and, as always, efficient in taking over control.

"We will strike when they go too far," repeated Chiang, and the young men groaned and muttered and talked of taking matters into their own hands. Anyone would have thought the country on the verge of revolt, but he would have been wrong.

Hu Han-min came back at last from Europe and listened in stately disapproval, but at least at closer quarters, to Chaing's representations that his proper place was in Nanking. Hu did not agree. If he deigned to come, he said—and he would not promise to do so—there would have to be some very searching changes made in

the government setup. Those secret police, for one thing . . .
Chiang let him talk, and kept his temper and persisted. Hu was still
one of the big three, and he counted in the Party. The suggestion
was even made, quite seriously, that Chiang give up his post as
Premier to the older man. Hu was tempted and nearly disarmed.
As Premier he would be in a good position to play watchdog for
the nation's liberties. He would probably have accepted, but then
something happened that took the minds of both men off such questions as appointments in a peaceful government. It was the South
again, the ever-restless South.

In June 1936 the trio—Chen Chi-tang, Li Tsung-jen, and Pai
Chung-hsi—sent a telegram demanding that Chiang go to war
against Japan. Almost immediately they followed it up with the
expedition that was *de rigueur* in these cases, Kwangsi soldiers into
Hunan and Kwangtung men aiming for Fukien and Kiangsi. Chiang
dispatched troops to meet them and turned, as he had done on
former occasions, to the Governor of Hunan, requesting him to
refuse permission to the Kwangsi troops to cross the province.

This time there was a new Governor; Ho Chien, who had fought
with Chiang in the anti-Communist campaign. His name was well
known to Chinese Reds because of his ruthless methods. Mao
Tse-tung, especially, had reason to know him: Ho Chien's men had
killed Mao's wife. Before the Nanking troops had time to reach
contact with the Kwangsi vanguard, Ho Chien had sent his own
men to block the frontier at Hengchow.

It takes war lords a long time to change their minds and methods.
Li, Pai, and Chen, remembering old times, seem to have thought
they were still playing the same game, and that there would soon be
one of those thundering telegrams from Feng Yu-hsiang announc-
ing that his People's Army were waiting and raring to go at Japan.
Wang Ching-wei would be heard from, and Hu Han-min would be
glad to join in. Then when all the boys were together, they could
start making demands on Chiang Kai-shek.

Suddenly the telegrams began to arrive. They arrived by the hundred, and none of them was from Feng Yu-hsiang offering his heart and hands to help resist Japan. None of them was approving at all. From Singapore and San Francisco and Paris, from Nanking and the Northwest, from Chinatown in London and Liverpool the wires flooded in, telling the southern war lords to give it all up and go home. Now was not the time, said the Chinese of the world, for that old foolishness.

Then at the beginning of July the nation was electrified by another piece of news. Every single one of Chen's fighting airplanes, forty of them altogether, had been flown from Canton to join Chiang Kai-shek in open rebellion of their leader. Chen was still staggering from the effects of this blow when his second-in-command, General Yu Han-mou, quietly took off by plane from the airfield, and the next thing they knew was in Nanking offering his services to the Generalissimo. His defection set off a chain reaction in the Kwangtung army; generals started jumping out like popping corn. A few days later Yu Han-mou set out on the homeward march as commander-in-chief of Kwangtung's troops, specially appointed by Chiang Kai-shek. They didn't have to fight with their provincial brothers; nobody tried to resist them. Chen Chi-tang ran away to Hongkong. Nanking felt as if an old, long-aching tooth had been pulled. Joyfully the C.E.C. met and voted the autonomous committee of Canton out of existence.

But Kwangsi was quite another matter. Li and Pai were toothaches just as bad as Chen had been, but they weren't so accessible; they lived in a natural fortress of provincial mountains. The nation expected Chiang to follow up his Canton triumph with an attack on Kwangsi, but it was disappointed. He did try rattling his saber; no results. In the end they all moved a little way in toward common ground; Li and Pai consented to announce that their troops were now a part of the National Army and accepted posts in the Nanking government, whereas Chiang gave up all insistence on a more practical sign of co-operation such as actual central control over Kwangsi military affairs. These affairs remained as they had been, in the hands of their own masters. There were glad outcries from Nanking about unity and co-operation, and all the rest of it. And anyway, Kwangtung had been settled.

Something else was settled, too. Chiang Kai-shek at last announced that China would resist if "any nation" should try to force upon her the recognition of Manchukuo. He knew that his army and its equipment were by this time in excellent shape. Also, Abyssinia had just been overrun and occupied by Italy. Abyssinia's fate was a fascinating study to the Chinese. Here was an independent country of non-Europeans suddenly overwhelmed and turned into a colony by a country that was breaking all the laws which, as the Chinese had been piously assured by the League of Nations, could never, never be smashed. And what were the other Western countries doing about it? Nothing at all. The lesson was obvious.

For a while the eager resist-Japan party was chastened and quiet.

Up in Sian, someone else felt chastened, though not necessarily quiet. The Young Marshal was thinking bitterly about Italy, and doing a lot of reorientating. When Italy raised her legation to an embassy, Chang Hsueh-liang's transports were a little moderated by the knowledge that his government had already been well and truly bilked by the Italians. Plane dealers had then rushed in on the good will of Italy's friendly action and sold several shipments of their merchandise to Nanking. Business was excellent for munitions makers at that time, when Chiang was quietly building up an air arm that was meant to be at least as good as Japan's, but the Italians got the cream of the orders—until the crates started arriving.

At first when they were unpacked everything looked more or less all right, though the young Chinese pilots who had been trained abroad wrinkled their noses a little: the models, they pointed out, were lamentably old-fashioned. But China wasn't a wealthy nation; she couldn't expect to buy the latest thing, and no doubt these were as good as anything Japan could show. Soon, however, their moderate judgment had to be altered. The planes quite simply were no good at all, and there had been worse cheating still—cases of alleged spare parts were full of junk that had nothing whatever to do with the planes. All buying from Italy stopped sharply; the Generalissimo did most of his ordering after that from the United States and Britain. The Young Marshal's friends had let him down. The Young Marshal had lost face.

Abyssinia's fate soon after this gave him more food for thought. He was stuck up there in Sian, working with Yang Hu-cheng, a Shensi general who was supposed to be helping him in the anti-Communist drive, but who really wasn't very keen on his work. Yang had a lot of political theories. They discussed things— Fascism and democracy and the rights of man—and Chang Hsueh-liang, always eager for new ideas, was impressed. They talked about Japan and the great wrong she had done him, and the further wrong she was doing everybody else: Clearly Japan and Italy were tarred with the same brush, just as clearly as that he had been wrong about Mussolini and the gay young Edda.

The Young Marshal's men seemed to be getting more and more unhappy. There was a good deal of talk about the uselessness of what they were doing—fighting in this tiresome, desultory fashion against people who were, when all was said and done, their own Chinese brothers, whereas over there in Manchuria the real enemy had it all his own way.

On top of everything else came the news that Japan and Italy, with Germany, had signed the Anti-Comintern Pact. Japan had promised to recognize Abyssinia's status as Italian property, and in return Italy—oh, betrayal of all Hsueh-liang's friendliest feelings! —was recognizing Manchukuo. Well, there you were; that was Fascism, naked and shameless. And here was he, the Young

Marshal, wasting the best years of his life, and the lives of his devoted followers, in a footling war against Communists, who seemed to have the right ideas. He was betraying his own men; he had promised to take them back to "Tungpei," the Northeast, but all that happened was that they steadily drifted farther and farther away from home. Surely something was wrong somewhere; surely Chiang Kai-shek didn't realize the great mistake he was making.

# 9 THE INCIDENT 1936–41

A number of other military leaders, too, were convinced that breaking point had been reached. Hu Han-min died suddenly, but he had followers. It seems strange that they should not have realized the Generalissimo was of their mind: no one but a madman would have planned to remain non-combative until he was squeezed to death. But it was a tense period and Chiang Kai-shek had never been a communicative type.

By this time, more forbearance with Japan was almost impossible. Yet the Japanese, like Chiang's generals, evidently did not realize that he was getting ready to act against them. They crowded the Kuomintang back and back. Every so often a Japanese national in China would be killed by a mob or murdered by some unknown hand: within a year the toll amounted to seven of these unfortunates, and after each occasion the Japanese Ambassador insisted on tighter and yet tighter controls. Their demands for more "economic co-operation" were an old story by this time. In 1936 the Japanese diplomats in Nanking complained that Chinese schoolchildren were being taught to hate Japan; they demanded a revision of Chinese textbooks forthwith. Their insistence that Manchukuo be recognized mounted to a pitch of shrillness. While they talked in terms of diplomatic courtesy—or at least in what passed for courtesy—to the Foreign Minister in Nanking, they permitted and even encouraged large-scale smuggling in the North. Customs barriers and the whole tariff system upon which China's revenues depended were being wiped out. Goods came in untaxed; silver flowed out freely, as it had done ever since America went off the gold standard. Foreign brokers made fortunes out of the disturbed situation, while Nanking's coffers were drained.

For months the Generalissimo parried Japanese demands with what appeared to be indifference. All conversations between their representatives and his government were carried on through lesser lights. The crucial moment when his attitude suddenly stiffened was not marked by any drama. He left it to the Foreign Minister to say one day in October 1936, almost casually, that China rejected Japan's demands separately and distinctly and wanted abrogation of the Tangku truce. This jolted the Japanese; they had not realized the moment of decision was so near at hand. They retired to chew it over. Perhaps, they thought, it was only a passing mood on Nanking's part.

But it was not going to blow over. Signs of a change in Chiang's policy were next perceived in the North, where Japanese expansion was now moving in its customary methodical manner to the region of Suiyuan Province. Here the invaders incited the Mongols who roved the plains above the border to cross over and claim adjacent territory. The Chinese resisted. Chinese had resisted before, always with the same disastrous results; this time it was different. They were better equipped and altogether in good heart. They drove back the Mongols, recaptured territory which had long been in enemy hands, and occupied Pailingmiao. There had not been such a thrill of pride in China since Hankow extraterritoriality was abolished. The rejoicing was loudest, as is usually the case, at the farthest point from the actual battlefield. City clerks in Canton and Shanghai whooped and rallied, and turned again to their ordinary peacetime pursuits. Resistance in Suiyuan was nice for the ego, but it didn't really impinge on life. In Sian, on the other hand, this crumb of hope was really only a crumb. The Tungpei men grunted and went on complaining.

For more than a year the routed Reds had plodded their way on the Long March to the Northwest. According to their rather scanty reports they were heroic and angelic the whole time. Villages turned out to do them honor; only the satanic Nationalists tried to impede their progress, as usual always in the most unfair manner. (An American writer indignantly describes Chiang Kai-shek flying over their retreating ranks merely to gloat.) According to equally prejudiced Nationalist reports the Reds were a scourge on the countryside, snatching food from starving village children, commandeering houses by the dozen, and laying waste the farms. One jaundiced foreign observer merely said wearily, "A plague on both their houses." Though nobody loves an army, the Reds on the whole behaved better than the hordes of war-lord mercenaries.

Toward the end of 1935, as the vanguard neared the northwest provinces, Yen Hsi-shan sprang to attention, for the Reds were obviously headed in the direction of Shansi. Yen had never come out definitely for or against them. He had treated with this or that local Red leader in his time; an unusually conscientious war lord, he was attracted by some of the Marxist theory. But Communism, flourishing and benevolent in its early phases of agrarian reform, was one thing; a large military band of refugees was quite another. Shansi was much better off without them; Yen was in full accord with the Generalissimo on this point, and when the first Communists to arrive made tentative gestures toward settling into Shansi, he sent them about their business. There were a few battles in the southwest of the province. The Reds were all driven out before the end of March 1936.

They settled down in Shensi next door, in Pao An, a desolate territory where there was no resistance from the few farmers who

occupied it. From March until December they stayed there, re-
cuperating from their ordeal and reorganizing. They announced
their soviet republic and sorted out the situation. They claimed to
number about fifty thousand in all, though on other occasions they
said that their ranks had shrunk during the Long March from ninety
thousand to five thousand.

Moscow was acutely interested in their whereabouts. Like Chiang
Kai-shek, the Russians viewed with alarm the rapid progress of the
Japanese. They did not wish to do anything about it themselves, but
they decided on a change of policy for the Chinese Communist
Party. Clearly it was time to stop harrying the Generalissimo and
help him instead. When Mao's rival, Chang Kuo-t'ao, protested
against being forced into such a sudden reversal, he was reminded,
as even the best Communists must be from time to time, that he
must take the long view. Mao Tse-tung didn't protest against the
new policy, and in the final showdown that is why the big men in
Moscow allowed him to wrest complete control from Chang
Kuo-t'ao.

In August 1936, in Moscow, a proposal was approved and
adopted: there was to be a national revolutionary struggle against
Japanese imperialism "and its Chinese servitors." In October,
Chiang had occasion angrily to reject the united-front conception
during a hurried visit to Sian to interview Chang Hsueh-liang. The
Reds captured Yenan in December and moved in close to the
Young Marshal's headquarters.

Chiang's visit to the Young Marshal on the twenty-second of
October was in response to an urgent call for help and advice. The
Generalissimo found Chang Hsueh-liang co-operating well enough,
on friendly relations with General Yang Hu-cheng, who headed the
Shensi forces, but neither man was attending to what should have
been his chief duty, fighting and suppressing the Communists.
Hsueh-liang explained that his men were unwilling to carry on any

longer with the campaign. They had been reluctant since the beginning, agreeing with the Reds, with whom they were fraternizing
nowadays, that the real war should be with the Japanese and not
with them at all. Moreover, the soldiers were convinced that Chiang
was using them where he should have been employing his own
Nanking troops, favoring his people at their expense.

Recently the troops had acquired an even more cogent argument
against anti-Communist action. They knew that the Reds had made
a handsome offer, that in return for cessation of hostilities and a
rightabout of objective they promised they would give up their
aims. No more attempts to undermine the Kuomintang, no more
anti-Nanking propaganda, no more of anything except earnest co-
operation against the Japanese. In fact, they wanted to stop being
Communists. Could anything be fairer?

Nobody realized how well convinced the Young Marshal himself
was by these arguments. Chiang seems to have taken his talk as a
statement of his men's feelings rather than his own. Nor did the
Generalissimo know that Chang's colleague Yang Hu-cheng was
already converted. Chiang treated his two generals like prefects
who have failed to keep their dormitories in order. He blew up in
one of his well-known histrionic rages, so often used to good effect
in military conferences. He pounded the table and insisted upon
more action along the lines already laid down. Then he went and
spoke to some of the cadets himself in the Sian Military Academy.
Chiang's oratorical style and content have never been flexible, to
put it mildly; he hammered it in again and again that the Reds were
the enemy and Japan only a secondary menace. The students flared
to anger. Some leaped to their feet and argued with the Generalissimo and assailed his theories; altogether there was a most spirited
row, and nobody felt at all calmed down by its sequel, when Chang
Hsueh-liang expelled three of the insurgents.

Just to show how unmoved he was, Chiang repeated the whole
speech at another school at Loyang on his way home. But still he

was not satisfied that he had stamped on the mutiny, and he sent word to his secret agents that they should redouble their watchfulness in Sian. As one immediate result, three of the hottest-tempered local firebrands disappeared overnight. The Army seethed with anger. Chang Hsueh-liang raided the party headquarters, found the students, and restored them to the school.

On October 31 Chiang would be fifty according to Chinese count, and fifty is a very important age in his country. Months ahead of time the government collected contributions for a fleet of airplanes, China's birthday present to the Generalissimo. There was a big ceremony at the Nanking airport, with a fly-past of new planes spelling out the national hero's name and age. Thousands of spectators crowded the field; the only ones missing were the Chiangs themselves and a few other V.I.P.s who had been called to Loyang for an emergency military conference. Yen Hsi-shan met them there, and Chang Hsueh-liang, and many more. "I must tell you," the Young Marshal had written, "that I cannot control my army much longer."

Chiang's diary, which was soon to become famous, gave no hint in the entries for the first week of December that he foresaw danger to himself. But he was wary of the general situation. One of his best divisions had been sent to Sian to encourage the others by taking the field against the Communists. They were promptly ambushed and overpowered. Moreover, Yang Hu-cheng's troops, though they were Shensi men and not aggrieved exiles like the Young Marshal's forces, had held an unofficial vote and decided unanimously that they must fight Japan and leave the Reds alone. On the seventh of December, therefore, Chiang, with an assorted set of generals and bodyguards, flew up to Sian for a conference.

He went to lodge at Lintung, a hot-springs resort on Lishan Mountain, with his guard and the leader of the hated secret police,.

who was his nephew. The hotel wasn't big enough for the whole party, and the subsidiary generals and officials were put up in town, fifteen miles off, in the Sian guesthouse. For several days there were interviews, with much squabbling and jockeying for position. As life would not have seemed normal without a student demonstration, on the ninth a parade of youths started out to march to Lintung from town. The police, ordered to break it up, fired in the customary wild manner and wounded two of the children.

Chiang's secret police reported that a mutiny was brewing. The Red secret police reported in their turn that Chiang's police were planning to break up the mutiny. Back and forth went the rumors. The boiling of the town was almost audible, like that of a giant teakettle. Foreign interpreters of the Communist point of view were tipped off, and started to gather, mostly from their watching posts in Peking, with freshly sharpened pencils at the ready.

The evening of the eleventh arrived. There had been a stormy conference among the Shensi commanders, some of whom were averse to waiting for action from the Kuomintang. They must hurry up and mutiny, they insisted, or they would find themselves imprisoned before they knew it. Yang Hu-cheng was especially determined, and at last, before dinnertime, he had his way and the mutiny was agreed on. He and Chang Hsueh-liang had been asked to dine at Lintung with Chiang Kai-shek, but the Young Marshal presented himself alone to Chiang and explained that Yang was entertaining the smaller fry in Sian. He seemed ill at ease, ate with small appetite, and took his leave early, after introducing Chiang to a general, Sun Ming-chiu. Sun was really there to spy out the land.

Sian is a cold country, and this was December. Outside, the bare, rocky land was covered with a light snowfall that would probably be there until spring. It was still dark, very early in the dawn of December 12, when the *coup* got under way. The Generalissimo had waked up as usual at five o'clock and started the day with his exercises. He was just beginning to get dressed when he heard shots at the front gate. Most of the guard on the hotel were Chang Hsueh-liang's men; Chiang had brought only his own bodyguard and twenty extra soldiers. Two of his personal guards went out to investigate; they did not come back.

Chiang decided, with anger but without undue surprise, that a few of Chang Hsueh-liang's troops had revolted as the Young Marshal had long warned him they might. He did not appreciate the full extent of the mutiny. Even when his lieutenant sent word back to the bedroom that the attackers had penetrated as far as the second gate into the hotel, he did not understand that this was a big matter. The lieutenant also reported that the back of the hotel grounds were not yet cut off, and so with two of his men the Generalissimo, just as he was in nightshirt and no shoes, ran out a back door and made for the wall gate at the side. Somewhere in the excitement he lost his false teeth.

The wall gate being locked, they ran around inside to a point as far back of the building and up the hill as they could reach. It was only about ten feet high, as Chiang said in his memoirs, and apparently easy to get over. They scrambled to the top and jumped off. In the dark they did not see that the drop would take them straight into an empty moat, much lower than the inside level. Chiang fell thirty feet to the bottom and injured himself badly. For several minutes he couldn't move. Then the guards helped pull him out of the ditch, and with their aid he walked painfully to a little outlying temple where some of his men were stationed. They took turns helping him beyond that, up the hill.

Chiang was in acute pain and it was terribly cold for a practically naked man to go mountain climbing, but even now he wasn't really worried. Moving slowly as he had to, it took him half an hour to reach the top of the hill. In the gathering daylight his party was plainly visible to the watchers below, and firing suddenly commenced from all sides, killing some of his companions. Chiang began to realize the scope of the affair. He and the surviving guards hastily took refuge in a cave halfway down the mountain slope. For nearly an hour and a half they hid there, listening to their pursuers running back and forth, searching. They heard firing in the hotel, and then the firing ceased. Then somebody spied the Generalissimo and cried out to his companions. Chiang overheard them arguing as to whether or not to shoot him before they took any other action. They weren't quite sure who he was.

"I am the Generalissimo," he called. "Don't be disrespectful." He added that they should kill him; it was a suggestion he was to make repeatedly throughout his durance, not hysterically but in a spirit of propriety.

But they did not seem inclined to kill him. The superior officer who came running to handle the affair was that same General Sun Ming-chiu who had been brought into his apartments and introduced by Chang Hsueh-liang the previous night. He knelt down— "with tears in his eyes," noted Chiang—and courteously requested the Generalissimo to go down the mountain. Chiang wanted to go into the hotel to put on some clothes and lie down to rest his back, but when through the doorway he saw that the place was wrecked and corpses lay all over the floor, he changed his mind. One of the corpses was that of his nephew, who was summarily executed as soon as the rebels got hold of him.

Throughout the proceedings Chiang scolded Sun Ming-chiu as if the general were one of his own erring cadets. He was outraged, furious, shocked; he was anything but cowed. He demanded that the Young Marshal be brought to him. Sun replied that Chang was in Sian, and very politely requested His Excellency too to go into town, where he would be more comfortable. Chiang told him to hold his tongue. Sun saluted, manifestly unmoved. At last Chiang agreed to go into town. No one had as yet explained exactly what was up or who was in the conspiracy.

The Generalissimo noticed that he was taken to Yang Hu-cheng's headquarters. "A feeling of doubt arose in my mind," he said. Why

Yang's place? Then he saw that the guards wore the armlets of Yang's army, and he remembered that Yang had not come to dinner the night before. No doubt he was already imprisoned, reflected Chiang, and his troops taken over by Chang Hsueh-liang. Even now the possibility of the general's being actively engaged in this rebellion never entered his mind. . . . "Yang is an old comrade of our Party and has been in long association with the revolutionary movement. It was my strong conviction that he had taken no part in the revolt."

News of the snatch sent China into a panic. The generals and statesmen who made up the Generalissimo's party had been surrounded and efficiently arrested while all hell was popping at Lintung. Many of their names were included, arbitrarily, in a message Chang Hsueh-liang now sent to Nanking informing the government briefly of what had happened and outlining an "eight-point program" that they wanted Nanking to promise to follow in exchange for their lost leader including: reorganization of the government; an end to civil war; immediate release of certain political prisoners; release of all political offenders in China; guaranteed liberty for the people to hold meetings and organize.

Nanking did not at first consider the program. The stunning news of Chiang's capture overshadowed all bargaining possibilities. No foreign observer had ever before seen anything like it in China for unanimity. In provinces like Kiangsi, where until ten years before the people couldn't have cared less who was head of the government, everyone took the event as a blow. Children were sent home from closed schools to chastened households. The treaty ports were silent and worried. In Communist territories there was rejoicing, but in all the rest of China there were sorrow and apprehension, and much indignation against the Young Marshal. Chiang's personal appearances and wide travels had accomplished the miracle: China was a nation at last.

For two days the Chinese were in mourning; they were sure the Generalissimo had really been killed, and that the reassurances from Sian to the contrary were lies. In Nanking the reaction became more complex as the days went by. Chiang's enemies grew confident enough to stop pretending. A slow, dignified dance of politics began; the boys were circling for position. Pro-Chiangites, however, denounced the conspiracy with a vigor and unity that startled the men who had the Generalissimo in their power. Chang Hsueh-liang in his usual emotional mood had convinced himself that his new Communist friends were correct in saying the country would undergo an immense upsurge and fly to his support. It is always a shock to find that you have fallen under the spell of your own side's propaganda, and he was shocked. Even Yang Hu-cheng, who had been the mainstay of the whole affair, was taken aback. What on earth were they to do next? Chiang was no help at all: he had gone to bed, testily repelling all overtures. He would have no truck with rebels. The only thing they could do with him, he said over and over, was kill him.

One heart especially was consumed with anxiety. What on earth, thought Donald, was his young fellow up to? He took plane immediately to Sian on December 14 and was enthusiastically greeted by the villain of the piece. If anybody could resolve the puzzle, the Young Marshal said, it would be Donald. The Australian was permitted to see Chiang and telegraph to Madame that her husband was alive and kicking. But he couldn't talk directly to the prisoner. The best interpreter, he insisted, would be the Young Marshal himself. Until now Chiang had refused to talk with Chang Hsueh-liang at all. Donald's presence gave him a tactful way out of the impasse, and soon the three men were earnestly conversing.

The worst was over; the worst had indeed been over ever since the first moment of capture. The real danger, as Madame soon discovered in Nanking, was from Chiang's enemies in the capital; they were exploiting to the utmost their chances of doing away with him through too much zeal. The Central Political Council nominated Ho Ying-chin commander-in-chief of a "punitive expedition." A number of the Generalissimo's birthday planes bombed a town in the Loyang–Sian Railway, where Tungpei troops were encamped. The next place to be bombed, it was announced, would be Sian itself.

This was bad news. Chiang was now engaged in long conferences with the Young Marshal, and in a wry way enjoying the obvious fact that he had regained his ascendancy over the emotional general's loyalties. He was not yet master of the situation: Yang Hu-cheng—it still amazed Chiang to realize it—was stubbornly inimical. Still it was clear that nobody in Sian meant to kill him. Things might yet be arranged in the manner Chiang preferred to clumsy force, if only the meddlers in Nanking could be held off. Three days after Donald's arrival, on the seventeenth, a man from Chiang's party was released and sent down to Loyang with a letter for the Kuomintang that said, in effect, "Lay off." Chiang added that in all probability he would return to Nanking within two days. He enclosed a reassuring word for Madame.

The government grudgingly ordered bombing to cease until the evening of the nineteenth. In actual fact hostilities weren't resumed then. Instead, T. V. Soong flew off that afternoon on what was carefully announced as an unofficial journey to Sian while Mayling fought the authorities fiercely, with all the strength and steadiness at her command, to keep the Army's planes at home. The Kungs and other pro-Chiangites stood at her side. The opposing party hesitated, considered wistfully their chances of getting by with outright defiance, and at last submitted: no more planes, they agreed, until further notice. After all, one could not be sure, even with all-out bombing, of hitting the Generalissimo fair and square, and say what you will it would *not* look well if one failed. . . .

What sort of horse trade was accomplished during the thirty-six hours of T.V.'s visit nobody would say, but he reappeared in Nanking with Donald, bright and well, after the week end. The situation, though still under control, was not exactly settled. Quantities of Reds had moved openly into Sian and with the all-out support of Yang Hu-cheng's troops joyfully set up a new government. As far as they were concerned, *Der Tag* had arrived. Chang Hsueh-liang was by this time past the middle of his indecision, woefully conscious of his wrongdoing and altogether a Chiang man once more. But it was going to be a ticklish business, said T.V., to handle Yang Hu-cheng. He brought a special message for Madame from her husband; on no account was she to put herself in danger.

Mayling was not sure about that. Donald was positive she would be able to help a lot if she were to go to Sian. He had limitless faith in her courage and brains; all the fervor of his gnarled, hardboiled, fundamentally sentimental nature went out to Mayling, always, and he felt there wasn't anything she couldn't do when she tried. The young fellow was attached to her, he argued. That would help. Her journey would give reassurance to the nation. She was the only person in the world who could handle "the old man" in his stubborn fits, and he was certainly being subject to stubborn fits at the moment there in Sian, lying in bed with no teeth and a wrenched back.

Mayling liked the danger of the idea, and the drama. She was Chingling's sister; Chingling, who had insisted on risking her life with the mob when Sun Yat-sen was in danger in Canton. Courage was considered a very good thing in the Soong clan. On the other hand, if she were to leave the beleaguered fort in Nanking, could she depend on those she left behind to hold back the dogs of war? It was tricky. But she would go: of course she would go. She packed a few clothes and a small revolver and Chiang Kai-shek's spare dental plate, and said that she was ready.

In bare outline the kidnaping story sounds fantastic enough to Westerners, but we do not really enter cloud-cuckooland until we study the fascinating little details that fill in the picture. There is, for instance, the diary. Everyone in the Kuomintang was aware that Chiang kept a diary; it was as much a part of his daily routine as his morning exercises or his prayers, and in its way it had become quite famous. Sometimes he gave diaries to his high officers, printed in the manner he preferred for his own. Chang Hsing-hai says that they "have a page at the end of each week where the keeper of the diary is supposed to make a strict moral analysis of himself. This is followed by another page where he is supposed to set down a plan of his activities for the next week. There is also a sheet at the end of each month where the owner of the diary is supposed to make a final examination of himself for that period."

If this sounds stuffy to my unregenerate readers, they can console themselves with the reflection that Confucius said, "I examine myself daily on three points: whether in transacting business for others I may not have been faithful, whether, in relationships with friends I may not have been sincere, and whether I may not have thoroughly assimilated and put into practice the instructions of my teacher." On top of all that, there were Chiang's daily prayers. On the whole, the diary made very edifying reading for Chang Hsueh-liang and Yang Hu-cheng. At least they said it did. Whether Yang really did undergo amazed shock, as he claimed to have done when he saw the Generalissimo's irreproachable sentiments set down in ink on the page, I am not sure. He said he had not been convinced until that moment that Chiang really did dislike the Japanese as much as he himself did. He said he had not believed, until he read the diary, that it was Chiang's ultimate aim to fight the invaders. He said his heart melted in surprised admiration. Maybe.

At any rate, the diary gave the insurgents a dramatic and heroic reason to back water and let the Generalissimo alone rather than strike him down for the vicious tyrant the Reds said he was.

Madame, T.V., Donald, and the man who had brought out the message arrived at Sian late in the afternoon of December 22. For all Donald's persistently offhand manner, Mayling felt tense as the plane circled for a landing, and the men were probably nervous as well. She handed her revolver to Donald and gave him directions to shoot her if anyone showed signs of seizing her; he gravely agreed to do so. But when they landed, everything was quiet and courteous. The Young Marshal looked subdued, but he was easy in his manners. Donald pocketed the revolver.

The Generalissimo writes that when he saw his wife, "I was very much moved and almost wanted to cry." He declared that he had read in the Bible only that morning, "Jehovah will now do a new thing, and that is: He will make a woman protect a man."

Conferences resumed and much more progress resulted. A number of tacit agreements were made which will probably never be admitted by the Chiangs in detail. Chang Hsueh-liang claimed to Mayling, excitedly and in injured tones, that they weren't trying to make the Generalissimo sign anything. All they wanted, he insisted, was to talk with him, and he wouldn't even do that. Now, however, with his trusted interpreter to back up Donald and T.V., Chiang Kai-shek was more forthcoming. Somehow, in what roundabout words it is impossible to know, certain conclusions were arrived at. Chiang promised at last to believe that the Reds meant to hold to their new program of co-operation in return for open defiance of Japan. He would sign no treaty to this effect, but his captors decided to trust him.

Not without a struggle, however. Yang Hu-cheng was disturbed on two counts. He didn't have the implicit faith in Chiang that the Young Marshal had (which was never, incidentally, betrayed). Nor was he certain of his own fate now that the mutiny was collapsing. Chang Hsueh-liang would be all right, he pointed out, because he was among friends, but what of himself? Until the last minute, Yang wasn't quite sure whether he should not, after all, hang on to Chiang Kai-shek.

However, he did not, and Christmas Day marked the end of the kidnaping episode. Chiang and his wife returned to Nanking, accompanied by the remorseful Young Marshal. Firecrackers popped unceasingly for hours on end. Young men marched and sang in the streets. Up in Sian, the new government sorrowfully struck tents and melted away. In Nanking the Generalissimo went to bed. In the midst of the rejoicing, people asked each other what it all really meant: what had Chiang promised?

Nobody was able to say, but events were soon to spell it out for them.

During Chang Hsueh-liang's one interview with the press, which was fated to be his last appearance as a free agent, he explained that he had done wrong and was ready to stand his trial. He had come to Nanking because it wouldn't have been safe to stay in Sian after his championship of the Generalissimo. He was not particularly safe in Nanking, either, during those angry, revengeful days, but the Chiangs had promised they would use their influence to get lenient treatment for him.

"I am by nature rustic, surly, and unpolished," he wrote in his apology, "due to which I have created an incident at once impudent and illegal."

Awaiting trial, he was held "in soft detention" in T.V.'s house. Chiang Kai-shek was busy with some breast-beating of his own. Within three days of the return he submitted to the C.E.C. his resignation from his posts on the ground that he was unworthy to hold them. He castigated himself severely. He had allowed the Army to get out of hand, and so the responsibility for all the fuss was his alone. He had been guilty of overconfidence and rash behavior. (His error of judgment genuinely bothered Chiang: he scolded himself in his diary over and over for having been careless.) As far as the C.E.C. was concerned, of course, the resignation was purely a gesture, and it was indignantly spurned. Again the Generalissimo resigned: again the resignation was rejected. Everyone behaved very nicely.

Finally Chang Hsueh-liang was tried at a special tribunal and sentenced to ten years' imprisonment and five years' loss of his civil rights. The imprisonment was not arduous. The young fellow's movements were regulated, but within a permitted orbit he was free to live as he had done in the pre-Japanese days, with his concubines accompanying him. Justice had been served, but the Kuomintang was slightly apprehensive for some months; how would the fierce Tungpei men take the loss of their leader?

They accepted it. The majority of them had already been weaned from their feudal allegiance, and though they still loved the memory of the Young Marshal, they now had the Red Star. Besides, their Marshal was a long way off. The years went by and memory faded. Nobody went out of his way to remind the Tungpei army of Chang Hsueh-liang's name. The Kuomintang takes care of him. He went to Changsha when they evacuated Nanking, and to Chungking after that; he went through all the vicissitudes of the government during the war. He is a free man, technically speaking, for the ten-year term has long since run out. But he remains silent and untroublesome in a Taiwan retreat. He plays tennis: he plays golf. When you come to think of it, he is one of the most dramatic of China's tragedies, but you don't often think of it.

The government would no doubt like to be free of him, as he would like to be free of them, but he has nowhere to go.


Nationalist troops occupied Sian in February, three days after Yang moved his men and the Young Marshal's out of town. The Communist government had long since melted away, and foreign journalists were left to mourn the cause they so wistfully admired. All they had left was the immunity conferred on them by their third-power nationalities and a sympathetic public waiting in the

West. A good deal more than their Chinese Communist friends had, at that.

Yang Hu-cheng finally submitted to Chiang and went abroad. The Tungpei army was moved to Honan and Anhwei. Everybody who co-operated with the Communists, in short, was now cleared off the scene, leaving the stage uncluttered for the Reds themselves.

Though Chiang's health called for immediate rest and the C.E.C. had already commanded him to take sick leave, he postponed the day of reckoning as long as possible. There was simply no time to go to bed. He hadn't signed any agreements in Sian, but there were agreements in the air nevertheless, and it was an urgent matter to get them down in some sort of shape. Early 1937 saw a dignified procession of gestures between Nanking and the Reds, all presumably impromptu, yet most certainly agreed upon in advance. First the Kuomintang was told that the eight-point program must, of course, be rejected, and then everybody in Nanking set about accepting its outstanding principles in other words. Chou En-lai made two visits to Nanking, without advertisement, to discuss matters.

The Reds continued to hold fast to the new line laid down in Moscow. They were no longer interested, they reiterated, in accomplishing the downfall of Chiang and the Kuomintang. On the contrary, they said Chiang wasn't bad after all. They accepted without demur the conditions stipulated by the Kuomintang; the Red Army was to be disbanded and the members thereof were to join the Nationalists; the soviet republic in the Northwest was to be dissolved; there would be no more Communist propaganda and no more class struggle—for the time being. Mao Tse-tung, even during the time when the wildest claims were being made in the West as to the purity of his intentions, did not himself utter a lie on the subject. In his protestations of amity more than once he included the phrase, "for the present."

For the present, then, the Chinese Communists declared themselves Communists no longer. Thus without breaking his pledge to uproot Communism from China the Generalissimo was technically correct in accepting the reconverted converts into Nanking's good graces. Later a "People's Political Council" was set up as a national Parliament to permit the Reds a hand in governmental decisions without being a part of the Kuomintang inner sanctum.

The capitulation of Nanking stimulated newspaper commentators abroad to produce millions of words of commendation. China was united at last—she was maturing—everything was going to be absolutely all right. How handsomely Mao Tse-tung had behaved!

Chiang paid little attention to all the comment; he was beginning to be just a wee bit disillusioned about foreigners' brain power. As soon as the situation was fairly well sewed up, he went into a Shanghai hospital for an X-ray examination. His back had not mended as it should and he was growing thin and weak. The doctors commanded complete rest and relaxation, so Chiang went back to the hills of Chekiang.

The Communists knew there was not much time left. So did the Japanese. So, of course, did Chiang Kai-shek, and he grudged the time spent in convalescence. At last, however, he regained his health, and though under Mayling's anxious eye he didn't dare to overwork quite so outrageously, he was soon back in his old routine. Hoping that the Japanese would still wait a little longer, he agreed with the Reds to hold a general meeting, a "National Salvation Conference," in the autumn of 1937.

It was one of the consistent policies followed by the Reds, whether Russian or Chinese, that they never admitted the close connection between their parties, but Nanking's relations with Moscow on the diplomatic level now began to improve, in a manner parallel with those between Nanking and Mao Tse-tung. Only a year before, in March 1936, Russia had concluded a defensive alliance with Outer Mongolia which directly contradicted her earlier agreement of 1924 that China held sovereignty over Mongolia. Nanking was not pleased. Now everything was friendly. Moscow seemed determined to back up the pledges made by Mao.

Japan observed the honeymoon with misgiving. The moment had come for another stroke, the Tokyo militarists decided, and on July 7, 1937, it took place.

Lukouchiao, or Marco Polo Bridge, is near the village of Wanping, just southwest of Peking. At that time it was occupied by a number of men from the Chinese Twenty-ninth Army under Sung Cheh-yuan, the general who had been dislodged by the Japanese from his command in Chahar. Wanping was one of the numerous places along the uneasy northern front at which you would have expected something to happen, with Japanese troops living close by. Later the Japanese said that one of their men went astray in the village during maneuvers, and when they tried to find him they were wantonly attacked by the Chinese. Japanese troops in Peking were quickly mobilized, and reinforcements were sent from Japan.

When the thing broke, Chiang Kai-shek was at Kuling, a mountain-top resort where he liked to spend the hot summer months. He received the news calmly, but it was clear from his message to the nation that he felt uplifted and excited. The humiliation of the Sian mutiny was forgotten. He wasn't overconfident, but this was *the* test, and he felt that China was ready for it as she had not been in all the years preceding.

For nearly three weeks attempts were made to handle the affair through diplomatic channels. For the first time Chiang was able to indulge in the luxury of making demands. He knew they wouldn't be met, but that was not the point. He asked Japan to admit responsibility for the latest upset, to apologize, and to pay indemnities. That gesture done with, he turned to his nation and made a formal promise. China would not make any settlement infringing on her sovereign rights or territorial integrity. No alterations would be tolerated in the status of the Hopei-Chahar Council. No more local officials would be shifted at the behest of any foreign government. No restrictions on the positions held by the Twenty-ninth Army would be tolerated. The period of Japanese expansion in North China, he said, had come to an end.

Japan forthwith attacked.

It was the fashion among foreign observers, during the years preceding Pearl Harbor, to laugh at Chiang's technique of defense. There was something ludicrous, we found, about his continued withdrawal. Each time the Army retreated the Generalissimo made a statement pointing out that he had ordered the retreat, and that it was a part of his whole "strategy of depth" or "defense in depth" to give way so that the Japanese might tire themselves out and venture farther and farther from their bases. There was really nothing else he could have done against an army so much better equipped, as the Japanese were. Today we can see it his way, but in 1937 and 1938 we laughed.

And yet the defense of Shanghai was not at all laughable; it was admirable. The Japanese threw their main weight against the army here, for Chiang's chief line of defense clearly must be the Yangtze Valley, and Shanghai was the gateway to Nanking and all that lay beyond. North China, he had decided, must make shift as best it could; the Japanese already had their feet in the door there. For three months, hampered as they were by the neutral third-party settlements in the city, the Chinese held out against the enemy around Shanghai. Four hundred and fifty thousand of them were killed in that period.

The Generalissimo contradicted the boasting of his information officers, of whom wartime convention demanded assurances to the public of quick victory. He said repeatedly that they would hold out and, if necessary, retreat (he knew they would have to retreat), and that the war would last at least three years. The Japanese, on the other hand, said they would mop up the entire situation in six weeks. Some of them actually may have believed this, but the scale of their preparations indicated a less optimistic viewpoint.

Until Shanghai was given up a steady stream of traffic flowed along the Shanghai–Nanking road. During a motor trip between the cities, the British Ambassador's car was shelled by a Japanese plane and the Ambassador himself was seriously wounded. Japanese bombers also attacked British and American gunboats in the river. Foreigners, taking their constitutional rides around the suburbs of Shanghai, were fired on and badly scared. But the Western powers satisfied themselves with diplomatic protests of medium-strength severity. Madame Chiang and Donald were involved in an incident when their car, speeding on the road from Nanking to Shanghai during an air raid, got out of control and overturned in a ditch. Mayling suffered several broken ribs and a slight concussion, but she carried on with the day's program.

In the meantime the Reds were being as good as their promise, busily and cheerfully going about the process of incorporation into the Nationalist forces. In September the C.E.C. decided how the troops were to be realigned. The Eighth Route Army joined the Nationalist Eighteenth Group Army and was sent to the "Second War Area" in Shansi under Yen Hsi-shan's jurisdiction. The rest of the troops were lumped together as the "New Fourth Army" under their own general, who was directly responsible for them though he was answerable to a Nationalist general. The New Fourth Army specialized in the guerrilla warfare the Reds knew so well after their years in the wilderness, and when the Eighth Route Army was formally incorporated—in April 1938—they moved south to Nanking and Hankow, there to start operations under the flag of the Republic.

"They made trouble from the start," said one of their Nationalist colleagues who is now working out of Taiwan as a guerrilla. "I was in charge of commissary transport between Nanking and Wuhan, and the Reds were so busy filching ammunition and snarling up my orders that I began to wonder which side it was safer to turn my back on, them or the Japanese. They never had any genuine intention of co-operating. Co-operating with the Reds was a standing joke with the rest of us."

However, none of this situation was publicized and for several years the West didn't suspect it. Chiang and his closest advisers had the idea that it would react unfavorably on the Kuomintang if this fretful question were to crop up once again, after it was supposed to have been settled and the settlement had been greeted with such enthusiasm overseas. Censorship of news—all news—about the Chinese Communists became a habit at Nationalist headquarters, and ultimately this habit boomeranged.

It is easy to understand, however, why Chiang took the attitude he did in 1937 and 1938. The Red problem must be allowed to rest, he felt, until the time came when he could not possibly continue to ignore it. He must stand by the agreement he made after the release from Sian. At first he had no reason to regret his decision, for after the Lukouchiao incident he found himself the recipient of profitable attentions from Moscow. In August 1937 he signed a treaty with Russia in which the Russians repeated the promise already made by Chinese Reds in Sian: they would lend no more support to "independent" political and military forces within the country. Russia and China agreed not to make war on each other, either alone or as allies with other powers. No other power making war on either of these nations was to be aided, directly or indirectly, by the other.

Benefits of a nation-wide dimension were soon to stem from this pact; in the meantime there came a personal and very welcome sign of released pressure from Moscow. Chiang Ching-kuo was sent back.

The first inkling of this development was a cable, signed with Ching-kuo's name and addressed to his mother in Fenghua, saying that he was on his way home across the Sinkiang trail, bringing with him his Russian wife and children. None of his family—his father, his mother, or anyone else—had known for certain, all those years since 1927, whether he was alive or dead. During the infrequent periods when Madame Sun was on speaking terms with her brother-in-law she conveyed reassurances, but these statements lacked conviction. Now he was coming back hale and hearty. His mother in Fenghua wept for joy, and the town went wild. Chiang himself controlled his transports as a superior Confucian must, but there was no doubt of his delight.

Ching-kuo arrived. He had grown into a stocky, bristle-haired man, shorter than his father and with no resemblance to him in build. He had the gait and manners of a Russian. His Chinese was halting and he spoke only the dialect of the South, where he had lived as a boy. His handsome blond wife didn't speak the language at all. She looked puzzled and out of place in her Chinese dress, and one cannot help feeling very sorry for her in those trying first weeks, responsible for the care of two clamorous children among the alien corn.

It developed that Chiang Ching-kuo not only looked Russian but felt that way. Twelve years in Moscow and Siberia without any contact with his own people had sent him back in an uncertain, chip-on-the-shoulder mood. It wasn't long before he was at outs with both Chiangs. He had been brooding about the domestic situation; he refused to call Mayling "Mother." Within several days he departed to Fenghua with his wife and children and set up housekeeping with his mother's clan. However, a few months straightened out the worst of the confusion, and as the Japanese War continued father and son patched it up. By the end of a year they were good friends; by the end of two years they had forgotten there had ever been bad blood.

On the national scale, too, Moscow continued to play Santa Claus. It was clear that the Russians had no intention of joining in the war personally, but they were eager to provide the tools and let Chiang get on with the job, within the limits permitted by their Chinese deputies. China was furnished with a credit of one hundred million dollars (Chinese currency) and a four hundred-strong fleet of bombers and pursuits complete with pilot instructors. A fleet of transport trucks began running back and forth across Sinkiang and the eastern reaches of Russia. Litvinov at the League Assembly pleaded with the Western powers to do something about Japan. With virtuous horror he retailed the aggressive actions of the island empire—the attack without warning, the invasion, the blockade of the China coast. Russia was China's only champion for two years; incidentally, every word Litvinov said was true. The League reacted as the Russians had known it would, with the usual formal condemnation, for which the Japanese cared nothing, and futile committee recommendations. China had long since learned that the League had no teeth with which to defend anybody. Litvinov's gesture had no effect, but the situation seemed clear-cut. Chiang and the Chinese Reds were presumably as one.

Chiang was directing the defense of Shanghai from Soochow when the position in the treaty port became untenable. The Japanese poured in men and material until they outweighed the defending army, and though they lost sixty thousand men they continued to supply troops. Shortly after the Chinese order to withdraw on October 27, more Japanese landed south of the city in Hangchow Bay. After that there could be no step-by-step Chinese retreat, but only all-out flight. The way between Shanghai and Nanking lay open to the invaders, but the Japanese paused to send out a feeler, by way of the German Ambassador, for a peace offer. None was forthcoming, and they started again on the inland road.

Chiang prepared for the worst. Some of the government offices were immediately transferred to Hankow, and the most important of them he sent farther west, early in 1938, to the Szechuan capital

city, Chungking. He had sized up Chungking during his flying tours
in earlier years and noted it as being virtually impregnable. There
were difficulties in carrying out this movement, for the war lords
were suspicious and jealous of their position in that remote country. But it had to be done, and Chiang reflected that an advance,
guard of government officials might well save him trouble later on.
With what remained of the government, a shadow organization, he
and Madame settled in at Nanking to wait for the blow.

They were gloomy, anxious days. The Chiangs knew that the
important part of the struggle was not among the soldiers, grievous
as their losses were, but over in Europe and in Washington, where
China was appealing for help and getting only diplomatic shuffling
in reply. The matter was "indefinitely postponed" at the Nine-
Power Conference in Brussels. The British felt that they could not
afford to antagonize Japan, and in America, though public opinion
was mildly indignant against Japanese action, nobody had yet organized it. Japan had been nibbling away so long at Chinese territory that we had got used to it, and were disinclined to pay
attention to more of the same. It is odd to reflect that popular
feeling might never have risen as high as it later did if the task
of disseminating anti-Japanese propaganda had not been shouldered
by American leftists, who knew their job and did it superlatively
well.

But in spite of their efforts, in the late days of 1937 Europe
thought China ought to write off her losses, settle again with Japan,
and stop bothering people.

Donald's reminiscences of the Generalissimo at this point are
vivid. He had never been able to feel close to the Chinese leader,
chiefly because of his stubborn whim never to learn to speak the
language. Mayling was their only point of contact: Mayling was
Donald's shining star. He often declared her a better man than

anybody else in the government, and if there was a hidden barb in these words for Madame's husband, this was natural. Donald was smitten, in his peculiar antiseptic fashion, by his pupil and thought she wasn't appreciated as she should have been.

But now, as third man in the party that fled before the Japanese vanguard with courage and as much dignity as one can muster in the act of flight, Donald found himself tardily beginning to appreciate Madame's husband, too.

At the end of November the three of them flew away in the family flying boat to Hankow. News soon arrived of the sack of the capital city and its attendant horrors. The Japanese were later to admit that the occupation of Nanking was one of the greatest disgraces ever incurred by their army. For a few days the Western world was shocked out of apathy, and for years afterward psychologists were trying to explain the reason for these excesses. There was a theory that the men were so intoxicated by their speedy success in attaining Nanking that they got out of hand; the three-day license customarily permitted a victorious Japanese army lengthened out to three weeks, or even more, before the officers regained control. It is more likely, however, that the soldiers were still fuming with rage at having been held up at Shanghai, and Nanking was at once exhaust and revenge.

When the turmoil died down, the Japanese set out to follow the Chinese to Wuhan. Europe and America regarded this fact with dismay. Japan did mean business, then!

During their travels together deeper and deeper into China, Donald was puzzled and amused by the Generalissimo's habit of "humming." It was his only comment on the adverse situation, and Donald noticed that it seemed to soothe him. If the Australian had been interested in the private tastes of his Chinese friends, he would have known what Chiang was doing. Poetry in China is recited in a kind of chant. Chiang was repeating to himself, for solace and inspiration, the thoughts of the warrior poets who were his models of deportment.

The troops and civilian refugees adapted themselves with Oriental readiness to a life of extreme discomfort in Hankow. Houses were crowded, funds were short, prices soared. Yet they settled in some- how, and Chiang even started one of his academies going again, and continued to give the cadets his long, repetitive, and—it must be admitted—platitudinous lectures on the good life for hours on end.

Chinese have a nervous trick of filling in the pauses in their speech, those same places where the American says "uh," with the two words that mean "this"—"chih ke," or as it is pronounced, "jerga." Chiang often uses it when he is making a speech. Its use would sound in translation something like this: "We must then exert ourselves heroically to make this, this, this, Republic of China wealthy and mighty, and to make this, this, this, this people's liveli- hood more healthy. . . ." To while away the hours as they stood in the sun while the words poured on, irreverent young officers would count the number of times they heard "chih ke" in the course of the morning. Afterward they compared notes and argued about the differing results. As time went on they laid bets on it in advance, rather like a ship's pool. Yet with all Chiang's foibles, they loved him still. The more the Army was held up, the more fervently they clung to the symbol of their leader.

The news grew worse. A war lord who had once been induced to desert Feng Yu-hsiang and had been rewarded with the leader- ship of Shantung, now turned coat again and submitted to the Japanese. His action aroused more wrath than surprise in Hankow. It was the nature of the beast, and because of shortages and the size of the problem the Kuomintang could not have hoped to hold Shantung forever anyway. But he must not be allowed to get away with arrant treason: he was tried and executed. North was gone;

now it was the turn of South. Near the end of October 1938 Canton
fell to the invaders with scarcely a shot. The same monetary blan-
dishments that had tempted the Shantung war lord, it was said, had
turned the scale here. Indeed the easy conquest of a city that had
shown it could be tough on occasion indicated that the gossip was
well founded.

As the fall of Shanghai had menaced Nanking, so did Canton's
loss leave the way wide open to Hankow.

"We will move on," said the Generalissimo. But he and his wife
postponed their departure, amidst the bustle and exodus, until the
last possible moment. Much to Donald's nervous irritation, Chiang
strolled about the airfield while the plane was readied, "humming"
the whole while, mysteriously drawing strength and solace from
ancient boasts.

The ineffably patient Dr. Hollington Tong (*Dateline: China*)
shows how the Western idea of propaganda ran up against Chiang's
old-fashioned prejudices. The superior gentleman ignores the
opinion of inferior people. To adapt his behavior and ideals to
the standard of barbarians would be to lower himself. The Generalissimo would not have put it that way, but it is the way he felt.
Good manners in China involve a lot of camouflage, courtesy, and
gentle surface mannerisms calculated to hide all ugly emotion. But
between themselves this surface is ignored. We don't mean it,
necessarily, when we sign our letters, "Yours sincerely." Chinese
don't mean it necessarily when they talk about their own unworthi-
ness. It shocks them, nevertheless, if someone drops that talk and
puts up a boastful front. And so, when confronted as he was, time
and again after the beginning of the war, with the Western conception of propaganda, when told that he and his people should
speak up and boast nakedly, Chiang resisted. The Information
Ministry had to fight him every step of the way.

There were difficulties in the opposite direction as well. Some-

times Chiang lost his temper with foreigners. Thumping the table
was all right within the family circle, as it were, but really, when
it came to talking like that to outsiders——

"When the Japanese were approaching Hankow," says Dr. Tong
rather sadly, "the British Chargé d'Affaires delivered to us ten
conditions drawn up by the Japanese as the price of their agreement
to a neutral zone in Hankow. . . . The Generalissimo was greatly
displeased by the willingness of the British to transmit such demands from our enemy and unburdened his mind frankly in an
interview with the British Chargé at which I was interpreter."

Tong demurred and failed to interpret the full strength of the
Generalissimo's speech. Chiang persisted. "I sought the support
of Madame Chiang," confesses Holly. "She spoke to the Generalissimo in support of my position and they had a quarrel."

Poor Holly apologized to Madame; she said it didn't matter,
that she would stand by him. "After all, a little quarrel between
husband and wife will not do any harm."

She was unable to soothe her husband. Dr. Tong then appealed
to Chiang's secretary-general, who agreed with him. "This made
the Generalissimo so furious that he called in Chen and told him
that he was chicken-hearted and had no conception of state-craft."
Chiang turned on Holly and repeated the accusation, adding, "You
cannot be a diplomat. Your action has made me very angry."

He gave in at last on the matter of the British chargé, but Chiang
has never, *au fond,* learned to love the British very much.

An important part of Chiang's strategy of retreat was the
"scorched earth" policy. (It was China, actually, who invented the
phrase and the practice.) Shanghai escaped the last-minute torch
because of those awkward foreigners whose property rights had to
be respected. But in Nanking the Chinese started burning and
breaking with ever-increasing enthusiasm. Such machinery as could
not be transported inland, such rice as was still green and grow-

ing, such oil as was waiting in the tank, must be blown up or devastated or burned. Civilians? Let them come along inland with the Army, said the Kuomintang, and build anew behind the natural protection of Szechuan terrain.

A good many urban civilians did this, but the peasants did not take kindly to the idea. The scorched-earth policy made excellent propaganda for the occupying Japanese troops, and better for the Reds. But even they could not have hoped for the propaganda Changsha was soon to afford them.

Changsha was one of the important stopping places selected by Chiang in his plans for retreating to Chungking. He was confident that the city could be held a long time, if not indefinitely: its history showed how hard it was to capture. Unfortunately Chiang himself was not there when the rumor spread, soon after the Army had begun to settle in, that the Japanese were moving straight on from Wuhan and would soon be battering at the gates. The panicky order was given that Changsha must be put to the torch. "Scorched earth" was supposed to be applied to a locality *after* the Army was again on the march, not several weeks in advance, but those were the orders, and they were immediately carried out. The true folly of the act lay in its irony: the city need never have been destroyed at all. The Japanese never did succeed in taking its smoldering rubble. When Chiang arrived, heads fell for this stupidity—literally.

In January 1939 the Nationalists made their final retreat to Chungking.

The combined influences of events and pressure from returned travelers were bringing about a definite change of attitude in America toward the Japanese incident. Europe was still indifferent: Hitler claimed all their attention. But now the Americans began to worry about what was going on across the Pacific. Roosevelt sponsored an appeal in January 1939 to collect a million dollars for suffering Chinese civilians, and the sum was quickly acquired.

Though the Chinese didn't expect direct intervention, they hoped to head America off any more economic co-operation with Japan. They wanted to stop Japan's purchase of scrap-iron, oil, gasoline, and above all shipping and weapons from Americans. As a result, at least enough public opinion was stirred up in the States to put across the idea of boycotting silk stockings. This was effective, as far as it went, but Japan continued to buy strategic materials.

Still working as one voice with the Nationalists was the leftist element. The Institute of Pacific Relations, strongly Communist in sympathy, kept tugging at American elbows, jogging American consciences, and talking loud about China. The party line was still ardently pro-Chiang: Japan was making headway far too fast to suit the Reds.

None of the clamor about oil and iron was likely to come to anything. American businessmen were jealous of British trade with Japan, and the English flatly refused to consider a mutual agreement to cut it off. They were not at war with Japan, they reminded America. Strictly speaking, nobody was. What was going on in China was still referred to, in Western diplomatic circles, as the Incident. Then came Wang Ching-wei's final defection. It is no use denying that this looked funny to us. The constant changing about, playing for position of Chinese leaders always seems funny to the Western eye. Through the years Wang had been moving about like Punch with the policeman, popping up now in Canton, now in the Northwest with Feng Yu-hsiang: delivering his broadsides by wordy telegram and popping down again to reappear, perky and smiling, back with the Nationalist Government.

But this time it was not funny.

Other hardy perennial opponents to Chiang had forgotten their rivalry and jealousy. Li Tsung-jen, Pai Chung-hsi, and the rest rallied when they were convinced that Japan was a serious threat; all of them did but Wang Ching-wei. Wang had tried so often to get to the top and had missed by so little and was so convinced of his rights as Sun Yat-sen's heir that he had become a monomaniac. Nothing mattered by that time except the struggle between Chiang Kai-shek and himself. He lost the ability to distinguish between allies. He was just as willing to take the help of Japan as that of some insurgent domestic general. What Japanese control of China —and himself—would lead to ultimately meant nothing to him. No doubt he was confident that when it came to that point he would be able to handle the Japanese: he would outguess them.

Wang had friends in Shanghai, people with connections in other countries, and they had told him in whispers, before his flight into the interior, that it was not too late. The struggle was not fundamentally between Japan and China, which were both, after all, Asiatic nations. It was a struggle between right-thinking men of both countries on one hand and this maddeningly tyrannical, inefficient clique on the other—the running dogs of Western imperialism. China would never be cured until Chiang was removed. What difference did it make, when you came right down to it, if it was Japan who helped the Chinese people to get rid of the tyrant . . . ? For a while Wang moved on with the Kuomintang, discontentedly shifting from Nanking to Wuhan to Changsha to Chungking, but he thought about these matters, and he corresponded secretly with his friends.

The Japanese were encountering a difficulty that usually faces conquerors suddenly possessed of a lot of captured territory. How to govern the country and yet continue to pursue the war? An immediate show of self-confidence and efficiency was necessary. The Japanese didn't mean to manage China like a colony; it would have been too big a job. They saw Asia of the future overseen by an omniscient Japan, divided by traditional borders yet united by international fervor; all the East was to be held together in the bonds of the Co-Prosperity Zone. To maintain this willing, loving spirit, the Japanese realized, they needed leaders from among the locals.

They tried for quite a while to find some leaders, but anybody who accepted a job of the sort was either assassinated very soon or turned out to be hopelessly incompetent or corrupt. It was a matter of education, the Japanese told each other wisely. In another generation that would all be arranged. At last, when their need was beginning to be genuinely awkward, they got Wang Ching-wei.

Everybody in Chungking seems to have been taken by surprise. For a long time no one had paid much attention to Wang. It was easy enough for him to get out. He went farther west, to Chengtu, on a routine trip; from there he flew down to Kunming, the capital city of Yunnan, and after a brief, unsuccessful attempt to bring the Yunnan war lord round to his way of thinking, he continued his outward journey to Hanoi in Indo-China. By the end of the year he was in Hongkong.

He sent a telegram to Chiang suggesting that China accept Konoye's peace terms. Chungking's reply was a denunciation. In time Wang set up his own Kuomintang in Shanghai, with the tight sort of administration and secret-police activity that are so familiar to occupied communities. In 1940 he was formally installed as "Chairman of China."

Lots of Russians came to Chungking. Those at the Soviet diplomatic headquarters were important enough, but the really interesting group stayed at an airfield a long way off, nearer Chengtu than Chungking, and trained pilots to maneuver the planes that had been brought from Moscow on an indefinite term of loan. They were all the outside aid China had.

Chiang's attention was divided between maintaining a working government in extraordinarily difficult circumstances, keeping the peace with suspicious Szechuan dignitaries, holding on to his tenuous friendship with Yunnan's war lord, Lung Yuen, upon whom so much depended, and carrying on what was left of the fighting war. As far as the West was concerned the international situation remained, for the time being, static; in Europe the dogs of war were growling, but in Chungking the worst had already happened. That sort of suspense, at least, was a thing of the past.

One of the inconveniences of life in the wartime capital was the lack of day-to-day supplies necessary for modern governments; telegraphic equipment, and typewriter spare parts. Things like this had to be flown in from Hongkong or brought across the Burma Road, and they were prohibitively costly. But such vexations were as nothing compared to the air-raid hazard. Chungking was placed in an excellent position as far as foreknowledge of the raids went; the city usually had an hour's warning when Japanese planes were on the way. It was also well supplied with rock in which to tunnel for safety, and after the first few tragic raids had taught the populace what bombing meant there were caves dug for everybody. But the city had no effective defense, either in the air or on the ground. Coping with the Japanese became a grim routine of carrying valuables into the caves, sitting underground for hours, and then carrying the valuables back to where they came from if that place still existed.

North China was being "consolidated." In Central China the enemy, by the end of March 1939, had penetrated as far as Nanchang and took over a burned, blackened prize of a capital city. By September he had attempted to capture Changsha, but failed. Japan's lines were overextended and seemed likely to remain that way indefinitely. But change, as the Japanese high command was well aware, was on the way. War was declared in Europe in September, but in Chungking the only thing that mattered was the state of China. The Japanese got in as far as Ichang, just the other side of the Yangtze Gorges from Chungking itself. There they stuck.

In Europe things began to hot up, and suddenly nobody remembered the phrase "phony war." Holland, Belgium, then France. But still the Chinese had their own troubles to think about. The Reds had begun to get restive again. When Stalin signed the Nazi-Soviet

Pact he hinted that the attitude of Russia was likely to change in lots of other respects as well. As if at a signal, Chinese Communist unrest followed. The New Fourth Army in Anhwei fired the opening shot of the campaign.

The story as reported by indignant leftist foreign correspondents was that the Communists were being picked on, that they hadn't had the square deal that was promised them in 1937 and were merely trying to call the world's attention to their plight. They were disgracefully ill fed, it was said, and ill clothed, and kept short of ammunition just because they were Reds. The facts do not quite bear out this interpretation.

When the armies were reorganized after the agreements of 1937 the Reds were assigned to the "Shen-Kan-Ning Border Region," the area comprising Shensi, Kansu, and Ninghsia borders. Using guerrilla tactics, they constituted an important defense against the Japanese, more effective than the Nationalists with their positional-warfare technique. In recognition of this fact their area of operations was enlarged and they established another region of their own at the borders of Shansi, Chahar, and Hopei. In both these places they set up their soviet type of government, with the Nationalists' knowledge and even, in a grudging way, their approval. The government also paid them a subsidy. That was in the agreement.

Friction soon developed between Kuomintang and Communist troops over the matter of equipment. The Reds claimed that they outfitted themselves at the expense of defeated Japanese troops; the Nationalists soldiers said, on the contrary, that the Reds picked up *their* rifles and munitions after lost battles and kept them for their own use. Inevitably there were also charges and countercharges of slacking on the job. The clash between Nationalists and the New Fourth Army followed an attempt by the Reds to take control of an area that was policed by the Nationalists. Clearly and simply, the Reds were out of bounds. Chungking thereupon disbanded the New Fourth Army, but the struggle continued just the same.

The American writers who were given the Communist angle on the story forgot that according to agreement there should have been no separate Communist angle at all. If I seem to labor the point about American correspondents, it is not due to the common occupational disease that leads writers to write about writers. It is because their influence on international developments at this point can hardly be exaggerated. Except for the Institute of Pacific Relations, they were the West's sole source of information on China. The shrill small voices of missionaries were ignored, because the missions, though they knew their stuff, weren't organized to speak as one. But the Institute of Pacific Relations was, and so was the fourth estate.

The struggle went on and on, not as a violent civil war but on the scale of one of Chiang's running battles with war lords in the old days. Red sympathizers among foreigners reported it as testimony to the tyranny with which the innocent victims were being hustled around. Kuomintang sympathizers among foreigners didn't report anything about it because they weren't permitted to do so from Chungking. The government stubbornly refused to allow anything at all to be sent out on the subject, assuming that if they ignored it so would everybody else. The adverse story, and only that, was printed abroad. It took a long time for Chungking officials to appreciate the uses and abuses of publicity.

One of the few men who could, perhaps, have shaken Chiang Kai-shek's convictions on this subject, and the only one who would certainly have persisted in trying, was no longer there to do his job. William Henry Donald, faithful friend and gadfly, was a war casualty. As long as China versus Japan was the only war that impinged on his conscience, he had been all right in Chungking. He had his house and his typewriter and his daily work with the Chiangs, and everything seemed normal. But outside in the rest of the world life was not normal, and it got less so every day. Belatedly Donald began to remember that he was British. It riled him that the

Germans of the legation in Chungking were free to go about like everybody else. Chiang still kept those few German military advisers who had survived the country's vicissitudes and observed the customary diplomatic courtesies toward their compatriots.

"China is not at war with Germany," Mayling would remind Donald in exasperation when he protested.

What with the constant battering air raids and suspense, tempers were running short, and as Donald grew older he was less and less easy to get on with. He had always prided himself on speaking straight from the shoulder, and very irritating this virtue could be. Now he took to picking up the gossip of discontented officials who complained about the Kungs' alleged graft and brought it to Madame like a dog carrying into the house a particularly malodorous bone. It was not the sort of thing he would have believed in earlier days, much less repeated. Mayling didn't like the bone and spoke sharply. Donald brooded.

During one of the long foggy periods in Chungking weather, when planes couldn't get in to provide their own sort of release for taut feelings, Chiang retorted in writing to one of Donald's complaints about the Germans, "I am not at war with Germany."

"I am," said Donald. Sorehearted, he left Chungking by way of Kunming and Indo-China and took to his yacht in Hongkong and started cruising in the South Pacific. Pearl Harbor caught him in Manila, but that is another story. Donald disappeared from the Chinese scene, and his understanding of Western-style publicity disappeared with him.

For the last year before Pearl Harbor, however, the Generalissimo's good press more than balanced the bad. As the cold war became less chilly and finally melted and boiled up in the blitz, Chungking began to attract lively attention in America and England. In 1940 Britain had closed the Burma Road in deference to Japanese opinion. Three months later she thought the matter over and opened it again. Chiang's opinion of Britain correspondingly sank to an all-time low for that period of three months, and then came up a little.

The Chiang household was in turmoil. Just as Moscow had signified a new era of friendship and union by sending back Chiang Ching-kuo, so the entire Communist complex now hinted at a similar state of affairs by permitting Madame Chiang's sister, Madame Sun, to make her appearance in the family, arm in arm and the best of friends, presumably, with Mesdames Kung and Chiang. She even allowed herself to be photographed at a reception with the Generalissimo, though it went against the grain to do it.

It took a lot of will power for her to remain in Chungking, even for the short time she was there, under a series of Japanese air raids. Chingling didn't like the air raids. She liked them even less than the other Chinese, who had to get used to three years of them. But duty is duty, and in other ways she was able to do a lot of useful work, implying to the faithful that she found her position, living as she did in the Kung house in a hotbed of capitalism, most distressing. The circle of Chou En-lai held indignant meetings to discuss Chingling's position among the enemy.

"Hardly more than a prisoner," they told each other hotly. This was not true, but it was dramatic. At last she was permitted to go back to Hongkong, where it was quieter. The gesture had been made. Up in the Northwest the Communists went on, quietly spreading out.

For perhaps the only time in her post-revolutionary history Russia got a genuine shock when the Germans betrayed the pact and attacked her. It was one war she had not foreseen quite so soon. The Japanese attack on China and the later one on America were there plain and clear in her crystal ball. Only her own future was obscure. In the flurry that followed the West held Moscow's attention for some months; Russia found herself allied with England and America, to the astonishment of all three, and the Far East naturally went by the board. This did not halt Mao Tse-tung, however; his program was always laid down well in advance, and in China infiltration, indoctrination, and sabotage went on as happily as ever.

Not only Moscow foretold the Japanese action at Pearl Harbor. Chiang Kai-shek was sure something was in the wind, and he kept saying so in messages to the U. S. A. Embassy. But toward the end, in that last fortnight before December 7, the picture was confused in Chungking, just as it was in Washington, by Tokyo's offer to talk matters over with the American State Department. Americans seized on this as a chance, and Chungking was very worried that there would indeed be a chance for a settlement at their expense. The choice offered to Washington was that in return for peace the Americans should force through a treaty between Japan and China by which Manchukuo be recognized and the other Japanese conquest accepted.

However, America did not give way. The Japanese attacked; the fire flared up. Germany and Italy declared war on America. Chiang, on behalf of China, declared war on Germany, Italy, and—at last—on Japan. The devious ways of diplomacy have seldom led to more of an anticlimax.

# 10 STILWELL VS. CHENNAULT 1941–43

Chiang now embarked on a new sort of life, heavily involved with foreigners. He held diplomatic discussions with
the leaders of the United Nations, and military powwows with
Western generals. In these unfamiliar circumstances he did his best
to live up, more than ever, to the Confucian ideal of the gentleman.
Seldom did he permit the mask to slip. Stilwell, however, was to be
there when it happened.

And Chiang had a good deal to control. His emotions at the beginning of the all-in war must have been enough to flood a weaker-
willed man. In spite of all the talk about the common struggle of the
United Nations, Pearl Harbor was bound to mean different things to
different countries. To the U.S.A. it was pure shock. To Britain it
was like the pricking of a large, painful blister. To the Chinese it
was relief that surpassed Britain's. Until that last minute it had
looked as if Japan would carry her point: Kurusu's trip to Washington had scared them to death.

The practical advantages of the situation were brilliantly clear:
America was in, and on China's side. What was purely impractical,
and plays no part in documentary history, nevertheless shouldn't
be ignored. Chiang had the intoxicating sensation of being justified
at last. These Western people who had been so impatient of Chinese

strategy, who had laughed as the Nationalist Army retreated and talked scornfully of the Japanese, were now in speedy retreat from those same islanders. In Hongkong, Singapore, and Manila foreigners were fighting for their lives—and fighting against Asiatics. If the Japanese were proud of Chiang Kai-shek for having withstood them so long and put it down to the training he had received at their hands, so Chiang was probably proud of the Japanese, much as he detested them, for putting Asia on the West's prejudiced map. Let the foreigners handle it for a while and see if they could do any better against the Japanese than the Chinese had done. It did not look from where he was standing as if they would.

Before the end of December, America had swung into action. As our only defense in the Far East, China must be supplied with munitions and other help. The usual route from Hongkong had been cut off; the British were obviously fighting a losing battle there. From the new avalanche of supplies visualized by the strategists in Washington only the Burma Road was left, that much-contested life line. It had always been a source of trouble. It was long, difficult to keep in repair, fantastically dangerous, and too narrow to permit much volume of travel at a time.

Just before Pearl Harbor there had been formally organized in Chungking a group of American aviators who worked on volunteer status for China and the Chiangs under Colonel Claire Chennault. Chennault was instructor at the Air Force Cadet School. Some of these men had been flying in China ever since the Kuomintang first began buying American planes, having come over to demonstrate the merchandise and remained to pilot and teach. Others had hurried over to join up as they were released from their volunteer posts in Spain. It was a familiar joke that pilots from both sides of the Spanish War were likely to meet and work side by side in China. But political convictions were not important to them and they got on well enough with each other, mercenaries of the twentieth century.

As traffic on the Burma Road swelled in volume and got itself mixed up, as cargo was lost through pilfering and trucks broke down from mishandling, the air freight service into Chungking became more and more urgently important. The backbone of its organization was American, and it had been in action for months before the Japanese attack. Halfway down the road, over the border in Burma, was a plane factory backed by American and Chinese capital. Thus China had one asset ready to hand, a trained nucleus of an air force. In double-quick time the handful of men, called the American Volunteer Group or "Flying Tigers," was incorporated into the U. S. Air Force.

Aside from all this it was America first in Chungking, for the very good reason that, among the United Nations, America was the only one to take China seriously. Chiang had envisaged a joint military council including Britain, Canada, New Zealand, and Australia—the Commonwealth group—with Russia and the Netherlands. But Russia promptly contracted out of the Asian side of the war: Ambassador Litvinov explained to the U. S. Secretary of State, Hull, that his country's energy was entirely taken up by the struggle with Germany. She would have no strength for coping with Japan, at least not for the time being, but he left open the possibility that Russia might join in against Japan later, when the German problem had ceased to press. This was bad news for the other United Nations, who had been counting on Siberian air bases from which to attack Tokyo.

Chiang suggested a meeting in Chungking of United Nations high brass, empowered to make plans for an all-Asia strategy of war and the defense of the widespread threatened area: China, Hongkong, Singapore, the Philippines, Burma, and the Dutch East Indies. In his opinion there should be a joint general staff based on Chungking, and it seemed to the Americans that some such arrangement would be a good thing. On December 22 General Brett for America and Wavell for England finally arrived in Chungking and joined a few lesser dignitaries for a conference. But Washington had learned that it is one thing to make these large, over-all plans and quite another to break them down into the working details that mean everything in war. Where were they to begin? Hongkong was practically lost and the positions of Singapore and the Philippines were very shaky. With Russia refusing to play, the answer to Japan could not be an immediate air offensive against her mainland. Should the Allies rush a joint army and navy to the East Indies? Or did Burma and Malaya come first? What about the threat to India if Burma was neglected, and what of Australia?

And there was a ticklish question that could not be thrashed out in the open. Some members of the conference, chiefly Britain, could not see Chungking as the focal point of their defense. They felt that Chiang didn't matter enough. His resources couldn't compare with theirs, and it would be wrong to give him a powerful voice in the allocation of their pool of men and material. America argued that China's geographical position gave her importance in the scene. But the British with their history vis-à-vis China of genial condescension had long since written her off, and they had strong objections to thinking again at this crucial moment. Churchill was in Washington putting up a battle against Chiang in which worried exasperation had to be hidden by tact. He was later to say in his book, *The Hinge of Fate,* that he found an "extraordinary significance of China in American minds" which he considered "strangely out of proportion." "I said I would of course always be helpful and polite to the Chinese, whom I admired and liked as a race and pitied for their endless misgovernment, but that Roosevelt must not expect me to adopt what I felt was a wholly unreal standard of values."

This was hardly an auspicious beginning to an alliance sure to be sorely strained anyway over the limited material available. How much Chiang heard about Churchill's arguments is unknown, but he could not have remained very long in ignorance of the general tenor of British sentiment.

The President smoothed it over, sending word to Chungking that as Australia, Britain, Holland, and America would have a supreme commander of their forces in the Southwest Pacific theater—Wavell—Chiang ought to act as Wavell's opposite number and command the China theater, including Siam and Indo-China, combining action with the Briton by means of a joint planning staff. Chiang accepted this adroit compromise and requested that Roosevelt appoint an American to be chief of the joint staff under him. And that is how Joseph Warren Stilwell happened to be sent to Chungking.

Would things have been different if someone else had been given the appointment—a less irascible, uncompromising character, someone who tried to understand the special problems he was bound to encounter? Stilwell seems to have been chosen partly because in 1935–39 he had served a tour in China as military attaché. What no one seems to have noticed in the rush was that even then his reports showed a strong dislike of Chiang.

Late in February he started out on the mission. By this time America and Britain had outlined their general strategy. Germany was to be defeated first, while Japan was to be approached from the east, across the Pacific, with whatever ships that could be spared. She must be contained, in the meantime, along the line of defense from Australia to India and Burma. The Japanese already encamped in China were to be bombed from Chinese airports, and supplies would be brought in over the Burma Road and stock-piled against a future push to drive them out. British and Dutch naval units were to guard the ports of Australia, Burma, India, and Ceylon; on land the troops were to be contributed by all the United Nations (except Russia), supporting an American force.

In Washington and London it looked all right, or, if not all right, at least as good as it could be at that stage. But in Chungking the picture was not so satisfactory. Held at any angle before the eyes—upside down, sideways, or right side up—the fact remained: China

came last. And what if in the meantime the Japanese decided not
to play the role of sitting duck there on the Chinese mainland?
What if they moved farther inland?

However, objections from Chungking didn't carry much weight.
The worried leaders of American and British armed forces only
retorted that perhaps it was not absolutely essential to defend
Chungking anyway. General Marshall, for one, was dubious as to
the importance of Chinese air bases; he shared Churchill's misgivings about Chinese fighting ability. At the most charitable it
could not be denied—nobody was trying to deny—that the Chinese
were tired after their years of struggle. The Generalissimo mentioned the fact frequently in a marked manner. However, Stimson,
the American Secretary of War, urged that the China theater be
considered as of first importance, and Roosevelt agreed.

Stilwell was to supervise and control all U. S. defense aid for
China. Under the Generalissimo he was to command all U. S. forces
in China and such Chinese forces as might be assigned to him. He
was to represent the U. S. on any international war council in China
and act as chief of staff for Chiang. He was to improve, maintain,
and control the Burma Road in China. Like other arrangements
made under the pressure of early events some of these were outdated very soon. Even before Stilwell set forth, Rangoon was in
grave danger and Lend-Lease material intended for China was
diverted for its defense by the British.

Stilwell set out with a full set of prejudices. He was a man who
leaped from prejudice to prejudice, and was seldom without a bag
full of them. For one thing he heartily disliked the British, having
already decided that they were getting too much out of Roosevelt.
In this he was merely voicing the opinion of a large number of his
colleagues in Washington, but Stilwell was perhaps unique in the
catholicity of his disapprovals.

"Besides being a rank amateur in all military matters, F.D.R.
is apt to act on sudden impulses," he wrote in his diary. "On top of

that he has been completely hypnotized by the British, who have sold him a bill of goods. It took the disaster in Hawaii to stop the flow of *all* our stuff to the Limeys. What they have gotten must be simply enormous. . . ."

Shortly before his appointment on January 1 he had observed:

"Trouble with unified command in Far East. Not as between British and ourselves, but among the British! The 'Senior Service' [British Navy] sits disdainfully aloof. Nobody can command *them*—it isn't done. The arrogant Royal Air Force will have none of it. . . .

"Chiang Kai-shek acting up. Ho Ying-ch'in and he think the U. S. Air Force should come right over and protect them. Also that they should get everything they ask for. [China] peeved over British grab of *Tulsa* cargo for protection of Rangoon. Chiang Kai-shek ready to send 100,000 men into Burma, but Wavell refused the help."

On January 24 he wrote to the War Department:

"The British have one brigade east of Rangoon and one more on the way. That's what they thought sufficient to hold Burma. And the SUPREME COMMANDER, Wavell, refused Chiang K'ai-shek's offer of two corps. [He] didn't want the dirty Chinese in Burma."

Could it be that loyalty to one of his allies was at last breaking in? No. The next day the general wrote, "The Burmese hate the Chinese *and* the British: maybe they are pretty right."

Comment on the ways of wartime alliances couldn't be more superfluous.

One of the first quarrels Stilwell stepped into was under way, hot and strong, before he arrived; a squabble about Chennault's position. The airman, as commander of the American Volunteer Group, wanted to be completely independent. Stilwell decreed that he must be subordinate to Brigadier General Bissell, and this set Chennault against him from the start. Air power was becoming the most important factor in China's defense. When Rangoon fell, the Road was cut off. But a new air lift was rapidly put into operation. Roosevelt was delighted to be able to present it to Chiang on a platter; in his mind it made up for the Lend-Lease material that had been promised to China and then diverted to hotter spots. The President was anxious about China's state of mind. Chiang had warned him that he could not answer forever for his people's capacity to resist.

Churchill insisted that this need not trouble Roosevelt; it would not make much difference, he said, if China did drop out of the struggle. But Roosevelt didn't agree. At the beginning of 1942 he was considering the latest request Chiang had made, for a loan of five hundred million dollars from Washington and the equivalent of fifty million more from Britain. It seemed a lot of money; was it all really necessary? Wouldn't it lead to graft and corruption? The Americans hesitated and rubbed their chins while Dr. Kung broke down the figures and explained how much was needed to pay the Army and shore up China's economy. An attempt to persuade Russia to enter the bargain met flat refusal. In the end the Americans decided to grant it, and the loan was authorized with no strings attached. "Later, when the memories of emergency grew dim and the feelings of friendship with the Generalissimo grew tired, there was regret that we had not been more stubborn. . . . Much of the proceeds were used up in measures conceived as brakes on the course of inflation in China and the decline of value of the Chinese currency. These failed. . . . The loan conceived in a rush of vivid sympathy and alliance turned later into a cause of fault-finding." (Herbert Feis, *The China Tangle,* p. 23.)

The feelings of Whitehall at being let in for this expense must have been inexpressible on the diplomatic level.

There had been one all-in conference between Chiang and the representatives of Britain and America a week after Pearl Harbor.

Thereafter so much high brass came and went in Chungking that foreign generals soon ceased to be any novelty to either the General-issimo or Madame. She usually acted as his interpreter, and a very demanding job it was, calling not only for accuracy, but a ceaseless flow of interpretation of less easily expressed things than mere words.

"In America this is the custom," Mayling would have to interpolate. "He is not being offensive; it is merely an idiomatic expression." Or occasionally, "I think he *does* mean to be offensive."

On February 10 Chungking heard startling news. Chiang Kai-shek was actually traveling out of China; he had that day arrived by plane in Calcutta, en route for New Delhi for a conference. In all he was eleven days in India. In spite of British reluctance to facilitate the meeting he had a talk with Gandhi. There was a slight awkwardness about that, because Gandhi couldn't come to New Delhi and the authorities didn't think it seemly for Chiang to go to him: they finally compromised and met in Bombay. Chiang also paid several visits to Nehru. Nehru was no stranger; he had visited Chungking in 1939, when he much impressed Hollington Tong by talking without interruption, save for the interpreter, all through a protracted air raid.

Tong was with the party in India, and he continued to be fascinated by Nehru. At a picnic, "as we grew more and more informal in our behaviour, Mr. Nehru took off his coat and began turning somersaults on the lawn. His daughter was upset at his lack of dignity. . . . We all felt that Mr. Nehru should have our moral support, so Mr. Chang Tao-fan . . . stripped off his outer coat and began to roll on the lawn himself." Nehru's daughter was so angry and humiliated that she refused to join the party at dinner. It was a homey little interchange that delighted the Chinese delegation. (*Dateline: China.*)

The interview with Gandhi had its effect. On the last day of the tour Madame broadcast the Generalissimo's message to the nation.

Chiang said that the British should give India her political freedom
as soon as possible. This speech was irritating to the British, but it
pleased the Indians, and the Chinese departed in a glowing haze of
good will. They professed themselves satisfied that India was genuinely anti-Japanese. In truth this fact was never to become absolutely clear: Subhas Chandra Bose, who mobilized resident Indians
in occupied Asia on behalf of the Japanese, was considered a hero
by the Indians at home, not a traitor. Nevertheless, Nehru was
charming; the Chinese were agreed on that.

They also agreed that Burma must be saved in order to shield
India from Japanese invasion as well as to regain the use of the
Burma Road. Chiang was more than willing to contribute troops to
this end, and he was startled when his offer was virtually turned
down. The British accepted only one Chinese division of seven
thousand men, the combined Fifth and Sixth armies. Like Stilwell,
Chiang construed this as a snub from the British—which in fact it
was. The incident didn't add to his love for the nation, and it in-
tensified Stilwell's Anglophobia. Later, when the first Burma campaign was lost, neither Chiang nor Stilwell saw reason to change his
mind on the subject. But common misfortune didn't bring these
two any closer together.

Lieutenant General Stilwell was traveling out from America
during the Generalissimo's trip. He was close upon Chiang's heels
in New Delhi, where he heard the news of Singapore's surrender.
On March 3 he flew to Lashio, and there met Chiang, who had gone
straight on from India to inspect the situation.

"Impressions of Lashio," noted Stilwell: "strained attention of
Fifth and Sixth Army commanders while Chiang K'ai-shek was
talking to them; sharp, clipped staccato voice of Chiang K'ai-shek
on upper porch of Porter House; hushed quiet below. . . ."

The reason for that strained attention and hushed quiet is re-
vealed in Tong's memoirs. That afternoon during the Generalissimo's daily nap, owing to some mix-up in arrangements, all

his English-speaking aides wandered off separately on informal tours of inspection. Scarcely were they out of sight when his telephone rang; headquarters wished to warn the distinguished visitor that an air raid was on the way. There the Generalissimo was with nobody to interpret for him, and there was H.Q. with nobody speaking Chinese. Chiang was in a rage when the Chinese returned. He had no time to tell them off properly; the Japanese planes were practically overhead. "We had barely time to scramble into a car and get out of town to a safe place before the raiders arrived," confessed Tong. (*Dateline: China*, p. 183.) No wonder the Generalissimo's voice sounded clipped and staccato. However, his greeting of Stilwell was cordial.

The ensuing two months moved swiftly and tragically. Angry echoes of that time still rumble through our post-mortem literature. The British editor of *The Stilwell Papers* says in chilly accents that the defensive campaign was doomed from the start and Stilwell showed limited vision in attempting it: "With Siam in Japanese hands . . . it was physically impossible to hold Burma south of Mandalay, because every position could be turned from the east. . . . As things stood in the summer of 1942, there were only two things to do: the first was to hold the frontier of India and the second to do nothing further, or if for prestige an offensive was considered imperative, to build up a sufficient force to drive the Japanese out of Burma *once their maritime foundations began to crack and crumble*. To attempt an all-out attack before this set in was little short of lunacy."

What concerns us is a different matter; the impact of Chiang Kai-shek on Stilwell, and vice versa. In *The Stilwell Papers* we see not only the portrait of the Generalissimo as Stilwell saw him—pigheaded, ignorant, dishonest, preoccupied with piddling little questions of "face," caring only for power, wildly disorganized in his military strategy, and, most damning indictment of all, hopelessly out of step with Western methods. We also see the American, at once keyed up by his responsibility and weighed down by it; full of nervous energy that went sour when it was frustrated; incapable —surely to an abnormal degree?—of appreciating that there are more points of view than one's own, and that the world is a good deal larger than America. Putting it simply, Chinese are not Americans. Stilwell must have known this in theory, but when he ran up against the fact it always surprised and dismayed him, and set him on the boil.

Most of the Chinese officers under him, he discovered, were inefficient or dishonest or cowardly. They wouldn't obey his orders. Often he suspected they had conflicting orders from Chiang. He stormed back and forth between Chungking and the rapidly deteriorating battle line, extracting promises, making demands, tearing his hair with exasperation over these impertinent people who not only didn't behave like Americans, but weren't even ashamed of their discrepancies. The inevitable defeat in May sent him with a handful of followers on the heroic march across the mountains into India, where—tired, ill, and in his way magnificent—he made the remark that went round the world: "I claim we got a hell of a beating."

Not once did it occur to him that the Chinese method, which he considered skrimshanking and cowardly and unfair to China's allies, the contemptible out-of-date traditional method of warfare, "defense in depth," which meant in blunt words simply running away until the enemy was tired out chasing you—not once did it cross his mind that sometimes the Chinese way might after all be the right one.

Anyway Burma was now in Japanese hands, and the only way in to Free China was by air.

While Stilwell railed against the inefficiency of his allies and swore to get Burma back no matter what stood in his path, Chiang and his people in Chungking were taking the defeat even harder. With them it was not only a matter of pride. What now was to stop the Japanese coming on into China whenever they felt like it? Not fear of the Western allies, for they had been shown up in Hongkong and Singapore and the Philippines, as well as Burma. The Japanese would attend to Chungking as soon as they had the time. And the Chinese feared they would be helpless to resist, for other people were getting the supplies that had been earmarked for them. Their disappointment and apprehension were so keen that American observers began to worry for fear Chungking would collapse altogether.

The U. S. adviser on Far Eastern Political Affairs, Stanley Hornbeck, was disturbed. The Chinese, he said, were receiving no reassurance anywhere. Things were going badly for their allies, and though the U. S. Government had promised to send goods to China, these goods did not arrive. How long would the Chinese go on accepting the situation? Once they concluded that they wouldn't get any aid, they would decide that it was not worth while to continue with their resistance, that the United Nations weren't sure to win anyway.

"From now on there is only one way by which we can make sure of maintaining China's confidence; we must deliver goods."

This opinion was shared by the President and most of the State Department, but it was simply impossible to get enough material ready and shipped before it was snatched away again to meet some emergency elsewhere. Nor had the question of adequate freight transport yet been answered. Then, in June, part of the Tenth Air Force in India, which Chiang had been assured was for China, was whisked off to the Middle East.

"Bang!" wrote Stilwell in Chungking. "Brereton to go to Egypt with all the heavy bombers and all the transports he needs. Bang! The A-29s are to be held at Khartum and diverted to the British. Now what am I to say to the G-mo?"

What he had to say did not matter, as it turned out; the Generalissimo had heard the news before he brought it, and had plenty in
turn to say to him. Madame, too, was full of reproaches. Stilwell
was angry with her, but in spite of himself he admired the lady; his
admiration shows in the diary through his acid remarks even when
he is being most catty.

Chiang had a reply ready and written out for Roosevelt. He presented "Three Minimum Demands": three U. S. divisions must be
sent to India for him, with five hundred combat planes, and there
must be a guarantee of five thousand tons a month flown in over
"the Hump," or "the ferry" as the flyers called the mountain range
they had to cross between Burma and Kunming.

"All by the end of August!" exclaimed Stilwell. "Utterly impossible."

It did look impossible. At that time all available planes, those
of the U. S. Air Force as well as the commercial Sino-American
line, the C.N.A.C., had succeeded in bringing in merely a fraction
of this, an average of a hundred tons monthly. The Generalissimo's
advisers had acquired what looked like a fantastic faith in aircraft
possibilities from Chennault, who was always claiming that the war
could be fought cheaper, with better results, if only everyone would
concentrate on air power.

The Chiangs followed up their ultimatum with explanations and
what Stilwell considered thinly veiled threats. They would have to
make other arrangements, said Chiang, if these conditions were not
agreed to. "China cannot go on without help. . . . The pro-Japanese activity is very strong."

In his anger at being bullied Stilwell forgot that what Chiang
said was in fact true, that China really could not go on much longer
without help. Even when he did recollect this unpalatable fact he
raged that it need not be true, that it was the fault of the Chinese.
Why wasn't their organization better? Why couldn't these people
behave like sensible Americans?

To make the situation more awkward for everybody concerned Chiang Kai-shek now decided that Stilwell was the villain; Stilwell stood between Chungking and Washington, and Chungking suffered at his hands.

In the Generalissimo's experience it was customary that matters of top importance should depend entirely upon the personality of the man, or men, who acted as go-between. That was the way his world went. Suppose that the representative of another power should approach the Chinese Finance Minister or one of his ministry with a request for a loan. Among Asians there was a certain pattern that would be followed. If the Minister or his official happened to like the applicant, or saw the chance of making something on the deal, the loan would go through. But if the ministry man didn't want to allow it, for no matter how personal a reason, it wouldn't go through.

As Westerners we deprecate this attitude and claim that personal considerations never affect our decisions of public interest, though in fact personality does sometimes creep in. The Chinese, however, are accustomed to the method and to their own attitude; they know no other. They are quite frank about it, in their way, but their way is obscured by conventional politeness, and so Westerners often do not recognize the situation in all its naïveté. Stilwell didn't grasp the fact that the Generalissimo was blaming him, Joseph Warren Stilwell, for the whole unsatisfactory state of affairs. Yet to Chiang it seemed clear that this bad-tempered officer was at the bottom of his troubles. Hadn't Roosevelt promised planes and all the rest of it? Were they arriving? They were not.

"What is being done amounts to disobedience of [the President's] orders," said the Generalissimo in Chinese to the uncomprehending Stilwell. (Madame was standing by to interpret.) "Less than ten per cent of what he agreed to give China has been supplied. I do not entertain any doubt that the President is sincere. What has been done is perhaps without his consent or knowledge. As chief of staff to me, you are responsible for seeing to it that the promised material is forthcoming."

Mayling didn't interpret this part of her husband's remarks. She, at least, realized that the American was not as resilient as her husband expected a chief of staff to be.

The censored interview was duly reported to Roosevelt, and Stilwell gleefully noted that F.D.R.'s reply was quiet and dignified and gave no satisfaction. Later he learned to his fury that F.D.R.'s message had never been sent, and he decided that T.V., who was being an absentee Foreign Minister in Washington, simply hadn't forwarded it. Stilwell was steadily being wound round with tentacles of suspicion. Like many another Westerner before him, he couldn't withstand the atmosphere of intrigue.

He was disappointed that the President did not simply take his irate advice to get tough with "the little dummy." Instead, Roosevelt sent Lauchlin Currie out to investigate the matter. Currie talked at length with Chiang, and also with Stilwell, and afforded both of them a good deal of relief merely by listening.

Chiang took a grip on himself and returned to comparatively cordial relations with his chief of staff. Before the peacemaker left he was invited with Stilwell to one of the rare Chiang social occasions, a quiet dinner with the family: Dr. and Madame Kung, the Chiangs, and Madame Sun. Chingling was now a resident of Chungking and one of the group: she had left Hongkong when it became untenable and was amiably supplying living proof of the united front. Stilwell noted:

"Madame Sun is the most simpatica of the three women, and probably the deepest. She is most responsive and likeable, quiet and poised but misses nothing, would wear well." (*The Stilwell Papers* is dedicated to her.) ". . . Chiang Kai-shek was late. He had been doing his evening prayers, which are not to be interrupted by anything. This is a new angle. Anyway, *he* takes it seriously, whether it's sincere or not. Maybe he is fortifying his intuition by communing with his Maker. He leans heavily on his supposed knowledge of psychology. . . . How do you move a guy like that? How do you get his point of view? He can hurdle logic and reason by using his 'intuition'; he dismisses proven principles and methods by saying that Chinese psychology is different; he jumps to a conclusion in keeping with a fancied resemblance to some former experience; and his obstinacy refuses discussion. He has lost all habit of discussion, in fact, because everybody around him is a Yes-man. No one dares tell him an unpleasant truth, because he gets mad. He's in a hell of a fix, and the best he can hope for is to maintain the present unsatisfactory balance of influence by fear and favor. He is not taking a single forward step, or doing anything concrete to improve the position of China, and so, incidentally, his own."

In Washington, Currie reported that the alliance between China and America was in danger; something must really be done soon to supply the material that had been promised so often. He also recommended that Stilwell be relieved. One must admit that he was right: either Stilwell or all the Chinese should have been removed from China.

The latter alternative was impracticable, and for reasons best known to themselves, the powers left Stilwell there, too.

In the calm that followed Currie's oil-pouring, Chiang was ready to consider the new Burma campaign. He had already modified his Three Demands. The Military Council drew up a plan with four reasons for retaking Burma:

"(1) to establish a base from which to start a counteroffensive against Japan; (2) to prevent Germany, Italy, and Japan from joining forces in the Middle East; (3) to open a line of communications from India to China so that large quantities of supplies could be brought into China, 'thereby enabling the Chinese to complete their plan for a general counteroffensive at an early date'; (4) to keep the Japanese too busily occupied to seize the initiative anywhere else in the Pacific." (Romanus, *Stilwell's Mission to China,* pp. 225–226.)

The plan was received with favor in Washington. The British were not enthusiastic, though for a time they did not oppose it outright. They felt that the importance of the four points did not warrant immediate attention, whereas their own problems did. Among themselves they accused Stilwell of the same fault he said they had —seeing only his own theater and ignoring the over-all picture.

A soldier without any personal reactions wouldn't do much good at his job, so we should not, perhaps, carp at Stilwell for his insistence on Burma. He was determined to get back, just as MacArthur was determined to return to the Philippines. And he had other, excellent, reasons. Burma must be recaptured so that China need not continue to depend on the miserable trickle of supplies coming in over the Hump, and the time to get it back was as soon as possible. To do this he must reorganize the Chinese Army.

There is no doubt the Army needed reorganizing. Most of the same difficulties faced a reformer as had existed ten years earlier, when Chiang had just begun to eliminate the war lords. The fact that the Generalissimo had done remarkably well in the time, considering the other tasks he was forced to shoulder simultaneously, was lost on Stilwell, who was either ignorant of Chiang's career or completely uninterested. All the American saw was that the Army wasn't unified, that most of the men were loyal to their provincial commanders to the detriment of the nation's welfare, and that there was a good deal of shortchanging in salary payments and grafting on commissary supplies. Stilwell decided that it was all the Peanut's fault. ("Peanut" was Chiang's code name for cables. Stilwell adopted it and finally preferred it to all the other epithets he applied to Chiang.)

"Troubles of a Peanut dictator," he wrote in one of his private summaries. "At first the Peanut thought that military and political functions could not be separated, so he combined the authority under the military commanders. *Now* he finds that it makes the boys too powerful, and he's been trying for a year to shake them loose, without success in Hupeh . . . Hunan . . . Honan . . . Kansu . . . Shansi . . . Chekiang . . . Yunnan . . . Why doesn't the little dummy realize that his only hope is the 30-division plan, and the creation of a separate, efficient, well-equipped, and well-trained force?"

The "little dummy" had never seen such a force, much less observed how it worked, but Stilwell in his enthusiasm didn't think of that. However, by dint of push and pull and getting at the Generalissimo in any way he could, whether through Madame or Washington, he made headway with his plan. He would take Chinese soldiers from the thirty divisions under direct control of the Kuomintang, *not* from the war-lord troops. He would train them in India, where most of them still remained after the flight from Burma; he would do this training on strictly American lines, so that they would not only be properly paid and fed for the first time in their experience, but would be in good shape for the Western type of offensive warfare.

Chiang did not enthuse about the project; neither did he turn it down. It was a new idea and needed digesting. He bargained: America must send a combat division of American men to help in the campaign; Washington must also increase his air force and air transport. The British must attack by sea at the same time the campaign was launched in North Burma, coming ashore in order to neutralize the Japanese at Rangoon. If these conditions were agreed to, said Chiang, he would consent to use not only that part of his army that was still in India. He would also send in other troops, the "Yoke Force" based in Yunnan.

His conditions entailed much arguing with Washington and the British. The solution never did satisfy either Britain or China. One would back out, and by the time that partner was reconvinced, the other would slide back. Driving these ill-matched allies in harness, Stilwell had his work cut out for him. His plans were realized after a fashion, before the end, but he had to wait and wait again for his revenge in Burma.

The summer was not without some light in Chungking's gloom. The Doolittle raid, though it ended short of its goal, had given Japan a lot to worry about. Now the autumn brought another high point on the Double Tenth, when America and Britain made a gesture that was, in Chiang's estimation, long overdue. On that day they announced that they were giving up their right of special privilege in China. Extraterritoriality was dead, or would be as soon as the treaty was signed early in 1943. True, at the moment no Nationalist was in a position to reap the benefit of this decision. Extraterritorial rights had weighed on the Chinese conscience chiefly in the treaty ports, which were now all in the hands of the Japanese. It was merely an academic gain, one more sign of China's new status among the powers. Chiang Kai-shek would have been better pleased with a larger share of the material that was being handed out to America's European allies. None the less it was a pretty gesture, and Chungking welcomed it with appropriate phrases of appreciation. Significantly, Chiang's message to Britain differed from the one he sent to America. To Washington he was merely conventional, but he congratulated the British, wryly, on "winning a moral victory over themselves."

Stilwell continued to tilt at the Chinese and British commanders, who remained obstinately unreformed, united only in a mystifying resistance to himself. Meanwhile the Reds of the Northwest were going about their business in a very different manner. Mao Tse-tung had decided that his people needed reorganizing, right down to the lowest echelons, and in to the deepest centers of human behavior. On February 1, 1942, he opened the movement that was to bring "brainwashing" into the scene—*Cheng Feng,* or "Ideological Remolding Movement." In a long lecture he explained something of this new idea. He said he had detected unorthodox tendencies in the Party. "We shall call the incorrect spirit in learning subjectivism, the incorrect spirit in the party sectarianism, and the incorrect spirit in literature party formalism. . . ."

During the year that followed thirty thousand leaders were trained to lead the reform, which was disseminated through the rank and file by means of cells, or study groups. The members of these groups analyzed their own sins and those of their companions, and testified to them in public confession. Unworthy leaders were thrown out without compunction. By the beginning of 1942 the effects of this program were showing in the rapidity with which the faith spread. It was not yet time for an open break with Chungking, but the implications were becoming clear. Little by little Stilwell was delicately introduced to the conception of a well-organized China in another place, whereas, it was impressed on him, the China he encountered in his official capacity floundered in a morass of outworn codes and corruption. The introduction was so deft that he hardly realized it had been accomplished for him. He thought he had known all along about the Communists, and that his good opinion of them grew up of itself.

However, he could point with justifiable pride to the organization he was accomplishing on his own hook, against tremendous odds, at Ramgarh in India. The Chinese commanders learned, to their dismay, that the payment and feeding of the troops were not to go through their hands. The soldiers, on the other hand, were delighted. Gradually they were being welded into a genuine modern force that would soon be able to conduct offensive operations. Stilwell found himself an ally from an unexpected source— Madame Chiang, who dropped in at Ramgarh on her way back from a diplomatic visit to Sinkiang. She was enthusiastic about the project and promised to work on the Generalissimo in order to get more genuine co-operation from him. In November, however, Madame went out of the picture temporarily, embarking for America on a sort of good-will tour.

Chiang's general attitude toward the Burma project, though on details he wavered, remained fixed. He was willing to let it go forward in the spring of '43 if the Americans and the British carried out their share of the bargain. His plan was to go on as before, sitting tight, waiting for the war material that had been promised, and keeping one eye on the Northwest. Every time Wavell hung back on the Burma question, Chiang too pulled in his horns. Stilwell flew back and forth between these two, urging, arguing, and trying to pick up the pieces whenever there was a row. The months wore on, and each seemed to carry with it some further postponement of the campaign: the British, preoccupied with crises on other fronts, began to think of it as a mere nuisance. Operations must start in March at the latest: the weather would render any later start completely disastrous. But March, it developed, was impossible. The whole thing was definitely called off for that spring. It would have to wait until autumn.

"Peanut says he won't fight," wrote Stilwell despairingly on January 8. " 'The Japs will fight desperately,' " he continued, quoting Chiang with all the savagery he could put into it. " 'They have had time to prepare. Our supply lines are not good. The British force is inadequate. We risk defeat. Failure in Burma would be disastrous. A combined land and seaborne operation is necessary. We can use the time by making an air offensive, for which *I* guarantee results out of all proportion to the force used,' etc. etc.

"Of course, next fall the Japs won't fight; they will have had no more time to dig in; our supply lines will be perfected; the British force will be 'adequate.' " Then, in a burst of spite, ". . . Chennault's blatting has put him in a spot; he's talked so much about what he can do that now they're going to let him do it."

Chennault had indeed convinced the Chinese that the answer to all their troubles, while waiting for something to happen elsewhere, was a much stepped up supply line by air over the Hump—more planes, more gasoline, and above all weapons for the army at home. In his eagerness he made vast claims of what could be supplied. Chiang was more than ready to be convinced, for this picture of warmaking fitted in with his own concept of patient waiting and defense. Stilwell for his part was so eager to prove his theory that he played down all aspects of aid through air. The army-versus-air-force battle that has been raging in all the capitals of the Western world since the beginning of World War II was thus reflected in war-bound Chungking. It was a bitter contest.

Frustrated, angry, hurt, and suspicious, Stilwell was all the more receptive to the constant suggestion that they ordered these things better in other lands; in Moscow, for instance, or Yenan. He wrote in his diary on January 19: "7:30 to Russian embassy for movies. Excellent. *A Day of War* . . . The Russians are O.K. . . . What a fight the Russians have made. The nation has obviously found itself. Twenty years of work and struggle. Results: tough physique; unity of purpose; pride in their accomplishments; determination to win. . . . Rugged young soldiers. Tough women. Every last man, woman, and child in the war effort.

"Compare it with the Chinese cesspool. A gang of thugs with the one idea of perpetuating themselves and their machine. Money, influence, and position the only considerations of the leaders. Intrigue, double-crossing, lying reports. Hands out for anything they can get; their only idea to let someone else do the fighting; false propaganda on their 'heroic struggle'; indifference of 'leaders' to their men. Cowardice rampant, squeeze paramount, smuggling above duty, colossal ignorance and stupidity of staff, total inability to control factions and cliques, continued oppression of masses. The only factor that saves them is the dumb compliance of [the common people]. . . . And we are maneuvered into the position of having to support this rotten regime and glorify its figurehead, the all-wise great patriot and soldier—Peanut. My God."

Yet what he was comparing was not two realities, but one reality against a propaganda movie.

# 11 CHINA OF THE BIG POWERS 1943

In one thing alone, Chiang Kai-shek and Winston Churchill
are alike. Both of them write in a manner that can stand a
lot of pruning. Fortunately their literary efforts are subjected to
the editing they need. Sir Winston's secretaries read and cut down
for him: Madame Chiang edits her husband. She has been heard
to say exactly what Sir Winston's secretaries say of him—that
Chiang repeats every single thing twice if not oftener.

The Generalissimo's literary style isn't often in a form where
the Western reader can judge for himself. He writes voluminously,
but usually this output appears in the form of speeches, and in
Chinese at that. On one occasion, however, he did publish a book
of considerable size: it appeared in its original Chinese in 1943,
and later was published in English under the title *China's Destiny*.
The left-wing press made much of their claim that Chiang's strong
anti-foreign statements in this book were played down in translation. Actually they were not so strong as all that. The book's
declarations of fondness for the Confucian ideal of government
mildly startled people who were determined to consider Chiang
an American gentleman with Western ideas of democracy. He did
emphasize the value of the old ways; he did sound bossy. One
realizes afresh, reading the book, how surprising it is that a man
of his background should have brought himself to modernize Chi-

nese schools as he did and further literacy for the masses. But he did not attempt to conceal his sentiments; he was not aware that he had anything to conceal. There is nothing sinister in *China's Destiny,* but it must be admitted it is dull.

At the time it first appeared, the West was reading a very different type of literature dealing with China. The American *Far Eastern Survey* in July 1943 brought out an article by one of the I.P.R. leading lights, T. A. Bisson, which asserted that two Chinas had "definitely emerged" from the ordeal of war, even before Pearl Harbor. "One is now generally called Kuomintang China, the other, democratic China." Americans, reading this, began to wonder why, in that case, they should be backing the undemocratic horse, and the wonder grew. So did the bulk of pro-left literature. Chiang's book came out in its English form in 1946 with a strange preface supplied by Philip Jaffe, editor of *Amerasia.* Here it is, said Mr. Jaffe. Here is the Nationalist creed in all its horror.

"The comprador-landlord-merchant-userer class, which today holds political power in China, is naturally in favor of preserving the semicolonial, semifeudal land and tax system that is the basis of their wealth and power." It was fashionable to talk like this in 1946. Whatever "semifeudal" might mean, nobody was going to question it or check up on the landlord system in China to discover that it was not at all, in fact, like the Russian landlord system whence the Jaffe argot came. Nobody even stopped to find out what that sinister word "comprador" meant. (A comprador is a merchant, a middleman for foreign import-export business houses in China.)

Four days after Stilwell wrote so enthusiastically about the Russian film, his President met Churchill in Casablanca for a conference on world strategy. Stalin sent his regrets, pleading as excuse that he was busy with his end of the war, but it was not necessary for Chiang to send regrets, because he wasn't asked. The U. S. State Department was uneasily aware that he resented this, but there it was: Churchill didn't want him. China's contribution to the war effort, said the Englishman, didn't place China's leader on that sort of footing: moreover, the Burma campaign and other questions bearing on China's future were to be discussed and this would be easier if Chiang were not there.

In the Generalissimo's absence, then, Roosevelt did his best for China. Advised by Stilwell, he tried to convince Churchill of the necessity of the Burma campaign, with accompanying British support in the Bay of Bengal. But Churchill would not agree. Let it happen, if it must happen, he said, late in 1943, after the monsoon. Subject to certain other eventualities. Britain would then be ready to supply amphibious support in South Burma. This agreement was relayed to the Generalissimo: two American generals, with one British one, flew up to Chungking to talk it over with him in person.

The Americans, at least, expected their news to render the Generalissimo happy and excited, but they were disappointed. Chiang received them in lukewarm fashion. The Burma campaign simply wasn't close to his heart, as it was to Stilwell's. All he really wanted was more supplies for the home front. He said he was willing to consider the Burma action, but other matters were more pressing. He wanted the American Air Force in China to be made independent under Chennault. This change had been requested by Chennault a year before and refused: now it was granted. Chiang also upped his earlier request to ten thousand tons of supplies flown in monthly over the Hump, and five hundred combat planes before November, which was the new provisional date for the push in Burma. The Western generals gave the Generalissimo a dissertation on shortages and the reasons for them. He must have heard it all before, and they noticed that he did not seem happy.

Stilwell kept tabs on the stories going around Chungking about Madame Chiang in America. "January 9: Rumors that Madame's

mission, whatever it was, has failed. What the hell is up? . . .
January 11: Madame has sent an S.O.S. to T.V. to come and help
her. She has apparently bogged down. The rumor here is that she
has 'failed her mission,' whatever it was." To his wife he wrote,
"Something has happened to May's trip. She had apparently planned
a Queen Marie tour of the States, turning on the charm all over
the place, and keeping the suckers in line. Now she's howling for
help, so maybe the higher-ups are getting hep and are putting on
the lid."

There was nothing so definite as a mission about Madame's trip,
and so no definite disappointment, either, but there is no doubt
that she expected to pin down the State Department to promise
more than they did. Even her old friend Donald could not have
asked more for her, however, than she got in the way of favorable
publicity. At first nothing was too good for the Americans to say
about her. Toward the end of her visit, however, she felt ill with
the urticaria which had long been making her life miserable at
intervals and was laid up in hospital. Moreover, her nephew, who
was acting as her secretary, failed (to put it mildly) to make friends
and influence people. The Red propaganda machine, going into
action on all cylinders, managed to make of Madame's visit, and
especially this hospital stay, a sinister affair. She used her own
sheets, people whispered, silk ones. Such swank! She had at least
fifty pairs of shoes and six priceless fur coats. Such extravagance
in a country of poor coolies! Within a few weeks people who had
never been nearer to China than Buffalo were talking knowledgeably
of the Soong Dynasty and the corruption of Chungking. Washington may have ignored this talk, though it seems as if not everybody
in the State Department did: Mayling herself was in no position
to ignore it. Her propaganda was being countered by a bigger, more
vicious sort. It is small wonder that she was, as Harry Hopkins
noted, "tired and depressed."

"Date with G-mo at 5.00," wrote Stilwell immediately after the

Casablanca conference. "He was sour as a pickle. Never one word of gratitude to the U.S. Just what he can get out of us."

It was a trying summer for Roosevelt, and for his State Department as well. More and more, the President took matters into his own hands, often making arrangements that the State Department knew nothing about. The China theater was only a small part of his problems. Stalin was clamoring to open a second front in Europe, and complaining bitterly about what he considered discrepancies in the U.N. war effort in Tunis. He refused even to discuss the Far East. As he grew more exigent, anxious advisers in Washington began to wonder if he might not back out altogether. Against this major threat similar hints from China fell on indifferent ears. There were disagreements from Britain, too, about allocation of war material; Britain *was* interested in the Far East, but British ideas of how to cope were often at odds with American. A new Burma Road was now in train, being built from Ledo in Assam, and the British were anxious that it should be completed.

Besides, when it came down to cases in China, there were many different opinions as to where help was needed first. Stilwell, as always, clung like a limpet to his plans for the Burma push. (Roosevelt was not at all satisfied with Stilwell's attitude toward Chiang. Even Marshall, who championed Stilwell, admitted that his protégé behaved in a strained, unpleasant way during his visit in the spring of '43 to Washington. Nevertheless, he argued, Stilwell knew the ground better than anyone else, and so had better stay on the job.) Marshall and Stilwell were against concentrating on building up China's air defense. If Chinese-based planes should strafe the Japanese to an annoying degree, they said, the Japanese were bound to advance on the airfields. You needed a good ground army to hold out against them, and China didn't have it. Her best troops weren't on guard where they ought to be, complained Stilwell. The Peanut was keeping them in the Northwest for his own

purposes, boxing in the Reds. He was absorbed in a totally unnecessary civil war. Stilwell declared, as he had often done before,
what was wrong with China's Army. Corrupt, underpaid, underfed,
badly led. It would be better not to stir up the Japanese to attack
on the ground.

But Chennault, who was also in on the conference, thought
otherwise. He was sure that with a really good China-based air
force the Japanese would never be able to come close enough to
take over. The planes could hold them off.

Roosevelt gave in to everybody, but in varying degrees. He sent
word to the Generalissimo urging him to consider the completion
of the new land route in Burma as one of their most pressing tasks.
He promised, himself, to send ten thousand troops and twenty-five
thousand tons of equipment to India for the Ledo Road. He told
Marshall that he thought they were neglecting the possibilities of
damaging Japan with an increased air force in China. Chennault
could go ahead with his program; of the stepped up tonnage that
was to be carried over the Hump, he would get the first 4,750 tons
of space and Stilwell the next 2,250, for equipping ground forces,
and so on. But the Generalissimo was still suspicious of the future,
still disinclined to commit himself to support of Stilwell's plan.
What help, he asked, had been absolutely promised for the Burma
campaign? Unless the British contributed that amphibious attack
in the South, the whole affair was sure to fail.

The President couldn't very well inform him of British intentions
because he wasn't yet certain of them himself.

Supplies were definitely stepped up that summer and Chennault
at first thought everything would go according to schedule, but
there were numerous disappointments. Because of these delays he
too was behindhand. Stilwell was smarting under a sense of grievance and this made him more than ever inclined to fall out with
Chiang.

"Nobody was interested in the humdrum work of building a ground force but me," he said bitterly. "Chennault promised to drive the Japs right out of China in six months, so why not give him the stuff to do it? It was the short cut to victory."

In June he thought he was to be proved right in his contention that China's ground forces were no good. The Japanese started on the long-feared push inland toward Szechuan, before Chennault had built up anything like the air force that he claimed would be necessary to hold them. They were halted at last, at Ichang on the Yangtze, just the other side of the gorges from Chungking. And then, in July, Chiang finally signed the three-power agreement to go ahead with the Burma plan. It began to look as if both Stilwell and Chennault were to get their way, after all. Even Chiang Kai-shek felt that better times were coming.

A pause seemed to hover over Chungking. Italy had surrendered. The world's tide was turning. At the beginning of August, Lin Sen, the gentle, harmless old President of China, died, and Chiang for the second time was named President, with the inauguration date for the autumn.

Stilwell was plodding away at the routine of his preparations, spending an occasional few days in India, checking up at Ramgarh. He had got quite used to quarreling with the Generalissimo. The take-off for Burma was not three months off, when a new influence suddenly came into his life, the Soong sisters, or at least two of them—Mesdames Chiang and Kung. They invited the general to tea and sounded him out. They talked things over, and expressed horror at his trials, and were generally much more "simpatica" than he had expected of any Soong sister but Chingling. Under their gentle treatment and the friendly noise of their twittering, Vinegar Joe in spite of himself felt his heart softening. He was still suspicious of anyone close to Chiang; he still snarled to himself when he got home. But he felt himself softening just the same. He recorded bits of conversation:

"Gave them the low-down on conditions in the Army and they were appalled. Told them about blocks and delays and who was responsible.

"Remedy? Make May [Mayling] minister of war. . . . Suggested northwest as source of drafts.

"May craves action. . . . Sis [Madame Kung] said she didn't know how I had the patience to carry on. We signed an offensive and defensive alliance."

Then, in the kindest way, the ladies warned him that he was reputed to be anti-Chinese. Poor Stilwell's feelings were so hurt at this piece of unreason that he lost his last grasp of Anglo-Saxon common sense. He did not see how firmly he was now enmeshed in Chinese intrigue. There is nothing so effective as someone who cuddles up to you and murmurs, "I think you ought to know the horrid things people are saying about you."

Doubtless the ladies only wanted to keep him happy while he fought. They saw that cat-and-dog relations between the Generalissimo and his U. S. chief of staff were doing China harm, and they knew, too, what Stilwell didn't, that Chiang wanted to be rid of him. This wasn't good, because no matter how much Roosevelt might discount his general's angry reports, Stilwell had the support of American Army commanders such as Marshall; *they* wouldn't forgive this insult. Day after day, then, the ladies gave Stilwell lunch or tea, and talked and told him things, and listened while he told them things. Sometimes "Ella," as he called Eling Kung, confided in him. ("It seems that Ella made Peanut fight at Ichang. . . . May says that without her insistence the Great Man would have kept on pulling out and God knows where we'd be now.") Sometimes May was the confiding one. It was May who admitted that Chiang Wei-kuo, the G-mo's adopted son, was opposed to Stilwell and reported stories against him. Both ladies disliked certain of the officers intensely; by a coincidence, the same ones Stilwell disliked. They called Ho Ying-chin "the unmentionable." The friendship flourished; confidences grew even more intimate.

"May let out that she has a hell of a life with the Peanut; no one else will tell him the truth so she is constantly at him with the disagreeable news. It can't be easy to live with the crabbed little bastard and see everything balled up."

This alliance continued for a month, and then one day, not long before the great Burma venture was scheduled to start, Stilwell got a shock. It should not have been much of a surprise, primed as he was with the Soong sisters' recent lessons, but it was. That day Mountbatten arrived with Somervell. They all had lunch together, and a long talk, and then "back to the house with Somervell, where he gave me the news: THE G-MO SAYS I MUST BE RELIEVED. The reason is that I have 'lost the confidence of the troops.' . . . (Somervell says that President Roosevelt has asked George [Marshall] to relieve me more than once, because I 'can't get along.' Nice backing.)

"The real reason is hard to guess. It may be with me out, nobody else will push the campaign. . . . Or it may be just the suspicious, jealous Oriental mind, listening to lies and thinking that it won't do to let a damned foreigner gain any more influence."

It should not have been so hard to guess the real reason. It has been summed up succinctly for the writer by a Chinese official who was on the scene at the time: "You see, Chiang is domineering. Stilwell evidently thought the way to deal with that was to outdomineer. He was supposed to be chief of staff to Chiang, but he acted more like commander-in-chief."

Anyway Stilwell seems to have thought until that moment that he was the only partner in the relationship who had been getting exasperated. Now he fired up: he would not be eased out so ignobly. He would go, oh, he would go. But somebody would suffer for this.

Once more the sisters took a hand. While Stilwell was still staggering and fuming and coping with a number of absolutely fas-

cinated Chinese friends and well-wishers, who hurried in as soon
as they heard the news and spilled more poison in his ears, he
received a summons.

"May called me over at 8:00. Ella was there. They are a pair
of fighters, all right, and Ella said there was still a chance to pull
the fat out of the fire. I was non-committal and calm and told them
I did not want to stay where I was not wanted. They talked 'China'
and duty, etc., and asked me to be big enough to stick it out. . . .
What they wanted was for me to see Peanut and tell him that I had
only one aim, the good of China, that if I made mistakes it was
from misunderstanding and not intent, and that I was ready to co-
operate fully."

Stilwell was persuaded. Followed an interview at which Chiang
was surprisingly mild. He administered a little patronizing advice,
Stilwell listened politely and agreed, and there it was, all fixed up
again. The unfortunate American, back again at his desk, scratched
his head and wondered what had been done to him.

"Now, why was Ella so sure it would come out O.K.?" . . .

A few days later the ladies told him triumphantly that they knew
now who was the troublemaker. It was none other than their brother
T.V. . . . "Ella . . . said she had to choose between 'her own flesh
and blood' and the good of China."

But the truth of the matter was not to be summed up in one
person or one situation. T.V. *had* worked against Stilwell, though
not to the extent Madame Kung implied—there was still little love
being lost between this sister and her brother. Officers *had* accused
the American of being anti-Chinese. What else were they to think
when he criticized their methods as freely as he did? The Generalissimo *did* have a grudge against him, partly in reaction to his
own grudge against the Generalissimo. But what had tipped the
scales in Chiang's mind was Stilwell's proposal in September,
during a long drawn out correspondence on the subject of using
ground forces to oppose a possible new push by the Japanese. Stil-

well suggested that they use the Reds, the Eighteenth Group Army in the Northwest, side by side with the Kuomintang troops. "At the worst it costs nothing in troops and little in supplies," he wrote to Chiang, "it makes use of units that are otherwise idle, and it will make plain the degree of reliability of the forces in the Northwest. If we do not move, the Japs will."

That had been his slip; that was the unforgivable sin. In Washington, where minds were being more and more made up on the subject of Chinese Communists by indirect methods, they had no way of knowing what a raw place their representative had touched. Stilwell himself didn't know.

(Surely it was an oversight or something similar that led the editor of *The Stilwell Papers,* Theodore White, to put the footnote he did on page 214? Stilwell, as already quoted, September 13, reported on a meeting with Madame: "Suggested northwest as source of drafts [for more men]." White's footnote carefully adds, "General Stilwell here refers to the approximately twenty divisions of government troops, stationed in the northwest, blockading the Communists." It is clear from the record that Stilwell was not referring to government troops.)

The Reds did not now confine themselves, as they had done previously, to locally aired grievances, nor did they trust their foreign friends to spread the word. They began to get very busy on their own account. Since early summer discussions had been going on between Chiang and Chou En-lai, and now a few cards were on the table. Chiang repeated his standing offer to allow the Communists a place in Chungking, like that held by other Chinese, if they would give up their separate government and hand over their armies to Kuomintang command. The Reds refused, saying that this would mean the end for them. This was a flat contradiction of their protests of unity made in 1937, but Chiang had long since gone past the capacity for pointing this out or for getting indignant about it, and the American commentators seem not to have noticed it. The Generalissimo demanded agreement by the end of August. Chou alleged that Chiang followed up his ultimatum by dispatching seven more divisions to the Northwest. Chiang denied that he had done so.

Russia now stirred herself and exhibited an overt interest in these proceedings that was very disturbing to Washington and London. In Chungking the Russian Ambassador complained to the American Embassy that the Kuomintang were trying to coerce the Communists, and that their troops on several occasions had actually fired on the Reds. In case of civil war, he asked, would the United States continue to send aid to Chiang?

And Russian newspapers began to show a marked change in their references to the Generalissimo's highest officers. They also spoke with significant emphasis of the superiority of Communist resistance to Japan compared with Nationalist prowess. In the States, Mao's admirers took up the cry. The Communists were the only people doing any fighting in China, they said. Chiang's troops were too busy threatening the Communists to attend to their proper business.

Once more, puzzled Americans asked themselves and each other what we were doing in China. Whose side were we on? Whose side should we be on?

American officials asked Chiang if he thought civil war was impending. Chiang denied it, and issued a statement: "I am of the opinion that first of all we should clearly recognize that the Chinese Communist problem is a purely political problem and should be solved by political means."

Washington was reassured, but left wondering. Who had been lying? On the whole it was simpler to believe that everyone had. But there remained more suspicion of Chiang than of the Reds. American Embassy officials thought that civil war still threatened. Our policy should be, they said, to watch out for it and try to avert it by urging on the Generalissimo a political combination in which the Reds could share. More democracy, said the Americans. More self-improvement: clean yourselves up. Keep the people happy, treat the Reds fair and square, keep your noses clean, and educate the masses. That way you can maintain peace.

In August, when Roosevelt and Churchill met at Quebec, the Chinese dropped the dignified silence in which they had been resenting Chiang's absence from Casablanca: this time they made a frank request that they be included. With some embarrassment, Britain and America again refused. If Chiang were permitted to attend they could not very well leave out Russia, and then they wouldn't have been able to make any headway, especially as the most important questions to be decided dealt with the Japanese aspect of the war, in which Russia was not a partner. However, Britain would have been against China's inclusion even with the Russian part of the matter discounted: Britain and her non-American allies were all against it. Nobody but America was in favor of China's having a voice in postwar settlements.

It is difficult to assess how bitterly the Generalissimo reacted to these high-level snubs because he maintained a smooth front. Motives and attitudes probably didn't interest him except insofar as they affected China's welfare. And it looked as if China didn't come badly out of the Quebec Conference. Though Molotov opposed her inclusion in the Moscow Declaration, Hull carried the day.

As far as the other United Nations were concerned, the high point of the conference was unrehearsed: a message from Stalin arrived just before they broke up. As soon as the Germans were beaten, he announced, the Soviet Union would enter the Pacific War against Japan. It was the first time he had definitely committed himself on this point and there was great rejoicing. But one sobering afterthought did occur to Roosevelt. When Japan lay supine, if Russia was to be in on the kill, where did that leave Russia's pets, the Chinese Reds? Obviously, in a very comfortable position. For himself Roosevelt had confidence in the Reds, but he realized that the situation was fraught with unpleasant possibilities for Chiang. On the whole, he decided, it would be as well not to reveal the news just yet to Chungking.

So Chiang was not notified.


On the surface Stilwell's relations with the Generalissimo had never been so cordial as when Chiang and a retinue of fifteen, including Madame, Hollington Tong, and the American, set out in November 1943 for the Generalissimo's trip to Cairo. They were going to attend what Roosevelt jovially referred to as "Chiang Kai-shek's Conference" with Churchill and the American President. There was a growing tendency on the part of these gentlemen to treat Chiang, whom neither had as yet actually met, as a being with a streak of childishness in his make-up. But Churchill complained, in his book *Closing the Ring,* that Roosevelt still persisted in taking these people seriously. Churchill had wanted to postpone the conference until after he and Roosevelt had met with Stalin in Teheran.

". . . The President, who took an exaggerated view of the Indian-Chinese sphere, was soon closeted in long conferences with the Generalissimo. All hope of persuading Chiang and his wife to go and see the pyramids and enjoy themselves until we returned from Teheran fell to the ground."

No, most decidedly, Churchill didn't understand. Chiang and his wife would not have enjoyed themselves at the pyramids, not in those circumstances.

Unfortunately for Hollington Tong and the rest of the retinue the Generalissimo was once again caught short without an interpreter when his old friend Lord Killearn called to pay his compliments. Killearn was that same Sir Miles Lampson with whom Chiang had vainly endeavored to talk English, years before, in Nanking. The two men were left staring at each other without means of communication; again poor Chiang was embarrassed.

Churchill and the Chiangs were introduced. The burly Briton

looked down at Madame and boomed, "Well, Madame, I suppose you think I am a scoundrel, a blackguard, an imperialist, out to grab more colonies and unwilling to part with what we have got?"

It was a pretty accurate summary. But Madame is *bien elévée*. She replied only, "Why are you so sure what I think of you?"

The conference went more smoothly than anyone had hoped; more smoothly, indeed, than later events warranted. Probably Churchill did not put up more objections to the proceedings than he did because he simply could not take the talks seriously. He was holding his fire for what he considered the real conference, with Stalin in Teheran. Pending possible upsets there, Chiang understood that the others agreed to the Burma campaign's starting immediately. Britain was to supply that amphibious force in the Bay of Bengal. Chiang would contribute not only the Chinese at Ramgarh who were to attack from India, but the Yoke Force in Yunnan, which was to march in from the east. He also believed that American troops would be supplied.

This agreement was contingent, naturally, upon what might take place at Teheran, and Chiang must have been shrewd enough to realize that Churchill, though he said little, was making reservations in his mind. But once again these Westerners were emphasizing what he considered the less important aspect of the problem. Burma was all very well, but he wanted quicker action to help his country, beset as it was by currency inflation, shortages, and great weariness. The Reds were a mounting worry. The Japanese stood threateningly at the gate of the Yangtze Gorges, though the United Nations were advancing against them in the Pacific.

However, it was pleasant and more to the point to be told that Roosevelt was in favor of returning to China all the territories wrested from her by Japan.

Chiang Kai-shek's Conference was soon over. Churchill thought that the Chiangs would remain in Cairo in order to hear the outcome of Teheran, but dignity, of course, forbade such a thing. The

Generalissimo and Madame departed immediately for Chungking, leaving Stilwell to hold the fort and send them word.

As Churchill had foreseen, a lot of Roosevelt's glowing promises to China had to be taken back when Stalin came into the picture. "Overlord," the all-important invasion of the European continent, was discussed and it pushed everything else into second place. Roosevelt struggled for Chiang's interests, but the best he could get from the British was a half promise to help out with amphibious action in South Burma in the autumn of 1944, when the big doings in Europe should have been finished. Chiang was to be given his choice: he could let the campaign continue immediately but without British support; or he could postpone the whole thing yet again.

In spite of these disappointments the Generalissimo was not completely disgusted with the Cairo Declaration. When it had been polished and published, he wrote to Roosevelt: "The whole nation is articulate to a degree that has never been known before in unanimously hailing the Cairo Declaration as a sure sign-post leading the Far East toward post-war peace."

Routine stuff, the cynical reader might say to himself. But Chiang had good reason to feel a lift in spite of everything. The future beckoned with genuine reassurance. China was to be given back Formosa, the Pescadores, and Manchuria, and oddly enough Stalin had not objected.

Chiang could not have realized to what a degree the President of the United States had been affected in his opinion of himself and the Kuomintang by the adverse comment that was now pouring into Washington from a number of sources. Most of these sources were themselves inspired from a common source, but Roosevelt didn't know that. The President was slipping into a role that he could hardly help enjoying—the all-wise father, sitting in judgment on his children and planning a new Jerusalem. This one was a good child and must be rewarded: that one needed a smacking.

And most of his entourage accepted this conception oɪ a President's position. His son Elliott, who was there, quoted F.D.R. in a conversation after the conference when they discussed Chiang Kaishek:

"He wanted very badly to get our support against the British moving into Hongkong and Shanghai and Canton with the same old extraterritorial rights they enjoyed before the war."

Elliott asked if the Americans were going to give this support, and his father said, "Not for nothing. Before it came up, I'd been registering a complaint about the character of Chiang's government. I'd told him it was hardly the modern democracy that ideally it should be. I'd told him he would have to form a uniting government, while the war was still being fought, with the Communists in Yenan."

Fresh from Teheran, back in Cairo, talking things over with Harry Hopkins and Stilwell, Roosevelt adopted an even more godlike approach. "How long do you think Chiang can last?" he asked Stilwell.

"The situation is serious and a repetition of last May's attack might overthrow him," said the general.

"Well then," said Roosevelt blithely, "we should look for some other man, or group of men, to carry on."

"They would probably be looking for us," said Stilwell.

"Yes," said the President, "they would come to us. They really like us. . . ."

# 12 VINEGAR JOE RETIRES 1943–44

Chiang didn't have many advantages in the bargaining game, but he was quick to recognize those he had and press them. Swiftly, while Roosevelt's conscience was still hurting, the Generalissimo made a new set of requests: the loan of a billion U. S. dollars, a firm undertaking on America's part to increase support of air forces in China, and an expansion of the Hump transport route to afford twice the supplies that had already been promised. He reminded Roosevelt that the Japanese were fully capable of concluding the obvious when they saw the U.N. armies busily employed in Europe. They would certainly take their chance to step up the attack in China, hoping to bring her to her knees before the Allies could get around to Chungking.

This time the Americans were firm and refused the loan. U. S. Ambassador Gauss, backed up by the Treasury, declared that money would not settle China's difficulties. Only hard-and-fast supplies could do that, and there could be no genuine stepping-up of supplies until a land route into the interior was opened. In other words, the Burma campaign. In yet other words, military operations which meant more help from the Chinese. ("These people are hanging back, expecting us to do everything for them," said the Americans.)

Chiang hesitated painfully about Burma. The Japanese might be too strong: his own troops might be inadequate on the offensive, no matter how much Stilwell reassured him. Now, or nearly a year hence? It was a question hard to answer. At last he determined to keep his cake and eat it very slowly. Stilwell, if he wished, might go ahead with his part of the proceedings, with full command of the troops he already had in India, but Chiang would not contribute more men until he saw what help might be forthcoming from Britain. ("These Americans want us to strip ourselves of all home defense," said the Chinese.)

Chiang asked for the American Army corps which had been spoken about in Cairo to help out in Burma. Roosevelt admitted that now things were different and he couldn't spare any troops from Overlord, but again he made a substitute offer. America was already supplying and training sixty Chinese divisions, with the promise to do the same with thirty more as soon as possible. Roosevelt upped that promise by thirty yet more.

Such anxious bursts of generosity on the President's part masked his increasing distrust of the situation. Other Americans didn't trouble to mask theirs. Ill-feeling was strengthened by a quarrel between the Chinese and the Americans over the rate of exchange; the Americans alleged that the prevailing rate, which was disadvantageous to them, was the price the Chinese extracted indirectly in return for the use of the Yunnan forces in Burma. The Chinese pointed out with mounting querulousness that their share of U. S. Lend-Lease was very small compared with that awarded to Britain and Russia. This elicited quick, angry replies. Said Mountbatten, "I do not see why we should continue to supply [Chiang] with munitions if they are to be used solely for internal purposes."

Stilwell, however, was satisfied. He had won the only part of the argument that interested him; he had permission to command the Ramgarh-trained men. "Can you believe it?" he wrote jubilantly. On December 20 he started off to India on the first lap of the campaign. Britain having refused to institute the amphibious landing, Chiang withdrew likewise from his half promise to contribute the Yoke Force to the operation. But Stilwell had an idea that the Generalissimo's determination might be shaken, and his colleagues in Washington agreed.

They appealed to Roosevelt. The President urged Chiang to reconsider and let Stilwell have the Yoke Force even though the British had failed to come up to scratch. If Chiang could see his way clear to do this, said Roosevelt, the ferry line over the Hump would soon be provided with enough transport planes to boost the monthly freight to twelve thousand tons. If he didn't, there would be no stock-piling for Chiang's use against whatever foreign—or domestic—enemy he might be worrying about.

The British added their voice to the combined temptation and threat. If the Yoke Force was not to be employed in the Burma campaign, said Mountbatten, then there wasn't any sense in going ahead with the Ledo Road, either. Long before it was finished the Japanese would have been driven out of their Pacific strongholds. The approach through Burma would be unnecessary; China itself (it was understood, though no one' said it) would be unnecessary. Why not just protect that part of the country through which the ferry operated and wash out the rest of it?

Chiang didn't like this argument. For different reasons Stilwell didn't like it either. "Louis welches on entire program," he noted furiously. "G-mo's fault of course." He was pushing his men hard in Burma, and they reacted splendidly. Through January and February they progressed, proving triumphantly that good training could make a modern army out of Chinese, that they were ready to submit to Western-style discipline just as if they had not learned their first lessons in the school of "strength for depth." Stilwell exulted, and his stock rose, and Roosevelt was impressed. The success of Stilwell gave the President weight when he argued with Churchill. The Chinese airfields would be vitally important when

Americans should succeed in landing on the coast of South China, he insisted: therefore, air force stock piles in China must be built up well ahead of time. Myitkyina in Burma, if the Sino-American forces could get it from the Japanese, would serve as an important strategical point in the supply line. The ferry over the Hump would have a less arduous road to fly, with lower altitude and a broader corridor for additional transport planes.

Churchill hated the whole idea of the Burma campaign; to him it seemed too long drawn out to be useful. But other events carried the day for Roosevelt's cause. Early in March the Japanese in Burma started a diversion; they attacked the British-Indian border near Imphal, two hundred miles south of the Chinese-Japanese battleground. It looked as if they might soon cut off Assam. Thenceforth the British had as much reason as the Americans to press Chungking for more Chinese troops under Stilwell. Press they did, but the Generalissimo continued to hold out.

This was not difficult at first, because as long as the Japanese retreated before Stilwell, Washington didn't insist too strongly. And it wasn't only Stilwell who was doing well: "Merrill's Marauders," with the Chindit Brigade, the Eastern Air Command, and the Fourteenth Air Force, all proved their value. But at the same time that the Japanese instituted their attack against Imphal they also showed new strength against Stilwell and these others. Stilwell's advance began to sag, and he clamored for more help from Chiang. The British chimed in. Where was the Yoke Force?

"Limeys have the wind up," said Stilwell with grim satisfaction. He hammered the War Department to get action somehow from Chiang. He was sure that if only the Yoke Force would start pushing in from the east as had been outlined in the original plan the Japanese would crumble. Finally he stirred up the War Department to put pressure on Roosevelt. The President should use the big stick that stood ready to his hand. He must cut off supplies to Chungking altogether if he couldn't get action otherwise.

Roosevelt didn't quite do that, but he sent an urgent message advising Chiang to reconsider. Refusing, Chiang made his usual replies—any of the participants in the argument could by that time have reeled them off for him word for word. The Japanese . . . The Reds . . . The Russians. Seven years of war and exhaustion. In short, no Yoke Force. However, to soften the refusal Chiang borrowed a leaf from Roosevelt's book and sent out two more divisions by air from Yunnan to India to reinforce Stilwell's troops.

This was not enough, said Stilwell; he sent alarmed messages to Washington. He needed the Yoke Force, he insisted. Again Roosevelt telegraphed to Chungking. After all, he reminded Chiang, that was why American money had been used to equip and train the Yoke Force, for use in this same action. The moral obligation was clear. Besides, if only Chiang would send them in everything would go so well! The Japanese would be defeated.

On April 15 the world witnessed a rare occasion: Chiang Kai-shek changed his mind. The Yoke Force would start out for Burma, he promised, before the end of the month.

As it happened, things had already begun to quiet down. That particular emergency passed; the enemy was turned back from the border near Imphal. Stilwell was glad to have the Yoke Force nevertheless. He managed to reach Myitkyina and captured the airfield, but after that the advance was stalled again, in spite of his reinforcements, by toughened resistance and monsoon weather. His estimates had been too optimistic.

It suddenly became alarmingly apparent that after all the Generalissimo had not merely been crying, "Wolf, wolf." For months he had said that the Japanese would seize their chance as soon as he committed his forces to fighting outside the country, and he was right. In May the enemy encamped in China suddenly rose up and began marching. They aimed to take the air bases set up by America at Kweilin and Liuchow, and there seemed little to stop them. Chennault's plan to hold them back with intense air activity didn't work; he had never been permitted to build up enough supplies to make it feasible. Chiang begged Washington to hurry up with the fulfillment of their promises, but he didn't get much reaction. Washington was nearly ready to write the whole thing off.

It was not only the Japanese threat that made Roosevelt sure the Kuomintang's days were numbered. Communist activity had now become so open that there was genuine doubt in his mind if the country as a whole did not want this change. The President was thinking in terms of American mentality; to him "the people" of China were politically conscious, capable of concerted opinion on such matters, and it now seemed more and more clear that what they wanted was the democracy offered in the Communist-dominated areas of the country rather than Kuomintang government.

This was not the attitude of the State Department as a whole, but in their way they arrived at the same conclusions. With them it was a matter of expediency. Soviet Russia had lately been more forthcoming as to Moscow's opinion of Chiang. Chiang had long made no secret of his fears of Russia. Russia, he insisted, was aiding and abetting the Chinese Reds. He wrote to Roosevelt in March about it: the Chinese Communist Party, while professing support of the government's policy of resistance against Japan, had for some weeks been secretly assembling their guerrilla units and concentrating them in North Shensi, "evidently preparing for an opportune moment to rise in revolt and take Sian, the base of our operations in the Yellow River Valley. The indications are manifest. Considering the matter objectively, it does not seem likely that the Chinese Communist Party would dare to make such a move without some understanding having been reached between the Soviets and the Chinese."

The Japanese were moving immense numbers of their forces from Manchuria to China, all too evidently confident that the Russians would do nothing to hinder this action. If the Russians meant to help the Nationalists, and not hold them back, they would continue to tie down these forces north of the border. Yet hadn't Russia, on the contrary, just signed an agreement with Japan over the fishery rights at Sakhalin? It was tantamount to an alliance against Chinese interests.

Chiang referred to a recent incident in Sinkiang, when Russian planes attacked Chinese troops who had crossed the border into Outer Mongolia—deserting from the Kuomintang, according to Chungking; deliberately violating the border agreement on behalf of the Kuomintang, according to the Russians. Washington studied the incident worriedly and decided that Russia had not been unreasonable. Evidently China was trying to "re-extend its authority over Outer Mongolia" when Outer Mongolia was obviously autonomous and ought to be left alone. Roosevelt told Chiang that the matter should be put away and forgotten until the end of the war. American annoyance with those difficult Chinese was heightened even more very soon afterward. Stalin was noncommittal in reply to a request that the Allies be permitted to use the Turkestan route to supply air forces in China. Considering how the Kuomintang was behaving, said the Russians, the request would have to be considered carefully. . . .

Altogether, Roosevelt decided, Chiang was being unreasonable.

It was June, and Overlord had swung into action when Ambassador Averell Harriman in Moscow sounded out Stalin's opinion of Chiang. Did the Russian leader not agree that the Chinese Reds and the Kuomintang should make it up? And oughtn't Chiang to liberalize the government? Yes, Stalin said, he did agree, but it was easier said than done. Chiang wasn't so bad, but he was poorly advised—surrounded by crooks and traitors. It was very foolish of him not to make it up with the Reds and fight the Japanese as a united nation. Why was he so worried about his Reds? He had no reason to be.

"The Chinese Communists are not real Communists," said Stalin, laughing merrily. "They are 'margarine' Communists. Nevertheless, they are real patriots and they want to fight Japan."

This was very reassuring to Washington.

Vice-President Wallace was already on his way to Chungking via Siberia, sent out by Roosevelt to talk the matter over with Chiang, to convey in person the essence of the latest directive. This was, generally speaking, that the Generalissimo ought to be nicer to the Russians and discourage Chinese propaganda against them. Never mind the troop movements from Manchuria; it wasn't the fault of the Russians anyway; they couldn't hold the Japanese if the Japanese did not wish to be held. Chiang would do better, on the contrary, if he put up more of a fight himself against the enemy and threw his crack troops into the fray instead of holding them back to blockade the Communists. Why didn't he make it up with the Reds so they could all fight the enemy together? The Chinese must also co-operate more than they were doing with Russia. America couldn't help China much more than she was doing at the moment because of European claims. Unless the Chinese Government managed to effect more cordial relations with Moscow, Russia wouldn't be inclined to help China either.

Wallace's journey, thanks to various subsequent developments in the States, is one of the most interesting bits of the history of Sino-American relations. He was accompanied by John Carter Vincent, Chief of the Division of Chinese Affairs, and Owen Lattimore. Whether because of the emergency of the Japanese advance or the fact that Wallace was, after all, Vice-President and sent directly by Roosevelt himself, Chiang abandoned the taciturnity that usually characterized his dealings with foreigners. He spoke volubly, and very frankly. Wallace's conversations with him were long. It has been pointed out by several commentators during the post-mortem that the Vice-President's state of mind was hardly likely to be sympathetic to the Generalissimo's attitude, no matter what Chiang said. Wallace had elected to come out to the East through Siberia and Outer Mongolia. He had stopped on the way to be entertained by the Russians and was full of his success with them. In any case he was already heavily biased in favor of the Soviet state. His mind was made up in advance: that is the argument.

In fact, however, even without Wallace's observations and advice to Roosevelt, American action would probably have been the same. Wallace was not alone in his opinions. In China he was surrounded and advised by State Department officials, most of whom had made up their minds to encourage a policy of softness toward the Reds. What would be interesting to know, purely as a matter of human interest, is not so much Chiang's impact on Wallace as Wallace's upon Chiang. We can make a guess at it from a report of one conversation between them, which was sent to the State Department:

"He [Chiang] said that the people of the United States did not understand the situation. . . . He said that the Communists desired a breakdown of Chinese resistance against the Japanese because this would strengthen their own position. Mr. Wallace expressed amazement at this statement. President Chiang admitted that the Communists desired the defeat of Japan, but held that they were now convinced that this could be accomplished without Chinese resistance. . . . Mr. Wallace referred to the patriotic attitude of the Communists in the United States and said he could not understand the attitude of the Chinese Communists as described by President Chiang. President Chiang said that the difference in the attitude of the American and Chinese Communists might be explained by the fact that there was no possibility of the American Communists seizing power, whereas the Chinese Communists definitely desired to do so."

Chiang added that in his opinion Americans were being prejudiced by propaganda and warned Wallace against the new party line based on Stalin's remark that Chinese Communists were not really Communists at all but agrarian reformers. He repeated what he had been telling Chou En-lai for many months, that if the Reds would allow their army to be incorporated in the Nationalist forces and would give up their separate government, he was willing to extend to them the same treatment as he did all other Chinese, with the right to maintain their political party. He wanted to warn Roosevelt that the Reds were the best propagandists in the world: the President must not be taken in, though American reporters in Chungking had already been misled. To continue pressing the Kuomintang to give in would only make matters worse. When Wallace brought up the matter of the blockade, saying that the Communists and the Nationalists should both be opposing the Japanese instead of each other, Chiang answered wearily:

"Please do not press; please understand that the Communists are not good for the war effort against Japan." The Reds would not be so useful against the Japanese, he said, as the Americans seemed to think. Why did the Americans keep talking about the government coming to terms with the Communists? Why did no one ever urge the Communists to come to terms with the government?

On the other hand, he thought it possible to make a deal with Moscow; indeed, he said, the Chinese Reds were even more Communistic than the Russians. Might not Roosevelt bring about better relations between his country and the U.S.S.R.?

Chiang spoke emphatically of the inimical relations between himself and Stilwell, but he didn't repeat his earlier request that the American general be recalled. What he wanted was an additional officer, someone more important, to act as his personal representative; somebody who would be able to communicate with Roosevelt direct, without going through the War and State departments—a liaison officer.

Wallace reported to Roosevelt, in sum, that the prospects of settling the Kuomintang-Communist dispute were very poor. Talks between the parties were imbued with prejudice, he found; the whole setup was extremely discouraging, and the Generalissimo was "bewildered in regard to the economic situation, unsure in regard to the political situation, and . . . distressed about military developments." It looked as if the Japanese would soon take over East

China with the American air bases, and he doubted if the Chung-king government would survive the shock. He recommended Chiang's idea of a personal representative appointed by Roosevelt. America must take determined steps immediately to save China unless she was prepared to write it off—determined steps militarily and politically as well. Otherwise there would be a political vacuum that would certainly be filled in ways the President would under-stand. Some sort of coalition was vitally necessary—Wallace was vague about this—but the emissary for whom Chiang was asking had better be appointed and sent without delay. And this man should not be Stilwell.

Prejudiced as Wallace was, he seems to have been stirred to something like compassion for the worried Chinese leader. He con-fessed later that he was "deeply moved by the cry of a man in distress."

Yet his one sympathetic recommendation, to play down Stilwell, was ignored.

In Chungking the customary wrangles between correspondents and government on such fretful questions as censorship and tele-gram priority had suddenly been suspended by a remarkable fluke. A Chinese Minister of Information, newly appointed, came to his first press conference badly briefed as to the Generalissimo's par-ticular phobias. Quite casually he gave permission to one of the American reporters to go to Yenan and see things for himself. The hubbub that grew out of this, and the clamorings of the rest of the boys, showed him that he must have made a mistake. But he had given his word and he was not allowed to go back on it. Behind the scenes he got hell from his superiors, but the correspondents would not let him off.

The question was first mooted in November 1943. The Ministry managed to stave off the actual journey until May 1944, but then they were cornered and the party set out at last. It was not exactly a cross section of American public opinion. There were six non-Chinese, one of whom was a Russian, the Tass representative. Another was a stateless member of the Communist Party, of Polish extraction. Two others, Americans, were strongly pro-Communist. Of the other two one was a Catholic priest and the other worked for a Kuomintang department. The other four, needless to say, reported overwhelmingly in favor of the Red regime. Those pro-Communists who could not speak Chinese did not feel hampered. Had they not adequate interpreters?

The nine Chinese newspapermen, who did speak the language, were not quite so impressed by what they saw. But then, said the American, they were, of course, prejudiced.

"The Chinese Communist Party has never wavered from its policy of supporting Generalissimo Chiang Kai-shek, the policy of continuing the co-operation between the Kuomintang and the Communist Party and the entire people, and the policy of defeating Japanese imperialism and struggling for the building of a free democratic China," said Mao Tse-tung. ". . . But China has drawbacks and they are serious ones. They can be summed up in one phrase—the lack of democracy."

What could be fairer than that? In a few days America's leading newspapers bloomed with reports about the splendid spirit in Yenan, the determination to resist Japan, the wonderful development of the land. Tough, well-fed, hardened troops. Democracy. Democracy. Democracy. . . . A few months later there were four new volumes in United States bookstores telling the same story.

The reporters had not yet won their permission to visit this paradise; they had hardly begun to fight for it in January, when John P. Davies, a State Department officer, first mooted the idea of an American military mission in Yenan. He thought the Reds might consent, just possibly, if Roosevelt hurried to get permission, but he counseled haste. As he pointed out, it would be highly advantageous if the mission could get in and find out for themselves how strong the Communists were and what Russia and Japan were doing in that remote territory. Besides, if American officers were right there on the spot, the Nationalists might be prevented from attacking the Reds and forcing them to give up their autonomy. Mr. Davies seemed to think the Reds needed such protection.

Roosevelt did ask Chiang hastily, as he had been advised, but the Generalissimo didn't take to the idea. Since that January correspondence, however, what with one development and another, Chiang's intransigent attitude had changed. In spite of all resistance the newspapermen had got through and were still in Yenan. The worst they could do was already being done. Therefore, though he warned the Vice-President that a military mission to the Northwest carried implications that would encourage the Communists to an undesirable extent, he consented. The American group went forthwith; they were greeted with enthusiasm by Mao Tse-tung.

"Any contact you Americans may have with us Communists is gold," he said to John Stewart Service, and proceeded to explain how very unreasonable the Kuomintang was being.

"How about going to China and fixing things up?" Marshall asked Stilwell.

It was the second of July, soon after Wallace had recommended Stilwell a recall. Marshall was fighting back effectively on his general's behalf; the War Department, touchy like most military people, resented criticism of their boy, especially in the light of his recent exploit in Burma. Moreover, they could point in support of their suggestion to Wallace's own statement. He had admitted that the situation called for drastic treatment if China was to be pulled out of peril. No other American had Stilwell's experience in the China theater. But this time, they said, he must have full authority over the Chinese forces; there must be no more interference from the top, no more hamstringing.

In their eagerness to reaffirm their trust in Stilwell, they ignored the danger of appointing to such a post the man who could write in his journal, at just that moment, "The cure for China's trouble is the elimination of Chiang Kai-shek."

Roosevelt too ignored it. He simply forwarded the proposal to Chungking. For his part, he was making Stilwell a full general, he said. What about it?

If, in Wallace's phrase, Chiang had been "a man in distress" before, what did he feel like now? The plan must have seemed almost grotesquely insulting, and mad besides. A foreigner to have complete command of his forces was extraordinary enough. But that it should be this particular man, Stilwell, who hated him, who had once nearly been recalled at his request, who constantly urged him to make it up with the Reds and let them fight shoulder to shoulder with the Kuomintang troops! A man who had no conception of what Communism really was! The Generalissimo didn't need a spy to find out what sort of thing Stilwell wrote to his superiors.

In a different department of his life, he now learned, there were other ugly criticisms. Chiang was not interested in gossip: it was Madame who heard it and told him, in great distress, that the talk about his private affairs was reaching such a pitch that she didn't think he could afford to ignore it any longer. Her missionary friends were advising her to do something about it. Everybody was talking all of a sudden; where the scandal came from it was impossible to say, but there it was everywhere, sprung up from the ground overnight. They were saying that he had a concubine, or two, or three; that he was openly visiting some woman regularly every day. They were saying that the Chiangs were going to be divorced. Mayling's pride was hurt.

It is safe to say that no leader has ever before taken control of a delicate situation in just the way Chiang did. It was just before his wife set out for Rio de Janeiro, there to meet her sister Madame Kung and try to find relief for her skin trouble. The Generalissimo did something extraordinary for him; he gave a big tea party, and invited a large number of foreigners and Chinese. When they were assembled he proceeded to make a speech. It had come to his attention, he said, that there were these rumors. He wished to deny them publicly, and to chide his friends and associates who had kept him so long in the dark about the matter: they should have told him before. "In leading my fellow countrymen, I rely not on power or position, but on my character and integrity. As a member of the revolutionary party, I must abide by revolutionary discipline. As a Christian, I must obey the commandments. Had I violated the discipline and the commandments either in public or private moral conduct, I should have been a rebel against Christ, against our late father Sun Yat-sen, and against the millions of my countrymen who have given their lives to our cause. Any one of them should impeach or punish me in accordance with discipline and the commandments."

"It was very impressive, and in a cockeyed way convincing," a foreign guest said later. "There he stood, talking in the most logical way, saying in effect that if he were guilty of such conduct he was unworthy to be the leader of China. But he *was* the leader of China. Therefore he could not be guilty of such conduct. Oddly enough, I was convinced."

In the hush that greeted this speech Madame stepped forward and said her piece. She declared that she had never for a moment entertained a doubt of her husband.

It wasn't exactly a gay tea party, but it made its mark. Fully two weeks must have gone by before people started whispering again that a divorce was in the offing. That was ten years ago, and they are still saying it.

Petty malice was one thing; the threat from Washington was quite another. With the Americans, Chiang could not afford the luxury of blowing up and speaking his mind. Instead he replied calmly; he said that he didn't like the suggestion. But if he had to accept it, the extent of General Stilwell's authority must be fully defined before they started; Communists should not be included in his command; and control of Lend-Lease material must be transferred to himself, for Chiang was afraid that Stilwell would give the best of the supplies, if he could, to the Reds.

In addition, Chiang reminded the President of his earlier request for some high-echelon officer to act as liaison between the White House and Chungking. To this part of the message Roosevelt replied without hesitation: he would certainly send someone, and was thinking it over at that moment. (Ultimately the choice fell on General Patrick J. Hurley.) The other conditions, he said, could be ironed out in the course of time. Communist aid would be valuable. But the main thing for the moment was speed: the Japanese were now past Hengyang.

Chiang didn't agree. Impatient with what they considered his stalling, the Americans went ahead anyway. They were keenly interested in furthering their latest idea, of a combined war council that was to include Communists. In the face of the unanimous approval of the State and War departments Chiang's hesitation to permit them to employ Reds in the actual fighting seemed to be 'way behind the times. The military mission to Yenan through their spokesman Service were reporting most encouraging things about Mao Tse-tung's men. It was Service's strong recommendation that the Communist army be aided by America: the Reds would be a great help against the Japanese, whatever the Kuomintang might say in objection to this plan.

Carefully Chiang talked it over in detail with Ambassador Gauss. In a long interview on August 30 he repeated his summary of the situation and his warning. Washington still did not seem to understand the danger. The Observer group in Yenan was merely making everything much more difficult; the Communists, encouraged by their presence and attitude, were slipping farther and farther out of the mood to compromise. The Americans simply didn't realize what the Reds were really after. "He thought we were acting in a way which could have very serious results," said Gauss in his report, "for the Communists were out to dominate all of China and to sovietize it."

The Ambassador listened patiently, but he was not impressed. It is not easy to figure out just what American policy was at this point, possibly because the State Department itself was not sure. If put to the question the members would have reiterated that Chiang Kai-shek was head of the acknowledged government, yet many of them felt, subconsciously, that a change was desirable and inevitable.

When General Hurley came out in August, he traveled by way of Russia; he visited Moscow on purpose to find out if he could what the attitude there was toward Chungking and the Chinese Reds. With Donald Nelson, who was going to Chungking with him, he interviewed Molotov. Nelson explained that his mission was to plan and organize production for China, with an eye to the situation after the war. What did Molotov think of the prospects of China's being unified? Molotov was most amiable. Russia's feelings for China had always been friendly, he reminded the Americans; it was the fault of the suspicious Chinese Government that Soviet proffers of friendship had been spurned. Nothing could be less true than that Russia was responsible for the Kuomintang-Communist friction. Hadn't he himself aided Chiang to get out unscathed in the Sian kidnaping affair? It wasn't Russia's fault that so many Chinese were miserable. Chinese Communists weren't real Communists anyway. Let conditions be improved in China, let the American Government give them a helping hand, and you would soon see how quickly they forgot Communism. Molotov seemed sublimely uninterested in the Chinese Reds; he wanted no part of them.

Hurley was sure Chiang would be overjoyed to hear the news,

but Chiang didn't seem to take much stock in it. . . . Well, naturally, the Americans concluded, he wouldn't welcome the prospect of reform, would he? It would mean loss of his own power.

"I judge Kuomintang and Kungchantang [i.e., the Communist Party] by what I saw," wrote Stilwell.

"[Kuomintang] Corruption, neglect, chaos, economy, taxes, words and deeds. Hoarding, black market, trading with enemy.

"Communist program . . . reduce taxes, rents, interest. Raise production and standard of living. Participate in government. Practice what they preach. . . .

"Chiang Kai-shek is confronted with an idea, and that defeats him. He is bewildered by the spread of Communist influence. He can't see that the mass of Chinese people welcome the Reds as being the only visible hope of relief from crushing taxation, the abuses of the Army and Tai Li's Gestapo. Under Chiang Kai-shek they now begin to see what they may expect. Greed, corruption, favoritism, more taxes, a ruined currency, terrible waste of life, callous disregard of all the rights of men."

On September 9, having arrived in Chungking with Nelson and Hurley on the seventh to discuss taking up his new command, he wrote, "Disaster approaching at Kweilin, nothing to stop the Japs. . . . It's a mess and of course all they think of is what we can give them. . . . What they ought to do is shoot the G-mo and Ho and the rest of the gang."

On September 12 Chiang agreed to appoint him commander-in-chief.

The points raised by Chiang when he first objected to the appointment had not yet been settled. That was up to Hurley, and now they were raised again, the subject of many a long talk. The Japanese resistance in Burma was turning into an offensive operation against the Yoke Force, which had been driven back to the Salween River it had recently crossed. Hurley told the Generalissimo that he must send in more men; the Generalissimo, on the contrary, was in favor of recalling those already committed. And there was still the fretful question of Stilwell's precise position. Was the American to have authority to reorganize the troops as he wished? That was what Stilwell naturally demanded, and what Chiang, equally naturally, was reluctant to grant. Moreover, the matter of the Communists could no longer be ignored. Hurley tried to persuade Chiang to lift the blockade of the Northwest so that the Nationalist soldiers would be free to turn against Japan, which in itself would be a major operation. He also asked that the Americans be permitted to equip the Reds themselves and use them in the fighting—what Stilwell had long been demanding.

Chiang preferred to risk that the Burma campaign be smashed and that threatened Kweilin be lost, with all the consequences involved, rather than give in on any of these points. In any case the Kweilin situation, as he and Chennault firmly believed, had been precipitated deliberately by Stilwell, who flew down to see it for himself on the fourteenth, declared the air base as good as lost, and ordered it to be demolished. Chennault believed that Stilwell held back help from Kweilin until it was too late. He declared that Stilwell was determined to prove himself right and everyone opposed to him wrong, that he intended to force the issue on Chiang.

Chiang also held out against the idea of a combined war council. It would mean a change, he said, in the structure of the government: to allow the Communists a voice in the council without insisting upon their subservience to the National Government would be fatal.

All this discussion was crowded into a few days, while the big brass and leaders of Britain and America were busy discussing the all-over plan of an attack on Japan in the spring of 1945. Roosevelt and Marshall, after a good deal of difficulty, had just succeeded in persuading the British that Burma must come first, when in the middle of the conference there came Hurley's and Gauss's reports that Chiang was going to pull the Yoke Force out of Burma. If he did this, all their diplomatic labor would have gone for nothing. For once Roosevelt was completely of Stilwell's way of thinking.

Everything came to a head in that rush of exasperation. The President felt he had been very understanding of China, generous in the face of tremendous odds. For months Stilwell had worked away, trying to undermine Chiang in Roosevelt's opinion, and Roosevelt had resisted. And this was the reward he got—this shilly-shallying, this open defiance of men who knew what they were talking about. Because of his personal dislike of those deserving people, the Communists, Chiang was imperiling the entire future of the Far East. He would lose the war in China for the United Nations if somebody didn't put a stop to it. Roosevelt thoroughly agreed with Marshall and the rest of the War Department at last: they would have to put the screws on Chiang Kai-shek.

Writing in the first person, the President told the Generalissimo that he must be prepared to "accept the consequences and assume the personal responsibility" unless he reinforced the Yoke Force in the Salween area and sent them forward in order to open the road. Chiang must also place Stilwell "in unrestricted command" of all his forces, or, again, face the consequences.

The President pointed out that as recent defeats in China had left Kunming in danger, the air route too might soon be cut off, and all China's and America's effort would thus be lost and wasted. He added a few comparatively sweet words about Chiang's farsighted vision and said he had been frank because it appeared evident "that all your and our efforts to save China are to be lost by further delays." But nothing could sweeten the bitter fact that he was laying down the law in most peremptory fashion to a proud man, the leader of a nation which still considered itself independent.

Roosevelt meant his words to be administered as a firm warning, not a slap in the face. To Stilwell, however, the message looked like a gift from heaven, a weapon specially fashioned for his revenge. It arrived on September 19. Stilwell put it in his pocket and set out happily to deliver it in person to the Generalissimo. Chiang was in conference at the time with Hurley, still wrestling over the question of Stilwell's limits of authority. Hurley knew that Stilwell was demanding "nothing less than full power, including the right of reward and punishment . . . and of appointment and relief. He [the Generalissimo] must accept the appointment of foreigners in some positions. . . . The Generalissimo must refrain from any interference in operations." Hurley believed that Chiang was just about to capitulate when the blow fell.

Stilwell asked Hurley to step outside for a moment, and with exultation showed him what he had in his pocket. Hurley was shocked. He wanted to break it to Chiang orally. He said, "You shouldn't now because of this firm language pile it on him at the time when he felt compelled to make every concession that we have asked. He has made them; he is ready to go; he is ready to bring troops down from the north to reinforce you on the Salween front; he is going to appoint you commander-in-chief."

Stilwell said, "Well, I am directed by the President to deliver this." Then he went in quietly and accepted a cup of tea, holding his fire for a few delicious moments.

He was about to have the message translated aloud by Chiang's aide—"I'm here to deliver a message from the President," he began —when Hurley interrupted, trying to make the occasion less painful. "Isn't there a Chinese translation written out?" he asked. Stilwell admitted it, and Hurley handed it over so that Chiang might read for himself.

There was a pause. Confucius's gentleman showed no change of facial expression, though Hurley said later that he looked as if he had been hit in the solar plexus.

"I understand," he said at last. He leaned over and put the top on his teacup.

"That gesture still means, I presume, that the party is over," said Stilwell. Somebody assented, and the Americans left.

"Mark this day in red on the calendar of life," wrote Stilwell. ". . . I handed this bundle of paprika to the Peanut and then sank back with a sigh. The harpoon hit the little bugger right in the solar plexus, and went right through him. It was a clean hit, but beyond turning green and losing the power of speech, he did not bat an eye. He just said to me, 'I understand.' And sat in silence, jiggling one foot. . . .

"I came home. Pretty sight crossing the river: lights all on in Chungking."

Once again Stilwell underestimated the degree of hatred he was capable of inspiring; once again he was to be surprised and indignant. It was the comparative stranger, General Hurley, who saw and understood the reaction of the Chinese. He realized that Chiang might give in on all the other points, but would never in the world, now, accept Stilwell as commander-in-chief. But Stilwell the veteran, the man of experience, was certain that they would have it all their own way.

A few days went by. The expected capitulation didn't take place, and in Washington, as tempers cooled, their owners began to think again. It was all very well to tell the Generalissimo to go it alone, but if he gave up now, all the Japanese soldiers in China, hitherto bogged down, would have to be dealt with by the other allies. In spite of Stilwell's plaints, Chiang did have his uses. . . . Stilwell, waiting for news, calmed his nervousness with such reassurance as sympathetic friends could give. "Madame Sun wants me to represent China at the Peace Conference," he reported. "Says I would do more for China than the Chinese. That I have a reputation among the Chinese people for standing up for them." He had a large following among the American newspapermen, too, and they all told him how right he was.

Then came the kickback. On September 25 Hurley broke the news. With certain reservations the Generalissimo accepted the idea of an American commander of Chinese forces. He was also willing to consider an amount of reorganization in the Army. But he wouldn't have Stilwell around any more. He had written to Roosevelt, "I cannot . . . confer this heavy responsibility upon General Stilwell, and will have to ask for his resignation as chief of staff of the China theater and his relief from duty in this area."

"Two years, eight months of struggle and then a slap in the puss as a reward," wrote Stilwell. Bitterly hurt—but why?—he listed the Generalissimo's crimes:

"Chiang Kai-shek is the head of a one-party government supported by a Gestapo and a party secret service. He is now organizing an S.S. of 100,000 members.

". . . hates the so-called Communists. He intends to crush them by keeping any munitions furnished him and by occupying their territory as the Japs retire.

". . . will not make an effort to fight seriously. He wants to finish the war coasting, with a big supply of material, so as to perpetuate his regime. He has blocked us for three years and will continue to do so. He has failed to keep his agreements.

". . . has spoken contemptuously of American efforts and has never said one word to express gratitude for our help, except in one message to the President, in which he attacked me.

". . . is responsible for major disasters of the war. Nanking, Lan Fang. Changsha and Hengyang. Kweilin and Lichow. Red blockade.

"*But* . . . is the titular head of China and has marked me as *persona non grata.*

"*Therefore* I cannot operate in the China theater while he is in power—unless it is made clear to him that I was not responsible for the September 19 note, and that the U.S. will pull out unless he will play ball.

"Ignored, insulted, double-crossed, delayed, obstructed for three years."

Stilwell had already suggested a compromise, in the first days after the message, when in spite of all his bravado he was slightly apprehensive about what he had done to his enemy. He had offered to go to Yenan and persuade Mao to do what Chiang had always insisted upon, accept the Generalissimo's authority. This strange man, who bullied like the grossest Communist caricature of American militarists, was really convinced by Madame Sun and others that he was spiritually akin to the Reds and could do anything with them. After this feat of diplomacy, he said, he would equip five Communist divisions and incorporate them into the Kuomintang army. But Chiang turned it down. Now Stilwell had an even more ingratiating suggestion. He was willing to sacrifice altogether his beloved hope of using Communists in the forces. He even offered to bring back the Yoke Force from Burma. Surely that was all the Generalissimo could possibly ask?

No, it was not all.

The American President was sorely perplexed, torn between the War Department's wrath and Chiang's incalculable resentment. The Generalissimo now made a statement to the C.E.C.: any American commander appointed in Stilwell's place was to be under his orders, and not over his head. If the Americans refused to accept these conditions, well, China would manage to get along by herself.

For Chiang this was gratifyingly worrying to Washington, but it also tore away the few strands of good will that might have remained. Stilwell's supporters in Washington had been angered enough by the request to withdraw their man; this repeated defiance sent them into a frenzy.

In the meantime the global picture changed and problems that had looked insoluble on September 19 were dwindling. The fighting in Europe was longer drawn out than the United Nations had counted on, and that meant that the big push against Japan could not take place on schedule anyway. American action in the Pacific, on the contrary, was going better than anyone had hoped, with less expenditure of men. Japan's air force showed signs of slackening. In the new plan, China's part would be merely to continue holding down Japanese ground troops. The question of who should command Chinese forces was no longer vital.

On October 5 Roosevelt told Chiang that he did not, after all, think it necessary or even wise for an American commander to be responsible for the Chinese Army, now that things there were in such a mess. Therefore it seemed to him quite reasonable that Stilwell should give up the post of chief of staff, remaining in China only as commander of the Chinese forces in Yunnan and Burma. Some third party would control Lend-Lease, and Hurley was to remain in Chungking.

Chiang refused to compromise. Stilwell must get out, he insisted, he must get out altogether. He retailed to Hurley his complaints against Stilwell. In characteristic Chinese fashion he did not confine them to what we would consider genuine grievances—Stilwell's attitude, his personality, and his penchant for lining up with Communists and fellow travelers. In Chiang's version Stilwell was responsible for practically everything that had gone wrong with any project with which he was connected. Stilwell had kept his air force short of supplies; Stilwell had lavished and lost his best troops on Burma; Stilwell personified all the failures of Sino-American endeavor. Though the Americans considered this fantastically unfair, the Chinese thought it quite natural. Didn't Chiang himself always declare that he was responsible for what went wrong in China, even when it was his own kidnaping?

In any case, now that the end of Stilwell was in sight, the Generalissimo was willing to take a milder attitude toward the rest of the affair. He quoted Roosevelt's statement that the U. S. Government should not assume the responsibility involved in appointing an American commander, because the Chinese situation had deteriorated. He said he did not altogether understand this statement.

"First: No matter what has happened . . . I cannot personally escape the ultimate responsibility for the future in the Chinese theater. Even the responsibility of General Stilwell's errors must be borne by me, since I allowed myself to be overpersuaded against my own judgment to countenance them. . . .

"Second: I cannot feel that the deterioration is so serious as the President suggests. After long years of experience and firsthand knowledge of the Japanese methods and strength, despite the defeats in East China, I cannot foresee any disaster fundamentally incapacitating China."

The War Department must have sighed sharply at this, and smitten their brows in exasperation—dramatic America, always going to extremes, faced with slow-moving China, always ready to wait, always refusing to admit that anything comes completely to an end.

Chiang continued. The statement, he said, was also distressing to him in another sense. "While I do not anticipate disaster, the situation in China is indeed critical. Aid is most needed in this hour of crisis. Yet the statement I have referred to appears to imply that aid will be withheld precisely because this crisis of the hour is upon us. . . .

"I am wholly confident that if the President replaces General Stilwell with a qualified American officer, we can work out together to reverse the present trend and to achieve a vital contribution to victory in China."

This message and Hurley's reports did the trick, finally. Clearly Chiang would never consent to Stilwell or any part of him. It really was, now, a matter of either Stilwell or the Chinese staying in China, and Roosevelt admitted it. He recalled Stilwell, appointing in his place, as chief of staff, General Albert C. Wedemeyer.

The exchange was accompanied by shrill screams in the American press. Stilwell had prepared for it on October 16, the day after Hurley notified him that the matter was settled. "Saw Teddy White and Atkinson and told them some home truths." On October 19 he entered in his journal, "THE AX FALLS. Radio from George Marshall. I am 'recalled.' So F.D.R. has quit. . . . Told White and Atkinson. They also were horrified and disgusted. Atkinson going home to blow the works.

"October 20 . . . Brooks [Atkinson] and White in. Teddy White has written a last article. . . . The Peanut offers me *China's highest decoration*. Told him to stick it up his—— Saw Madame Sun Yat-sen. She cried and was generally broken up."

There was a flurry of resignations, and wild excitement in America from coast to coast. Most people had a simple reaction; one of Our Boys had been grossly insulted.

Thinking of Yenan at this point, I am tempted to paraphrase the Hodgson poem:

> *Picture the lewd delight*
> *Under the hill tonight—*
> *"Stilwell!" the toast goes round,*
> *"Stilwell!" again.*

# 13 MANCHURIAN DOUBLE CROSS 1944–45

In his relief at getting rid of Stilwell the Generalissimo made every effort to prove that he could be as co-operative as Washington wished. Various changes were immediately set in train, following Wedemeyer's tactful suggestions, and reforms which the Chinese had hitherto stoutly insisted were impossible were now accomplished with no fuss at all. Chiang did a general overhaul. He appointed the efficient, modern-minded Chen Cheng Minister of War, a considerable step in the direction America desired. It was a considerable step in his own character, for that matter, to relinquish the claims of old friendship for the Army's needs.

Hurley seemed so successful with the Generalissimo that Roosevelt asked him to serve as Ambassador in name as well as act. Gauss had never played a very dazzling part in the post; perhaps the Chinese had obstructed him out of resentment. They were disappointed when he was first sent out to Chungking, not from any personal reason but because he had already served in the past as consul in China. The Chinese felt that they had been fobbed off with something inferior. In their world ambassadors did not work their way up, but burst upon the diplomatic scene full-fledged and glorious.

"We should have somebody more important," said Madame Sun discontentedly.

In an atmosphere of fresh good will, Wedemeyer at the end of October went to work armed with good manners and a clear understanding of the difficulties he was stepping into. With the one great exception of acceding to a coalition, Chiang was determined to minimize these difficulties. He was a completely different person, dealing with Hurley and Wedemeyer, from the man Stilwell knew. He assured the Americans that he would not recall the Yoke Force; on the contrary, he reinforced both armies in Burma and filled in the gaps which the campaign had left at Ramgarh. He repeated what he had said to Roosevelt, that all was not yet lost in East China. (Wedemeyer did not agree with him on that.) He even offered to Wedemeyer that command over his forces which he had so indignantly held back from Stilwell. But Wedemeyer had his instructions; he refused.

From the time he took over, the military aspect of the China theater improved. It was divorced from the Burma-India theater, as a part of Roosevelt's and the War Department's recasting, and Chiang was now in so malleable a mood that the executive side of the new arrangement slipped into action without a hitch. The American general Sultan managed the Hump ferry from the other side. Wedemeyer, after frankly disagreeing with the Generalissimo over Kweilin—he said, like Stilwell, that it had to be written off—argued that the Japanese would most probably aim next for Kunming. Therefore Yunnan must be prepared for defensive action and all Chinese forces should concentrate on fortifying it, even at the expense of Chungking if necessary. If the worst came to the worst the government would have to shift again.

Chiang hated the idea. He had begun the government's residence in Szechuan on good terms with the local lords, and had since managed, most adroitly, to maintain cordial relations. But the war lord of Yunnan was not friendly and had never been trustworthy. Chiang dragged his feet over the arrangements. Had Stilwell met such opposition he would have gone up in the air, but it was different now. Wedemeyer and Hurley didn't scream or bully, yet in a short time Chiang saw things their way and went along with the new plan.

In any case it was a desperate last measure, and would probably never eventuate. While the Chinese Army was strengthened and the kinks ironed out, while Wedemeyer simplified transport problems, persuaded recalcitrant generals to co-operate, and supplied new equipment, the Japanese threat ebbed away. By this time, the end of 1944, the Americans were bombing Japan itself, and battle by hard battle American naval and marine forces were shoving Japanese off the islands. Nobody in Washington was optimistic that victory would come soon. Island hopping would take a weary long time. But the Japanese could no longer afford to push ahead in China. And Burma would soon be clear, and already the ferry was bringing in over the Hump an amount of tonnage that would have been unbelievable in 1943. Nearly thirty thousand tons were carried across to China in December.

So the practical details of building up the Army, preparing it for the long fighting march to the coast which everyone still assumed would be necessary, were much less of a problem for Wedemeyer than gloomy prophets had said they would be two months before. But the problem of reconciling Chiang and Mao was as big as ever, and Wedemeyer, for all his tact, was committed to his government's policy as firmly as Stilwell had been.

Hurley was supposed gently to persuade Chiang to swallow the coalition, but he found himself being pushed. Many of his compatriots in China were working hard to convince Roosevelt that the Red forces were entitled to the new equipment we were sending in just as much as were the Kuomintang forces, if not more so. By this time the Red guerrilla exploits had been described so glowingly and often that in the average American mind these encounters took on the proportions of heroic major engagements, and Nationalist battles were never heard of. The fact was there was not an immense

amount of fighting done by either faction.            , .. ~ Reds were
becoming openly listless about the Japanese. But America wasn't
given this version.

Washington's attitude had settled into a worried longing to see the
Kuomintang-Communist dispute ended, with China "unified" before
the end of the war. Roosevelt still believed, because he wanted to
believe, that Stalin wasn't interested in the Chinese Communists.
Yet it seemed clear even to him that Russia would not refuse to
take them under her wing if they should come pleading for protection. His pro-Red advisers reminded him that it was dangerous to
"push the Chinese Reds into the arms of Russia." Far better, of
course, to shove them into a coalition with Chungking; unfortunately America could do the pushing only from the other side.
America could bully Chiang, perhaps; she couldn't do anything to
the Reds because they weren't beholden to her.

Hurley reasoned and reasoned with Chiang. He also went to
Yenan, with the Generalissimo's full consent, to talk it over with
Mao Tse-tung. He was nicely treated there—Americans in those
days were always nicely treated by the Reds—and he brought back
a set of proposals for a coalition that would be acceptable to Mao.
Chiang rejected them and drew up a set of counterproposals. Hope-
fully Hurley forwarded these to Mao. They were rejected.

"I told you so," said Chiang.

Hurley started all over again.

The Observer Mission was still sending copious reports to Washington about the excellence of the "so-called Communist" regime.
Its members were relieved and charmed by the fact that Mao's
domain was being run on principles that seemed to them truly
democratic, not at all like the way things were run in Russia. The
people were being allowed a voice in the local governing bodies,
there was a genuine redistribution of land, and nobody except really
unpopular figures seemed to be suffering. The Americans, like the
peasants, took it for granted that this state of affairs was to be

permanent. Mao did make an occasional statement in print, or in some Chinese speech, that sweetness and light was a temporary phase on the road to achievement of the traditional Marx pattern, but the Americans did not believe him. A number of State Department officials were sending in private reports; they were sure Chiang was hopelessly discredited and doomed unless he chose to ride the wave of the future and combine with the Reds. The people of China all wanted Communism of this sort, said the bright young Americans. If it had been *Russian* Communism it would be different, but it wasn't. And they were such nice people, anyway, and so friendly!

Wedemeyer's subordinates were as keen on the Reds as were the State Department officials. He had not been in China more than six weeks before their eagerness precipitated a crisis. Unknown to the Generalissimo, these enthusiasts approached the Reds with a plan by which they could utilize Communist-held territory. American paratroopers, working side by side with Red companions, were to go out on small guerrilla expeditions and capture outlying Japanese posts.

Wedemeyer put his foot down when he heard of these plans and Hurley was quick to help him do it. The Reds were disappointed and resentful; their friends argued that their behavior from that time on grew worse, and Hurley and Wedemeyer were bitterly blamed for ruining a promising amity. Hurley defended himself; such action would be tantamount to American recognition of the Communists. Stilwell may have wanted this, but it was different now. We were supporting Chiang and that was that.

Yet, while Hurley and Wedemeyer were being so meticulous about the Generalissimo's rights and dignity, the Yalta Conference was in the making.

The time had come for the fulfillment of Stalin's promise, made at Teheran, to come into the Far East war as soon as Germany should be accounted for. Germany was on the run and it was clearly only a matter of months before she surrendered. But the

Allies had not counted too much on Stalin's remembering his pledge, and he surprised everybody when he brought the matter up himself in September 1944.

Recovering swiftly from the shock, the other United Nations set to work at his behest, figuring out how much they thought Russia might contribute to the final struggle to eliminate Japan. At the time it was thought, erroneously as it turned out, that Japan was very strong, much stronger than she was in actuality after all those years of war. Evidently Stalin saw no reason to disabuse the Allies of this idea.

It seemed best that the Russians should handle the northern part of the affair while the Americans went ahead with their plan to land on the south coast after taking as many islands as they needed. Stalin continued to surprise: he now declared himself ready to act on a far bigger scale than they had ever expected. His estimates of the number of Japanese that would be encountered outdid the gloomiest Chinese and American apprehensions by a great deal. The other allies, therefore, produced an outline by which Russia would be expected to secure the Trans-Siberian Railway with Vladivostok, co-operate with the Americans in conducting air raids from the Maritime Province, cut off Japan from the mainland by sea, secure the supply route across the northern Pacific to Russia, and, most important of all, meet with and destroy the Japanese occupying Manchuria.

To all of this Stalin amiably consented. If the extra Lend-Lease supplies that he thought necessary could be delivered in time, he said, he would be able to go into action three months after Germany collapsed. The Lend-Lease supplies were to maintain his forces for something under two months, which was the period he said would be necessary for dealing a mortal blow to the enemy.

The list of material he said he needed was a staggering one, but the Russians explained that they must have it all for the hard task ahead; they would have to supply a million and a half men, three thousand tanks, seventy-five thousand vehicles and five thousand airplanes—nearly nine hundred thousand tons of dry and two hundred thousand tons of liquid cargo. Eighty per cent of it was actually delivered as promised, before June 30, 1945.

The conference to settle all this was scheduled for the beginning of February. Roosevelt was not at all well when he arrived. Harry Hopkins, who accompanied him, was also a very sick man, but there was nothing wrong with the health of the President's adviser, Alger Hiss. Yalta was selected as the meeting place because that was as far away from Moscow as Stalin could be persuaded to go. It was kept very secret for a lot of good reasons, and for other reasons that interested parties, had they known, would not have considered good at all. To advertise it would have been to tip the Japanese off. And to let Chiang Kai-shek know, as Roosevelt, Churchill, and Stalin agreed, would have been equivalent to advertising it. Nothing, they said, was ever kept secret very long in Chungking.

Chiang, in fact, was so innocent of the arrangement that in February he talked to Hurley about improving Sino-Russian relations. The Generalissimo had long thought that he might have better luck dealing with Moscow than with his own country's Reds. He had said this to Wallace and asked Roosevelt to act as "intermediary" between Stalin and himself. He even evolved the idea of sending his son Ching-kuo to Moscow as an emissary to hold conversations with Stalin. Later he decided, on Hurley's advice, that T. V. Soong would be a better envoy. Twice he tried to make a definite date for Soong with Stalin; each time Stalin put him off with some convincing excuse. The true reason for the postponement, the impending conference, didn't occur to Chiang. For a long time Yalta was that rare thing in diplomacy, a genuine secret.

If ever in all the grueling years the Generalissimo felt cheerful about the future he must have done so just then. The Japanese would soon be on the run; Americans were being polite at last; supplies were pouring in.

The Big Three had a lot of things to talk over; China was one of the least of their worries. Stalin's claims in the Far East were not even brought up until the fifth day, and he was very easygoing when the time came, just as amiable as he had been during the preliminary discussions with Ambassador Harriman in Moscow.

Naturally everyone was prepared for a request that Russia get some sort of reward for her commitment to the war against Japan. The main price she demanded was not unexpected. During the Teheran Conference Stalin had mentioned that his country badly needed a warm-water port, and Roosevelt had then suggested that Russia be given access to Dairen or Port Arthur. Chiang, when sounded out on this idea, had offered no objection. Stalin now spoke again of these ports; he wanted the right for Russia to lease both of them. Roosevelt pointed out that there were two ways to give Russia access; she could lease them as Stalin suggested, or she could share equal rights in them with the rest of the world—in other words, they could be made international ports. Stalin did not persist.

Another point was that "The former rights of Russia violated by the treacherous attack of Japan in 1904 should be restored viz:

"(a) the southern part of Sakhalin as well as all the islands adjacent to this part of Sakhalin should be restored to the Soviet Union. . . .

"The Kurile Islands should be handed over to the Soviet Union."

Strictly speaking, this was asking for more territory than had belonged to Russia before the Russo-Japanese War of 1904. By the treaty of St. Petersburg in 1875, when Japan was weak and Russia strong, Russia had grabbed southern Sakhalin from Japan and awarded the Kurile Islands in exchange. Sakhalin was rich in coal and fisheries, whereas the Kuriles were barren, wind-swept spots on the map that hadn't belonged to Russia any more than they did to Japan. Either Roosevelt and Churchill weren't especially aware of this unimportant bit of history, or they didn't care to go into detail on the matter. Naturally nobody was inclined to haggle on Japan's behalf.

There was also the matter of the railways in Manchuria. Stalin requested "the rights possessed by Russia before the Russo-Japanese War in the operation of the Chinese-Eastern Railroad and the South Manchurian Railroad providing an outlet to Dairen . . . on the understanding that China should continue to possess full sovereignty in Manchuria." But Russia in the days of the Czars had seized these rights by force and they had been contested by the National Government of China. Once again Roosevelt pointed out, as he did on the question of the warm-water ports, that the railroads could be controlled either by Russian lease or some less exclusive arrangement, preferably a Chinese-Russian commission. Like the other question this was left in the air.

None of these matters, least of all the last one, should have been decided without Chiang's co-operation, and Roosevelt paid lip service to this fact during the ensuing haggling over the wording of the agreement. On the final point, when other amendments had been made, he added, "It is understood that the agreement concerning the ports and railways referred to above requires the concurrence of Generalissimo Chiang Kai-shek." Beyond this shadowy reference nothing was said on the subject, and no alternative proposals were made in case the Generalissimo refused to give concurrence. Roosevelt asked when Chiang should be told about the arrangement, and Stalin said he would let him know. At any rate, they all agreed, he need not be told just yet. Stalin wanted to put a lot more men into the Far East first.

In the meantime the man whose fate was being sealed thus summarily was going about a task that had been neglected, if not forgotten, for many months. The period of "political tutelage" as laid down in the Kuomintang program had expired. It was time at last for the constitution, said Chiang. On March 1 he announced that a People's Congress was scheduled for November to prepare for the constitutional government in which all political parties were to have equality.

Outrageous, said the Communists. It was being done merely to pull the wool over the eyes of the people. They would have no part of it.

A large number of bright young men from Washington were now wandering about China, sending independent reports on the situation, making their own contacts and their own promises to friends they had picked up beyond the Red frontier. It was no wonder that the Communists ultimately tried to by-pass the Ambassador and make unilateral arrangements behind his back. Certainly they were given every encouragement to do so, and that is one reason Hurley resented it highly when the Red general Chu Teh calmly approached Wedemeyer, instead of the Ambassador, and asked for an official loan of twenty million U. S. dollars. That Wedemeyer behaved with perfect propriety and turned the matter over to him did not soothe Hurley. It seemed to him that this was the last insult. He went back to Washington with Wedemeyer for a conference, determined to have it out.

There he found even more reason to rage. Hardly had he left Chungking before a number of these State Department officials sent a telegram to headquarters strongly urging that Washington crack down on Chiang and insist upon equipping and using Communist troops. Otherwise, they declared, the Reds would turn to Russia just when America needed them most in the coming crisis. Washington's policy of supporting Chiang, they insisted, was merely encouraging him to remain stubbornly set against coalition. If he still refused, America should go ahead anyway and use the Communists. After all, if Chiang *would not* see reason . . .

By this time Hurley had learned of the Yalta Conference and its resulting agreement. The knowledge may have been worrying him, lending strength to his resistance; at any rate, he blew up over the telegram. He said that he couldn't work when his own staff was disloyal, that the others were trying to reshape government policy. Roosevelt and his advisers agreed that Reds should not be used until Chiang gave his consent. Then the more turbulent of the officials-without-portfolio in China were moved to other posts, and the rest were awed into silence for a little while. They were silenced partly because Chiang seemed to be showing up as a reasonable fellow. He had consented to permit Communists to accompany the Chinese delegation to the coming San Francisco Conference, at which the United Nations postwar organization was to be discussed. Mao had demanded that they appear as an independent body, but this Washington would not allow.

Hurley, with the guilty secret of Yalta weighing on his mind, visited Moscow on his way back to his post, intending to get permission from Stalin to break the news to Chiang. Chiang fully realized something was in the wind and had begun to ask embarrassing questions. The fact was the atmosphere had suddenly changed in Washington and the State Department was more than uneasy about that agreement. The innocents had just been brought up short by information received and checked through a private, preliminary investigation of the files of the pro-Communist magazine *Amerasia*. Someone had noticed things in one of its articles that should not have been there, things that were presumably secret and confidential. When the F.B.I. managed to get a look at what the editors had, they were astonished and dismayed. The awakening came in March, but open action had not yet been taken. In the meantime the editor was being watched, and it was slowly borne in upon Roosevelt and his aides that some of their young men must be supplying him with a lot of material.

Moreover, Stalin's behavior in other directions was illuminating.

Rumania had been taken over; Poland was clearly going the same way. Stalin's and Molotov's attitude altogether was not nearly so jolly as it had been heretofore. When a peremptory note came from Stalin, accusing the American Government of trying to make peace privately with the Germans in Italy, Roosevelt was deeply shocked. He had just sent his reply to Moscow, appealing to the Russians not to entertain such a spirit of distrust when his sickness at last overtook him and he died.

In those last troubled days he had a glimpse of the enormous mistake he had made.

Nevertheless Stalin and Hurley had a pleasant interview because Hurley was indomitably optimistic about settling the China question. He had arrived ready to affirm on behalf of his government a future policy regarding China that the Russians strongly approved: it suited them in every way. Chiang was to be persuaded to permit the arming of at least four divisions of Communist soldiers who would be added to the thirty-six Nationalist troops already in training. If he refused—well, the threat was not voiced at this interview, but the implication was there. They would be equipped anyway. All China's resources were needed, the men agreed, for the great all-out push against Japan.

And now, asked Hurley, what about letting Chiang in on the Yalta agreement?

Stalin had an excellent excuse for putting off the moment for another two or three months. He wanted to prepare, he said. It would not do for the Japanese to know what he was up to, and Hurley accepted this reasoning, even though as Stalin had already served notice on the Japanese that their neutrality pact was to be allowed to lapse, there would not seem to be much point in this continued caution. The Ambassador proceeded to Chungking. Faithful to the agreement, he said nothing even yet to the Generalissimo about those "pre-eminent" clauses.

Though he was not alarmed, however, other Americans were. Harriman and Kennan (who acted as Harriman's relief in Moscow) read his cheerful report and hurriedly wrote to Truman. They warned him against relying on Russia's good faith in dealing with China after the war. Yet even to them "after the war" seemed a long way off, and other worries were clamoring for attention. The State Department came to the conclusion that they had plenty of time to watch Russia and frustrate her plans. They knew in theory and from experience what she would do: take control through the agency of the Chinese Reds, masking her interest and avoiding outright intervention. But they were busy, and even at that point some of them refused to be convinced. In the meantime, it was decided, the original program must go forward. Come what may, China must be unified by coalition, both militarily and politically: it was too late to turn on the Communists at this date, who might in such case sell them out to Japan, or go on strike, or precipitate undesired action from Russia, or——

Far better wait. Deliver a knockout blow to Japan, and then deal with the Russian question. It was a remote, complicated matter for the newcomer Harry Truman to handle, and he left it to die-hards who insisted that all would yet be well. They argued that a unified China would naturally wish to be independent of Russia. A unified China would be friendly to America. Didn't the Chinese need the trade such friendship would bring? Everything would be all right if only Chiang would consent to that coalition.

Yet, considering what Mao Tse-tung was saying quite openly about the coalition, Hurley as well as the optimists in Washington seemed indefatigable. Mao delivered a report on April 24, 1945, at the Party's Seventh National Congress.

"There exist in China two different guiding lines," he said, "one of which helps to defeat the Japanese aggressors, but the other, while incapable of defeating the Japanese aggressors, in some respects actually helps them to undermine the anti-Japanese war. The passive policy adopted by the Kuomintang government toward the war with Japan and its reactionary policy of oppression toward the people have resulted in military defeats, the loss of large parts of territory, a financial and economic crisis, the oppression of the people, hardships in the people's livelihood, and the undermining of national unity. . . . But the movement of the people's awakening and unity has never been halted, it has been developing in a circuitous manner under the double oppression of the Japanese aggressors and the Kuomintang government. . . .

"Our regular forces have been expanded to the strength of 910,000 men, while the people's militia have increased to over 2,200,000. . . .

"The leading ruling clique in the Kuomintang has persisted in maintaining a dictatorial rule and carried out a passive policy against Japan while it has upheld a policy of opposing the people within the country. In this way the Kuomintang armies have shrunk to half their former size and the major part of them has almost lost its combat ability; in this way a deep chasm exists between the Kuomintang government and the people, and a serious crisis of poverty, discontent, and revolts among the people is engendered; thus the ruling clique of the Kuomintang has not only greatly reduced its role in the war against Japan, but, moreover, has become an obstacle in the mobilization and unification of all the anti-Japanese forces in the country. . . .

"Why did this serious situation come into existence under the leadership of the major ruling clique of the Kuomintang? Because this ruling clique represents the interests of China's big landlords, big bankers, and the big comprador class. . . . There are many indications that they have prepared, and, particularly at present, are preparing to start civil war once the Japanese aggressors are sufficiently driven out of China by the troops of a certain ally. . . .

"Many negotiations were conducted between us and the Kuomin-

tang government to discuss the way to end the one-party dictatorship, to form a coalition government, and to effect the necessary
democratic reform. However, all our proposals were rejected. . . .

"The New Democracy we uphold demands the overthrow of ex-
ternal national oppression and the doing away of the internal feudal-
istic, Fascist oppression."

Mao grew really eloquent on the subject of China's relations with
Russia. "We maintain that the Kuomintang government must end
its hostile attitude toward the Soviet Union and immediately improve the Sino-Soviet relationship. The Soviet Union was the first
nation to abrogate the unequal treaties and to sign equal new
treaties with China. During the First Kuomintang National Congress . . . and the subsequent Northern Expedition, the Soviet
Union was the only nation that assisted the Chinese war of liberation. After the war of resistance broke out on July 7, 1937, the
Soviet Union was again the first to come to the aid of China. . . .
We believe that the final, thorough solution of Pacific problems is
impossible without the participation of the Soviet Union."

Ah well, said Hurley, no doubt this could all be arranged later
on. The State Department opined that there was a good deal in what
Mao said. They felt they must not let Chiang get the idea that he
had a blank check. The Kuomintang must work toward a broadly
representative government and aim for stability, democracy, and
all the rest of it after the war. Americans must hold themselves free,
otherwise, to approve other arrangements. And when, a little later,
an all-out raid on the *Amerasia* offices disclosed the extent to which
espionage had been carried on, Truman submitted to advice that
a scandal involving Russia just at that time, before the San Francisco Conference, would be fatal. The affair was accordingly
hushed up.

Germany surrendered on May 8. Amid all the appropriate rejoicing the Allies still looked forward with apprehension to the

grueling battle they expected before Japan could be whipped. Once more Hurley reminded the President that Chiang had not yet been told the truth about Yalta and asked for directions.

The fact was that by this time, though the Ambassador's misgivings did him credit, Chiang knew the main clauses of the agreement, at least in general outline. How much resentment he felt after the first impact is impossible to say; he seems never to have expressed it to Hurley. Certainly he must have still felt confident that America would see him through the worst of the sorting out, once Washington realized how impossible it was to depend upon Russian good faith, and at this moment, all too obviously, Washington was realizing it. In the meantime the formal notification was once again postponed for another month.

But much reassurance was felt from some of Stalin's statements. Hopkins tried to pin down the Russian as to his exact plans and interpretation of the Yalta agreement, and Stalin was very easygoing and pleasant. His armies would be ready to get out of Manchuria by August 8, he said, within the terms of the three-month clause. Furthermore, he declared himself perfectly willing to cooperate with Chiang Kai-shek, who was obviously the man to unify China. Russia had no designs, no territorial claims, on Manchuria or Sinkiang or any other part of Chinese territory. Even if Soviet troops entered and occupied Manchuria, he would depend on Chiang to organize civil administration in the occupied areas.

It was therefore with relief that Truman at last, on June 9, had the long-awaited talk with Soong and broke the news to him in detail. At least he was able to preface the bald account of the Yalta agreement with all the pleasant promises Stalin had just made. Hurley was asked to tell Chiang Kai-shek when Soong arrived in Chungking. So Chiang, who knew all about it in essence anyway, was informed twice again before the official unveiling: once by private coded message from Soong in Washington, and once by the Soviet Ambassador.

Naturally the Generalissimo did not react in any violent manner to the American Ambassador's disclosures. He listened attentively to the interpreter. He sat quiet for a minute when the announcement was done. He asked for the speech to be repeated, and again listened carefully. Then he said that he was terribly disappointed.

He had three suggestions for modification all ready, however; anything, he implied, rather than leave him alone to face Russia. He wanted America and Britain to become parties to whatever agreement China might sign with Russia, so that the Soviet Union would have to live up to it. Port Arthur, he said, should be a joint naval base for all four of the powers; this corresponded to Roosevelt's earlier suggestion that it be an international port. He suggested that the matter of Sakhalin and the Kuriles be discussed by the four powers. But Hurley said that as all these matters bore on Sino-Soviet relations, he hardly thought that America or Britain could be expected to be party to agreements between the other two nations.

Some of Chiang's bitterest non-Communist critics among the Chinese have often referred to this interview and its outcome. At that moment, they say, he should have risen up in his wrath and refused to be a party to the Yalta agreement. To the suggestion that he would have brought abandonment and catastrophe upon the country if he had refused, they retort that catastrophe was inevitable, anyway. But this, surely, is being wise long after the event. Chiang still had reason to suppose that he could rely on the intentions of the non-Communist Western world, in spite of its patent ignorance of strategy. As long as he was not written off America's books, there was a chance, his only chance; he had no other road to follow. He could no longer play on Washington's fears that he might surrender to the Japanese.

The new "secret" of the atomic bomb must have played its part in all the interested nations' cogitations. Though nobody, outside the small circle of initiates, was supposed to know about it, both

Moscow and Chungking were well aware that something tremendous was brewing.

So T.V. set off for Moscow to talk it all over with Stalin, and the Americans now turned their attention to another matter that had lately been neglected—the political situation in China. Wedemeyer was worried. The encounters between Chinese Communists and Kuomintang forces were stepping up; in fact it was only by diplomatic fiction that China was not actually in the throes of a civil war at that moment. As the Japanese retreated there would be a rush between the two factions to occupy the empty country.

T. V. Soong found Stalin much less amiable than Hopkins had done; the Russian demands were in excess of anything that had ever been mentioned at Yalta. First of all, the Russian declared that China must recognize the independence of Outer Mongolia. Soong refused to commit himself on this. Stalin proceeded: the Soviet Government would refrain from aiding Chiang's enemies and would work with him, *but* it wanted to control Manchuria by means of a military zone including not only Port Arthur and Dairen, but a good deal of adjacent area. There was to be a naval base at Dairen for the exclusive use of Russian and Chinese navies. The railroads and their factories, workshops, coal mines, and so on were to be owned outright by the Soviet Union.

Chiang Kai-shek's suggested agreements, of course, were along directly opposite lines. If Russia recognized Chinese sovereignty in Manchuria and agreed to withdraw aid from the Chinese Reds and the Sinkiang rebels, he would agree to preserve the status quo in Outer Mongolia until after the war and then hold a plebiscite. The Soviet Navy would have the right to share Port Arthur with the Chinese Navy, but under Chinese administration. Dairen might be a free port (under Chinese administration) and Russia might have a lease on certain docks for merchant shipping. The railroads would be directed and managed by a joint Sino-Soviet company.

After that the bargaining began in real earnest. During its course Stalin declared flatly that he would support only the Nationalist Government in China. But in spite of the pleasure that T.V. politely expressed at this statement, they remained unreconciled on the crucial questions of Manchurian ports and railroads. On the same day that Soong took his leave the Japanese Ambassador to Moscow requested Stalin's services as mediator to arrange peace terms —any terms short of unconditional surrender. Stalin replied that he was too busy getting ready for Potsdam to grant an interview: they could talk it over later.

The occurrences of the next few weeks were of staggering importance and it is not surprising that the world leaders should have been swept off their feet. First was the atom-bomb try-out in New Mexico, which took place during the Potsdam Conference. There were terrifying reports of its power. The Big Three mapped out the zones of influence which each army should handle when the day of victory came. Korea, Japan, and part of Southern Manchuria were to be in the United States zone. On paper, therefore, Chiang had no reason to worry. He was probably not overtrustful, at that, but when Truman spoke to Stalin about Russian demands which seemed to be exceeding those granted at the Yalta Conference, saying that Dairen should be maintained as a free port, Stalin assured him that the city would have that status. Soon afterward, the Potsdam Declaration with its famous "unconditional surrender" terms was drawn up and signed, and sent on to Chiang for his signature. The Japanese ignored the ultimatum which was presented to them on July 26.

On August 6 the bomb was dropped on Hiroshima. Two days later Russia declared war on Japan; and on the early morning of the next day, without waiting for China's concurrence in the Yalta agreement, Stalin sent his armies into Manchuria. Within three days they were swarming all over North Manchuria and marching south, with no one to stop them. On the same day the Russian invasion began, August 9, the Allies dropped another bomb on Nagasaki, and the day after that Japan accepted the "unconditional surrender" ultimatum with certain provisos. On August 14 the Japanese Emperor declared the war at an end. That same day, several days *after* Soviet troops entered Manchuria, the Sino-Soviet agreements were signed. Both signatories promised "to act according to the principles of mutual respect for their sovereignty and territorial integrity and on non-interference in the internal affairs of the other contracting party."

In Chungking there was not much time for mutual congratulations, or the sort of celebration that went on in America and Britain. The world war was over, but Chiang's chief headache was still with him, and Russia herself had never before loomed so large on his horizon. However, for what it was worth he had Stalin's agreement to recognize him as head of the country; it now remained to deal with the great waste area that had been Occupied China.

Until the latest development it had been thought that the liberating American forces would land along the south coast of China, straight from the Pacific islands. Therefore as the Japanese were drawn out or beaten off, most of Chiang's troops had been sent to South China, there to await the landings. Chiang arranged with Wedemeyer that for the moment Wedemeyer take command of all landing American troops in the North, and he planned to move his Chinese in as soon as possible. Chinese civil government groups were to take over in good time, as things straightened out, and American troops were to avoid co-operating with Communists.

But Russian soldiers were pouring into Manchuria. The Chinese Communists were being reinforced by friends, and their enemies were still hundreds of miles away. It was a mad scramble to see who could get into the Japanese-occupied areas first, and the Reds had a head start. They were aided by Washington's directive to

American forces not to become involved in any major land campaign in any part of the China theater.

Wedemeyer was to help with the transport of Chinese troops to key areas. Americans were authorized to accept local surrenders of Japanese when necessary, turning over such places as they liberated only to agencies accredited by the Central Government; no action, however, must impair the principle that Americans shouldn't support the government in case of civil war.

Wedemeyer tried to hurry as much as possible, but the Reds were wasting no time at all. On August 12 they announced by radio from Yenan that the Japanese and their puppets should surrender to Communist forces. The Joint Chiefs of Staff, to whom Wedemeyer appealed for reinforcements against this danger, said that there were many claims elsewhere; they needed troops in Japan and Korea, and the most General MacArthur could spare for a long time to come would be two divisions.

In Moscow, T. V. Soong, with Harriman's help, was battling against a Stalin in a new mood; a Stalin who pretended to be surprised at any objection to his proposition that Russia manage the port of Dairen and control the area surrounding it. T.V. gave in at the end, more than the Americans liked, by acceding to a compromise; the Soviet Union promised not to exercise military authority over the city, the port, or the railways in times of peace. Soong said there was little else he could do as long as Stalin's troops kept advancing through Manchuria. Besides, Stalin had reiterated his promise to respect China's full sovereignty over Manchuria and permit Chinese civil government in liberated territory. Nevertheless American observers were uneasy, and pointed out in private dispatches that all these assurances meant next to nothing if Stalin wanted to trick the world. For years Russia had maintained her own lofty, diplomatically correct position in China while Chinese Communists did her dirty work. The same technique would doubtless be applied now. Hurley, however, was not worried on this account. The Chinese Communists seemed to be not a part of the same problem, but an entirely different and far more pressing one.

When General Chu Teh made the famous broadcast from Yenan he not only commanded the enemy to surrender to the Communists, but declared that the Reds were to occupy any city, town, or communication center formerly occupied by pro-Japanese forces. They were to advance northward to meet the Outer Mongolian armies which had recently gone on the warpath in defense of their autonomy. Red General Ho Lung in Shensi was to seize control of the Tatung-Pukow Railway. Chiang denounced this "abrupt and illegal action" and commanded the Reds to stay where they were, take no independent action against the Japanese, and await his orders. Chu Teh ignored him and broadcast again, this time denouncing Chiang as a Fascist chieftain. On August 16 he wrote identical letters to the American, British and Soviet governments, claiming that it was the Reds who had won the war against the Japanese while the Kuomintang did nothing. The Reds had liberated most of nineteen provinces. It was they, and not the Kuomintang, who represented the people. Yenan had the right to accept Japanese surrender and join in the peace conference, said Chu Teh, as well as share in the control of Japan.

Commenting on this note as he forwarded it, Wedemeyer warned Washington that civil war was rapidly approaching and quick action was necessary. Still hoping to handle the matter politically, the State Department sent Yenan a mutual statement from all three powers that Chiang was the recognized head of the state and Yenan's attitude was only obstructing China's unity. The Department harked back to the coalition plan, and Hurley even went to Yenan to talk it over. He came back, as usual, full of hope. But what must have mattered far more to Chiang than Hurley's report was that Wedemeyer was supplying speedy transport for his troops to North China.

The American general mobilized the air forces already based in the country, as well as the transport planes that had flown the Hump so many times. Great numbers of troops were moved in this way. Soon Chungking forces occupied Nanking, Shanghai, and Peking. Others were carried to Tientsin by sea. Fifty thousand American marines were landed at Tsingtao, Tientsin, Peking, and Chinwangtao to facilitate the evacuation of the Japanese. Though it was clearly understood by Chiang that since the war was over this American aid could not last forever, he was at least able to feel secure of his own strength in most places south of the Yangtze and isolated points north of it. North China as a whole, however, was swarming with Communists, and the policy that America must not mix in with domestic disturbances became less and less tenable as Wedemeyer brought in Kuomintang troops. From the American point of view they were there to accept the surrender of the Japanese, but each new shipment called forth more protests from Yenan. Soon the Reds reacted with more than protests. There was the affair of Chefoo, a port not far from Dairen. When the American cruiser U.S.S. *Louisville* and several destroyers approached Chefoo with intent to land some marines there and take it over, Chu Teh informed Wedemeyer that the Eighth Route Army was already in control of the area, and that a landing of Americans would be interfering in Chinese affairs. The Americans asked the Communists to get out. Chu Teh refused: Chefoo was close to his friends in the Russian zone, and very useful. If the Americans persisted in landing, he said, any resulting trouble would be their responsibility.

The two American officers in command of the little fleet, an admiral and a general, talked it over and decided that since there were no Japanese in the vicinity there was no military reason for landing their men. They were right according to the code; they had no justification for calling the Communist bluff. But the decision did nothing to clear up the situation, and similar incidents soon crowded in upon other of Wedemeyer's men.

The war was over and America expected soon to see all the welcome signs of this termination—the boys marching home and a swift decline in United States expenditure. On the subject of demobilization there was no argument. Even experienced generals watched with equanimity as American forces were disbanded as quickly as possible, almost before the Japanese were sent home.

Wedemeyer thought that the China theater could be "deactivated" by December 15, as far as the Army was concerned, and the marines in the seaports could go home even earlier, possibly from November 15. By that time, he was sure, the Japanese would have been disarmed and repatriated.

Wedemeyer's duty, however, was not fulfilled with the straightforward task of settling Japanese affairs; it developed that he had somehow inherited the responsibility of carrying out, or of persuading the American Government to carry out, a promise made by Roosevelt at Cairo. Chiang said Roosevelt had assured him of America's intention to help build up China after the war. And it was undeniable that the country was in a very bad way after eight grueling years. Food supplies had been disrupted, cities devastated, factories dismantled; and there were other pressing questions, particularly that of education, on which he needed help. There was also the matter of future defense, against neighbors who were unnamed. There was the Communist threat as well: it was out of fashion to talk plainly of the Red danger, but Chiang did talk of it.

Even in the glad rush to get home the Americans admitted the necessity of helping with China's rehabilitation. There were various methods of going at the job; loans and training of the National Army and Air Force. Lend-Lease was supposed to stop with the signing of the peace treaty, but a lot of equipment was still on the way to China or earmarked in the States for the hostilities that now would not eventuate. This equipment, it was thought, with much of the surplus material already in China, could be used to outfit a small army and air force cheaply and efficiently. Thirty-nine divisions were talked of: Chiang, however, wanted at least ninety. Truman told T. V. Soong that a small, well-equipped army on modern lines would be far better than a large, loosely organized, badly fed one. He also reminded the Chinese that the Generalissimo had promised to settle China's political difficulties politically: the military assistance furnished by the U. S. was not to be "diverted for use in fratricidal warfare or to support undemocratic administration." If Chiang took these words to heart he must have been sadly puzzled as to their exact meaning. Why keep an army if it is never in any circumstances to be used? In a fuzzy way, of course, Truman must have meant what Americans always did mean: hurry up with the coalition. But it takes at least two to coalesce.

One thing at least was becoming clear on the muddled scene of Manchuria. No matter what contemptuous remarks Stalin and Molotov may have made in the past about Chinese Communists, they seemed more than willing now to forget such ruderies and greet these social climbers as brothers. The Chinese Reds and the Russians were in constant communication, joyfully settling into Manchuria as if there had never been any talk of Nationalist sovereignty. Washington had already faced the fact that a rebellion in Sinkiang which had been worrying them was not genuinely settled, although on the surface the rebels there were willing to wait to discuss their independence and the Soviet Union—equally on the surface—was doing its part to keep them calm and quiet. But the Manchurian problem was nearer to the West and even more disturbing.

According to the agreement of August the Russian forces were to be completely withdrawn from Manchuria, except for stipulated places such as Dairen and Port Arthur and railway points, within three months after the cessation of hostilities. In fact they gave few signs of beginning the withdrawal as they had promised. Nor did they accept Japan's declaration of surrender; detached bodies of Russians continued to attack Japanese until an appeal was made to MacArthur in Tokyo to put a stop to the Russian offensive.

On the other hand, Chiang made his arrangements as they had been laid down in the agreement of August. Following the plan that Nationalist troops should be shipped in as Russians were shipped out, an expedition of Chinese were dispatched by sea in American ships, early in October, and the Russian General Malinovsky, commander of the Soviet forces in Manchuria, was advised that they would be arriving at Dairen. Then the trouble started. Russia objected to the landing of troops at Dairen on the grounds that it was a commercial port, and that allowing soldiers to come in would be a violation of the treaty.

America had bowed out; it was a matter to be settled purely between China and Soviet Russia, and the Chinese could do nothing. The U.S.A. was involved only insofar as American ships were carrying the Chinese. Stratemeyer, temporarily in charge of affairs while Wedemeyer was in Washington, told the Generalissimo, after two weeks, that something would have to be done soon, as the ships could not go on floating about indefinitely, weighed down with soldiers. He proposed disembarking them at Chinwangtao, the nearest Chinese port to Manchuria. But this would mean marching them a distance overland of some hundred miles even to get beyond the border, and Chiang hesitated. Malinovsky had suggested that though he had no authority to permit the Chinese to land at Dairen or Port Arthur, there was no reason why they should not disembark at the three other Manchurian ports: Antung, Yingkow, and Hulutao. Therefore, Chiang decided to send them on to Hulutao.

But now the Chinese Reds occupying Hulutao declared that they would not permit a landing there, and the Russians explained that in that case they couldn't "guarantee" a safe landing. The American ships duly steamed away toward Yingkow. There too they found the Chinese Communists busily engaged in preparing fortifications;

there too they encountered a refusal. The American Admiral Barbey, he who had run into a similar situation in Chefoo, again retired, and told the Chinese Nationalist commander to arbitrate. The Chinese, Hsiung, asked Malinovsky for an explanation, and the Russian was very glib. He wasn't responsible for the presence of the Chinese Reds, he explained. They had come up from the South, and what could he do about it? Let Hsiung talk it over with the Reds himself. This Hsiung refused to do. Malinovsky then said virtuously that he could not interfere in Chinese affairs. There was a quarrel: the Russians thereafter ignored the situation, leaving the matter to the Chinese Communists, who of course did not budge. In the end Barbey and his associate turned around and took their load to Chinwangtao.

Chiang behaved as circumstances made necessary, as if these delays and betrayals were merely small obstacles that could be smoothed over with diplomatic exchanges. He went on, getting his men into Manchuria as best he might, trying to build up those centers of civil government that Stalin had so cheerfully promised to respect and protect. He sent five hundred officials up to Dairen and Harbin. The idea was that the rest of the government, and the police and military guard, could be enlisted from the local population. Very soon, in spite of the Russians' courteous welcome, the Chinese from the South found out that they couldn't recruit anybody. Chinese Communists kept moving in on them, interfering with their work, and even with such public utilities as water and electricity. Finally the mission had to be withdrawn. All through this crisis Chiang found it impossible to communicate with Stalin. The Russian was not at home.

Malinovsky admitted that Chinese troops could be brought into Manchuria, if not through seaports, at least by air. But they were to come in only as the Russian troops withdrew, and these still gave no signs of withdrawing, though their deadline of December 3 was close at hand. Yet if they should retreat before the Nationalist

troops got there, the way would be open for the Chinese Reds.
Though all this juggling was transparently clear, Chiang went ahead
playing the game according to the rules. When the Russians kindly
offered to stay on until he could manage to get his troops in, he
accepted the offer. The Soviet troops, therefore, announced they
would stay on until January 3, 1946.

All the time the Communists flowed in freely, with full access
to the immense store of arms and equipment that had been left
by the Japanese.

Chiang's affairs at home in the government, through the past
few years, had been left to a routine that appeared superficially to
work as well as it had done early in the war. Actually it was badly
in need of overhauling. The Army *had* been overhauled, frequently
and painfully, because of American prodding, but civil affairs had
not received the same treatment. No man can do everything when he
is in Chiang's position, but Chiang had never admitted the truth
of this precept; he felt that he was capable of keeping an eye on
all the departments under his wing. During moments of strain such
as those that came on thick and fast in the years succeeding Pearl
Harbor, something had to go by the board, and that something
was the ordinary mechanical process of civil governing. It was a
crowded government, like all such bodies in exile. It was an uneasy
one, subject to the difficulties and temptations that would naturally
beset it, set down as it was in a backward community like Szechuan.
It was badly in need of reform; full of small grafters and weakened
by that plague of the distrustful East, nepotism.

In times of peace Chinese nepotism and grafting are usually
kept within reasonable bounds. But these eight years had been a
period of turmoil and neglect, and their growth had got out of hand.
Every grievance, every small outrage that could be dramatically
exhibited to the people was now snatched up and used by the
Communists to their advantage. Chiang's own stamping grounds

in Chungking and Nanking were seamed and cracked with resentment: there was no place in all the war-saturated land that was not in some way affected. China needed peace for a grand clean-up, but there was no peace.

Faced with this situation, Wedemeyer himself—and he was not as easily stampeded into panic as some of his predecessors had been —took an exceedingly grave view of the domestic situation. His tour of duty was running out, but the Communist threat had suddenly swelled up, as it were, overnight. Was America justified in simply walking off and leaving Chiang to do his own battling? Diplomatically speaking it was still possible to keep the Communist menace apart from that of the Soviet, but the Russians were in their way even more of a perplexity to America, for they could not be confined to the boundaries of Chinese domestic disputes. The American marines, then—should they be kept on, after all? Should they be empowered to take offensive action when necessary? This alternative was so dangerous that Wedemeyer didn't really contemplate it, but he realized that as the marines were at that moment stationed at ticklish points and carefully avoiding any complications that might be called domestic, they were a constant irritation to the Communists and Soviet Russia, while accomplishing no useful purpose. The general's opinion was that Chiang would be able to hold North China on his own, but would certainly not be able to manage Manchuria as well. He suggested that Chiang concentrate and consolidate, and cut his losses. But here they ran into one of the deepest disagreements of all their association.

Chiang could not possibly relinquish his claim on Manchuria. His whole career was based on the idea of a China united, once more in possession of the territory stolen by Japan. Since his earliest association with the Army the hope of a Free China had been fixed on restoration of her old status, before the Japanese began chipping away at the map. All the rest of it, the revolution and the long apprenticeship with Sun Yat-sen, and the war-lord battles, and the break with the Reds—all of it was a structure that was built around that central idea, China free and united. Chiang had no intention now, in 1945, of tamely giving up and settling into a nation that accepted its contracted limits—a nation that had merely exchanged one threatening neighbor for another—under a leader who had swapped more than three decades of struggle for nothing.

He determined to go on trying. If the men in Washington wanted him to continue talking about a coalition with the Communists, if they still didn't see what a waste of time it was, why, he would go on trying for that, too.

# 14 THE MARSHALL MISSION 1945–47

Washington did want him to go on trying. At that stage there was not much else they could think of to do. U. S. officials held a series of meetings about the situation at the end of November, and they decided to leave the marines in China for a while. They resolved to arrange a truce, if possible, between the Kuomintang soldiers and the Communists in disputed areas; they considered acceding to Chiang's latest request, to transport more of his troops to the North, and they would certainly continue, they declared, to press for the coalition government. Some of them thought it might yet be achieved if only the Generalissimo would be a little more reasonable.

Then Hurley administered a fresh shock to the State Department by resigning.

He had several reasons, but the most outstanding was that he felt he couldn't trust his colleagues in the Foreign Service. He considered it sinister that Acheson and Service, both of whom he particularly distrusted, should have been appointed to posts in Japan under MacArthur. Moreover, he had reason to suspect a leak somewhere in the State Department. Information that could not otherwise have got out was appearing in American leftist newspapers. In any case he was perturbed over the attitude toward his mission prevailing in Washington. More and more, it seemed to him, the Department leaned toward the Communists. He thought he detected an unseemly eagerness to push Chiang into a coalition somehow, anyhow, in order to get him off the public mind.

And Hurley had to face the fact that this solution was as far off as ever. After months of fruitless arguing, negotiations had stopped, leaving Mao and Chou En-lai still insisting that their army be permitted to participate in the National Military Council, retaining their identity as Communists. They would not consider reorganization in the Nationalist forces. They demanded the right to nominate the chairman of provincial governments in the Border Regions as well as those provinces they already controlled, the vice-chairman of yet six more, and the deputy mayors of Peking, Tientsin, and Tsingtao. They claimed of the seventy seats of the Council twenty for themselves as against forty for the Kuomintang, with four more to go to the crypto-Communist group called the Democratic League.

Hurley was convinced that he had come to the end of his rope.

General Marshall had retired from his post as Chief of Staff. With World War II wound up, the most important question in international affairs, in American opinion, was the Chinese dilemma, and it seemed good judgment to send the general himself out to the East as a super trouble shooter. Marshall had been Stilwell's chief all through the painful episodes that ended with Stilwell's recall. He had championed his man to the end, as a good chief ought to, and his impressions of the rights and wrongs of the Nationalist-Red argument were colored by what he had heard from Vinegar Joe. His feeling about Chiang Kai-shek was one of caution and suspicion mingled with a certain amount of reminiscent rancor.

He was preparing for the journey and discussing his proper policy with the State Department when the military affairs of Chiang's government took a sudden turn for the better. Some of the Chinese soldiers who had been barred from landing in Manchuria from shipboard managed to arrive after all, by rail. In a short time they drove out the Communists occupying Hulutao. Then they marched toward Mukden, and could easily have taken possession of it had not the Russians been there. Chiang began to wonder if he should not continue to move in troops and consolidate his position in Manchuria before he went ahead with any other task. Encountered on equal ground, the Communists did not seem formidable after all: his men marched ahead.

By the middle of December, Marshall was ready to embark on his task. First detail in importance, naturally, was that long-deferred truce that was to iron out all differences between Nationalist and Red, and unify China under a democratic government. Americans were to help the Chinese shift as many troops and supplies as were necessary into Manchuria immediately; this action, it was agreed, was called for by the Cairo Conference, the Yalta agreement, and the Sino-Soviet agreement, all of which asserted that Chinese should have sovereignty there. In spite of Wedemeyer's advice that North China be reinforced before Manchuria, Washington had come round to Chiang's belief that Manchuria should be taken care of first—certainly before the truce was settled.

North China was not forgotten. Marshall had his orders to assist in the transport of Chinese troops there, too, but not immediately: this move was to wait on the truce. If the negotiations failed, however, Marshall was not to feel himself bound to carry on with the North China plan. The decision was left to his discretion.

In the meantime the marines were to remain in North China, and the Soviet Union didn't like that. Byrnes explained one good reason for their retention: there were still many Japanese in the area awaiting evacuation, and Russia, if she was sincere about wishing to see a settled, unified China, would not object. But the Russians still didn't like it. Molotov reminded Byrnes that their own troops had remained in Manchuria at Chiang's special request: otherwise they would have gone long since. The Soviet troops were no longer necessary or even wanted in Mukden, Chang-chun, or Harbin; Chiang's soldiers were waiting for them to get out so that the Nationalists could move in. The Chinese Reds moved about freely under their wing and dug in where they liked. The Russians worked at top speed, moving everything movable from the factories which had been set up in former times by the Japanese and carrying all the machinery away to Siberia. When the Nationalists at last got in, they found empty shells of buildings.

By the time Marshall arrived in Chungking, the officials were busy getting ready for the move back to Nanking. Great things were in the air: 1946 was to see the beginning of that long-deferred thing, a constitutional government. Amid these preoccupations he was glad to note that Chiang had not put aside the truce. Once again the Reds were willing to try, and had sent a deputation; once again they were haggling about the Red Army's autonomy. Marshall had his orders; they boiled down to the old pattern. If Chiang proved unreasonable though the Reds were willing to give way, the American was to threaten to withhold all future aid. If the Reds were unreasonable whereas Chiang proved amenable, the Nationalist advance into North China was to be put into practice immediately.

Negotiations were resumed. Marshall took up where Hurley had left off, which was almost the same point where Hurley had begun: the difference was that the Reds had gained immensely in the interim. On January 10, as part of the machinery for the era of truce and coalition, the government called a "Political Consultation Conference," or P.C.C., with a council that included Communists. Of thirty-eight members eight were Kuomintang, seven Communists, four from the Democratic League, and nineteen from the other minority groups. The council discussed the future National Assembly to write a constitution, which had been so often postponed since it was first bruited in 1936. It was agreed to hold it on May 5 in Nanking.

In theory China was free again and could make a fresh start. Actually the country was badly crippled by the necessity of carrying on what was in all but name a civil war. There were no funds to spare for reconstruction and few resources with which to combat rapidly rising inflation. Of these resources, the most substantial were the formerly Japanese-owned properties, which had been confiscated according to the rules of war, along with those that had belonged to collaborators. In addition there was Formosa or, as the Chinese call it, Taiwan, which after fifty years of intensive Japanese development had been returned to Chinese ownership, somewhat damaged by bombing but still a valuable acquisition. There was also—until the end of June—Lend-Lease, and sometime after that, to take its place, U.N.R.R.A. But U.N.R.R.A. didn't come along in time, and once again the Chinese applied to Washington for a loan. A small one was granted, as a stopgap, but the sum of five hundred million that was requested had to wait upon events. If the Kuomintang could make it up with the Communists, said Washington, the money might be forthcoming. Until then, no.

"Many Chinese thought and said that this looked like an offer of a choice between modes of suicide," said Hollington Tong. But, he added, "the exhausted condition of China required that the Generalissimo go along with as good grace as possible in the futile negotiations."

There was a brief flurry over the choice of Hurley's successor. Marshall favored Wedemeyer as the obvious man, and both the War and State departments were agreeable to this until the Reds heard of it. Then Chou En-lai made a strong protest: if Wedemeyer stayed as Ambassador, the whole truce was off. In the end Marshall appointed Dr. Leighton Stuart of Yenching University, an honest, well-meaning man, but no ball of fire. Marshall had good reason for feeling amiably disposed toward the Reds just at that time, for he had actually succeeded in arranging a cease-fire. On the face of it everything was going to be all right now; all that remained was to decide on the details of the truce.

That, however, was the stumbling block. In theory the cease-fire began: in actuality the Reds never stopped working at the war for an hour. While Marshall had every reason for thinking that his firm handling of the situation was paying dividends—at the conference table all was as reasonable and constructive as anyone could wish —the Red leaders back in North China were shipping forces across the border to key points in Manchuria. Thousands of troops passed through Dairen and Port Arthur during the first month of negotiations and bargaining, and stood ready to move into the key cities at the word of command.

On February 15 Marshall presided at the signing of what looked like an all-important agreement, to integrate the Communist army with the Nationalists. One of the greatest obstacles to accord had been the matter of proportional representation; the Reds had persistently demanded a larger number of troops compared with the Nationalists than Chiang felt it safe to maintain. Now all objections seemed to melt like icicles in summer sun: Marshall was gratified to observe that where the Nationalists were willing to cut down to ninety divisions in the first phase of a year, the Communists would be satisfied with eighteen, and after that crucial period both sides promised to demobilize further.

Everything looked so calm, and events were proceeding at such a rate, that Marshall felt safe in leaving China on March 13 to report to Washington. The main part of his mission was accomplished. It only remained to arrange a commission to oversee the Army's amalgamation—in which, by special request of Chou En-lai, America was to play no part—before his task could be declared finished. Everyone had behaved beautifully. Soon China would be united and well on the road to rehabilitation, with friendly support from American banks making easier her climb toward the summit of true democracy. Mao and Chou would keep a stern yet just eye on Chiang: Chiang, presumably, would bow to their timely corrections and yet somehow maintain his position of superiority well enough to do the governing.

Marshall's back had been turned just a month when the whole picture changed. Now at last the Soviet troops were moving out of Manchuria. Within a day after they removed themselves from Changchun the Chinese Communists attacked, as if there had been no truce at all, and moved in. Harbin, Tsitsihar, and Szepingkai were to follow: the war restarted in full cry, with plenty of bloodshed. Marshall had to begin all over again. He came back, of course, immediately, and the strange game was taken up where he had left it, while in Manchuria the battle continued. As the Nationalists rallied the Reds seemed to give way. Again they filed out of one city after another.

Moving back to Nanking was a slow process. Much of the old capital city was badly damaged, and new quarters had to be found for the ministries. Chiang himself was one of the last to make the homeward trek, on May 1.

Determined to carry through the Manchurian commitment, he persevered with the double program of truce talk at the table and battles in the North. He may have been deluded, as the Americans were, by the success with which his army was now pushing the Reds around. Possibly he knew better; his intelligence service told him that the enemy was lying low only temporarily, and had taken possession of the great reservoir of arms left behind by the Japanese Kwantung Army. But he didn't cry havoc. What was the use of alarming the Americans? They were already on the verge of complete discouragement. It wouldn't take much to push them over into isolation.

Therefore, though the Reds still held all the cities along the South Manchurian Railway and had moved their capital from

Yenan to Kalgan, though a number of Chinese soldiers who had fled from the Japanese into Siberia were now in Manchuria training the comrades in the use of their newly acquired Japanese arms, the situation on the whole looked promising and Chiang said nothing of fears for the future. His army held the ostensible advantage in Manchuria for another seven months.

By that time, however, Marshall had developed his own insight into conditions, and collected intelligence that showed him a dangerous state of affairs. Now he regretted the policy of aiding the Nationalists to venture into Manchuria before North China was under control. He advised Chiang not to carry on with the Manchurian campaign but to cut his losses, pull in his overextended lines, and turn his attention once more to North China, which was imperiled through neglect. It took no prophet to observe that the Reds had reverted to their former guerrilla tactics, against which the old-fashioned Chinese soldiers were not able to hold their own.

Chiang did not agree. He suspected that Marshall's advice was not based on a detached point of view; he knew that the Reds had threatened to withdraw from the truce negotiations if the Nationalists occupied Kalgan, their stronghold. He was sure that the American was impressed by this threat and wouldn't scruple to hold him back in order to save the conference. Chiang had had enough of being held back. The end might justify the means in the eyes of Marshall. If the Nationalists could strike quickly and beat back the Reds thoroughly, why then the prospects of peace would improve and Washington tempers would be soothed.

Besides, it was tempting. Kalgan was easy. He simply gave the command and his troops moved in. Marshall too gave commands. After all, it was up to him, according to the terms of his directive; he was to use his discretion.

"General Marshall, infuriated by this disregard of his wishes," according to Hollington Tong, "cut off all American military aid to China. From that time for a period of eight months, all American shipments of military goods to National China were embargoed."

The facts are not quite so clear-cut. During the next year something under a billion and a half dollars' worth of aid went from the United States to China. But it was very slow in coming. Some of the delay was due to muddle. Some of the material got lost on the way through black marketeers—and not all of these were Chinese. Yet some delay, indubitably, *was* due to American policy.

While the fiction was still being preserved that the Communists were ready and willing to be integrated with Chiang's army, they had been promised by Marshall that their integration be preceded by "a brief period of United States training and by the supply of minimum quantities of equipment." American officers were assigned to the task and waiting in Shanghai to start work, but before any supplies reached the Reds from America—before Stilwell's old project came to fruition, many years after he advocated it—the anomaly of such a gesture seems to have become evident to enough Congressmen to bring it to a halt.

Finally Marshall had to admit defeat. In any case he was being appointed Secretary of State. He left China on January 7, 1947, summing up his frustrations and his theory as to their causes in a statement to the President. It was all due to extremists, he said, a "dominant reactionary group," and "dyed-in-the-wool Communists" opposed to them. (There was no more talk about their being merely agrarian reformers.) "Between this dominant reactionary group in the Government and the irreconcilable Communists who, I must state, did not seem so last February, lies the problem of how peace and well-being are to be brought to the long-suffering and presently inarticulate mass of the people of China. . . ."

The rot of despair had set in in Nanking; if not in Chiang's heart, where it mattered most, among the troops. As the Communists stepped up their guerrilla activity and spread the gospel, soldiers of the Nationalist Army slipped off and joined the other side in rapidly increasing numbers. Part of their discontent may have been due to homesickness; they had been in Manchuria a long time. But other soldiers had spent months away from home without feeling that they must desert in protest. It was more than that. They were tired of war and uncertainty and repeated disappointments; they were worked on by everything they read and heard; they were tempted by the glorious picture held out to them by the Reds. Ironically, Chiang's reforms of the past played a large part in the collapse. Under his government, schooling for the people had improved. The revolution begun by Hu Shih gave them a vernacular to use in print. A "basic Chinese" of eight hundred characters had been evolved under the Nationalist Government, and now many coolies and soldiers, whose fathers had been illiterate, could read the newspapers. What they read with their new education was mostly Communist propaganda, carefully written and toned down to be comprehensible to them.

Moreover, much of what the Communist writers alleged was true. Local government *had* broken down; corruption *was* increasing; the future *was* uncertain. The more grievances the people had the more eager they were to believe that it was the fault of their leaders, and that a change of government was the only way to improve matters. Workingmen of old China had seldom been receptive to such ideas because they were used to their lot and were trained to accept it—or, rather, had never been trained to expect anything else. It was different in 1947. They had learned to demand more of life, and the fact that it was the Kuomintang that had taught them this counted for nothing against all the ideas they were now getting from the Kuomintang's foes. Most of them, of course, even more than most people anywhere, were still led, still easily deluded, still dependent on more agile brains. But they were far more ready than they had been in the old days to switch their dependencies, and the new generation of Communist-trained intellectuals were there on the spot, showing them the way to go.

In the middle of this turmoil came Wedemeyer, who had earlier gone back to the States. The general was to spend two months traveling about, finding out facts, reporting on the situation.

His attitude was wary. Much of his former friendliness for Chiang had evaporated under the erosion of Marshall's report in January and the riots that took place in Taiwan in February. Taiwan was gaining new importance and had brought publicity of an unpleasant sort to the Kuomintang. When the island reverted to Chinese ownership, after the surrender of the Japanese, Chiang sent over a group to administer civil government, set the war-paralyzed industries going again, and generally put the place on its feet. He spotted its possibilities in case some place of refuge was needed in the future just as he had spotted the possibilities of Chungking in Szechuan years before. In the case of Taiwan he had a good historical example. Kwok Sing Ya or, as he is usually called, "Koxinga" had fled to Taiwan in 1661, when he was driven off the Chinese mainland by the army of the Manchus. It was Koxinga's people who settled down and gave Taiwan its Chinese cast of countenance, gradually supplanting the aboriginals and living like the Chinese they were until the Japanese took them over and superimposed their culture.

In 1946, when the mainland Chinese began coming in—officials first, with eager merchants in their wake—the Taiwanese greeted them with mixed feelings. There were naturally the call of the past and the knowledge of their common ancestry, but there were also apprehension and the mistrust of people who had been brought up to look toward Tokyo and the Emperor, to speak Japanese as their second tongue, and fight for Japan when necessary. A lot of Taiwanese had indeed fought for Japan. And Taiwan had not come out of the war unscathed; the bombings of China's ally, America, had been terribly effective.

The mainlanders' feelings were much simpler. They didn't like the Taiwanese, who had a bad reputation as dirty fighters during the war, and they were eager to make new fortunes in this island, which was by repute rich and exploitable. Followed a period of shameless carpetbagging and ruthless grabbing. The officials were not of a good stamp to begin with, and the National Government of China, over in Chungking and Nanking, was busy with other pressing matters. For the most part, Kuomintang eyes were turned toward Manchuria or Washington or Moscow. Taiwan was badly neglected and very badly treated. And there was, of course, a Communist fifth column eager and ready to work. In February a riot broke out in Taiwan, and then for a little while the world did survey the ugly scene and was shocked. Chiang removed the governor and put in a good man. There was a hasty house cleaning—it was easier to handle a small place like Taiwan than a great sprawling nation of China's size—and soon things were being managed much better; soon Taiwan was on its way to being a model colony. But in the meantime the affair had made a noise in Washington, and Wedemeyer could not have been proud of his Chinese friends.

His report on his mission, when it came out in September, was unwelcome to both the Kuomintang and the Communists. The general had not followed the usual pattern of swinging sharply Left because of his displeasure with the Right, but he spoke plainly and severely nevertheless. He said that the Kuomintang was characterized by "reactionary leadership, repression and corruption," and that the public had lost faith in it. However, even so, he did not believe that the majority of the people wanted to switch to Communism. The great mass of them were caught between misrule and totalitarianism. Yet moderates who represented this school of thought, he said, were not able to make themselves heard because of National Government repression. Wedemeyer urged that America take the initiative and aid Chiang quickly to stabilize the country. In spite of all the "corruption and incompetence" he said he observed, that would be the way to meet the wishes of the people, of whom "Some have become affiliated with Communism in an indignant protest against oppressive police measures, corrupt practices and maladministration. . . . Some have lost all hope for China under existing leadership and turn to the Communists in despair. Some accept a new leadership by mere inertia." But Chiang must mend his ways, or, rather, the ways of his subordinates. It would be no good otherwise. Reform, drastic and immediate, must go into effect.

Wedemeyer suggested a guardianship over Manchuria of China, Russia, America, Britain, and France, or failing that, a trusteeship established by the U. N. General Assembly. Otherwise, he added rather unnecessarily, "Manchuria may be drawn into the Soviet orbit, despite United States aid, and lost, perhaps permanently, to China."

The heartburning to Nanking caused by this report was sharp. Wedemeyer himself later declared that he had joined in too enthusiastically with the popular chorus in Washington. "It hurt, and it hurt deeply," he said. And there was the added indignity of his recommendation, which by this time had become routine, that aid be withheld if China did not mend her ways forthwith. To no other nation did America ever take quite the same attitude of "either— or," though others cost her far more in money and material.

Yet the recommendations would have been followed, if only Chiang had been able to do so. As usual he was held up by the feeling that it was not the time. If he looked too closely at, for instance, Mr. Wang's behavior and fired him, would not Mr. Wang's brother-in-law have taken umbrage; and wouldn't that mean opposition from the entire clique surrounding the Liu clan? Then there would be rebellion in an important section of the Kuomintang, and one thing would lead to another. . . . It was always not the right time. A little later, he probably told himself, as soon as the constitution was working, when China could truthfully call herself a democracy. That time was close at hand: for what it was worth, China was to have the vote.

The constitution had already been drawn up, and it went into action in December 1947. In essence it is rather like that of the U.S.A., though there is only one House, the National Assembly, instead of the two at Washington. The members of the Assembly, like the President and Vice-President, serve for a term of six years. The five Yuans were retained from pre-constitution days.

China's first general election of the National Assembly was held in November 1947 under the considerable difficulties of all-out civil war. Forty-eight per cent of the members elected were nonpartisan; forty-two were Kuomintang; the remaining ten were members of the "Young China Party" and Social Democrats. Five months later, in April 1948, the electoral college voted in Chiang Kai-shek as President of the nation. He had made the conventional attempt to bow out of the race, but it came to nothing, and everyone would have been amazed if it had succeeded. Li Tsung-jen was elected Vice-President, having run a close race against Sun Fo. There was a lot of talk about the buried hatchet, old enmities forgotten, and so forth, which is not without interest considering how soon the hatchet was to be exhumed.

That election stands out as the gratification of a national dream. Thirty-seven years on the way, it had arrived just in time for the record.

# 15 FLIGHT 1947–49

Disaster struck first in Manchuria. In one blow after another the Nationalists lost their best-equipped and best-trained men. Before the all-out drive in the autumn, it was already obvious that the moving spirit of dissension, there and in North China, was the Democratic League that claimed to be the gathering place of China's true liberals. League men stirred up mutiny in the Army, and wherever there was local unrest, especially in Peking, where the students in their usual way had begun again to riot, you found a League member at the bottom of it. Among the American observer team there were red faces at this development, but things had now gone so far that it didn't matter very much. No detail mattered very much in the path of the inevitable.

The early months of 1948, with Manchuria obviously slipping out of control, brought added distress to China itself. Inflation had gone so far that the government's requests to America for another loan now lost all vestige of conviction: the most wildly optimistic banker must have seen that loans would not meet the case. The cities were crowded to choking point with refugees from the North. Nevertheless there was one more American contribution when the Marshall Plan was drawn up in Washington; China must have her share, and an appropriation for economic and military aid, amount-

ing to something under half a billion, was approved in April. But
the material included in this agreement did not begin to arrive in
China until August, by which time a large part of Chiang's troops
were cut off and under siege in Changchun and Mukden. By the
end of October the remnant of this army was on its way out,
evacuated through Hulutao. Many were dead; many more had gone
over to the Reds. The Manchurian adventure was over, and Chiang,
in setting his judgment against Marshall's, had lost the argument.

Long before this the rot had spread to North China. Shansi was
battling for life, and no one was sure if Yen Hsi-shan would continue to hold out. In Shantung a chief general changed over to the
other side, taking his large army with him, and the governor soon
followed suit. Peking and Tientsin were next: their general resisted until 1949, but supplies that he had been promised were
held up and in his wrath and discouragement he too slipped away.

The Reds moved on south. Hsuchow in Kiangsu, commanding
the Yangtze Valley with Nanking and Shanghai, fell in December.

The stable of statesmen, generals, and ex-war lords who made
up the Kuomintang government began to fall apart. War with Japan
had held them together in a fashion that was, after all, highly
uncharacteristic; the old way of life had still beckoned as a possibility when victory should have come: they had faced the
tiresome lean years with all the philosophy of which they were
capable. Under the threat of Communism this spirit evaporated.
There would be no future for most of them if the Reds conquered.
One or two, like Feng Yu-hsiang, had reason to suppose they had
a foot in the door of that future; the rest did not delude themselves.
It was not surprising, therefore, that they should begin to look for
a compromise. It was the sort of thing they had always done, and
managed to survive by doing. Their squabbling over a peace movement was to plague Chiang's last days on the mainland. We need
not take the ins and outs of it too meticulously; no matter what ar-

rangements they made and remade, it came to the same in the end.
With Communists, the backsliders were to discover, there was no
compromise possible.

The falling Chinese currency brought matters to a head. After
vainly attempting various remedies, Chiang decided to battle the
immediate and most pressing evil of inflation, food shortages and
hoarding, by putting his son Ching-kuo in charge of the matter.
Ching-kuo used his vast powers with promptness and severity,
arresting and executing black-market leaders. It was only a temporary stopgap; all price controls soon had to be abandoned. But
Ching-kuo had proved himself resourceful, firm, and trustworthy.

Again Chiang thought of America. Even now it seemed unbelievable to him that Washington would stand by and calmly watch
China fall to the Communists. He did not entertain any delusions
about the feelings of the American leaders toward himself; he had
never believed much in their affection, and Marshall made no
secret of his opinion. There had been Stilwell, now dead but un-
forgotten, and all his critics in the Foreign Service. Yet surely, in
spite of all this, his early judgment of American mentality could not
be so grotesquely wrong: Mayling's missionary friends *must* know
what the average American thought of Communism. Innocent
Americans obviously were, but even the most innocent of nations
wouldn't take a risk like that—or would it?

Chiang talked it over with the few people he trusted. Somebody
ought to go to Washington and present the case more vividly than it
could be transmitted through telegraph and the lukewarm American
Ambassador. The choice was obvious; though other names were
suggested and discarded, it was Madame Chiang who determined at
last to shoulder the responsibility. She was doubtful: Chiang's
latest request had been ignored, and her own experience in America
had not been so pleasant that she was eager to risk a new test. But
there was really no one else so well fitted for the tricky mission.

Much against her inclination, she informed Marshall of her intentions.

The diplomatic procedure of the projected visit as he outlined it sounded an ominous note. The Secretary of State did not invite Chiang's wife, as she had been invited before, to visit the capital as a guest of the government. He would, of course, be delighted to see her, he said, as his personal guest. When Mayling arrived in Washington, though she wasn't exactly snubbed, it took rather a long time to get to the President. Nor did he greet with approval, or even with interest, her suggestions that America support Chiang openly against the Communists and supply Nanking with another general and lend a billion dollars' worth of aid every year for the next three years of the struggle.

Madame conquered her feelings and stayed on in Washington until it was quite clear that she would not succeed in any of these requests. Truman was polite, at least: the press was not. It was the worst rebuff she had encountered in all her life.

The end of 1948 bore a zombie resemblance to the old days when Chiang was still struggling on his way up, and seldom saw a month pass by without a denunciatory telegram from South or North. Once more, as in the past, the initiators of the denunciation were Pai Chung-hsi and Li Tsung-jen. Though Pai was now one of Chiang's most important generals and Li was Vice-President, the old rebellious Kwangsi spirit still survived. This time, plenty of C.E.C. members supported them in their arguments, namely that the President should try to make peace with the Reds and settle down with what was left to him in China.

Chiang would not agree. As twice before, he decided to resign rather than try to force his own will on a dissident government. The awkward fact that he could not resign so easily, now that he headed a constitutional body without any machinery for resignation, did not deter him: he walked out anyway and left Li Tsung-jen in charge as "Acting President." Let those who worried about protocol pick up the pieces and make it as legal as they could: he was angry; he would not stay.

"It isn't the Communists who have driven me out," he declared. "It's the Kuomintang." And back he went to his Chekiang village. Quietly, he had already made arrangements in Taiwan, setting a new government in order there. As governor he appointed Chen Cheng, his most loyal, honest general, and Chiang Ching-kuo was sent over to head the Kuomintang party. For himself the Generalissimo settled down on his old mountain top and watched events.

Li Tsung-jen promptly set to work arranging peace talks with the Communist heads.

He probably expected a settlement along the lines he had always been used to—a good deal of extreme talk on both sides, and then compromise. In his suggested terms there was talk of a neutral zone in which Shanghai would be included, and of course he already had Chiang's resignation to offer on a silver tray. But Mao had no time nor any use, now, for compromise; his reply was brusque and unequivocal. After the peace war criminals were to be punished, the government armies to be completely reorganized, the land system reformed, all capital confiscated, all "traitorous" treaties repudiated, and complete reorganization of China's legal system. It did not look as if he would relax any of these demands, but the Peace Party of the Kuomintang had a try, anyway.

A cease-fire was proclaimed, and Li accepted the Red proposal as a basis for negotiations. In spite of bitter quarreling among the National officials these went forward for a time. (The government prudently shifted from Nanking to Canton early in February.) But there was really no intention on the part of Mao Tse-tung to negotiate an easy peace. Why should he give any quarter at all to these people he had on the run? As a preliminary the Reds announced the names of the so-called war criminals: the Generalissimo with his wife and son headed the list. The forlornly hopeless conference began on the first of April, 1949, in Peking. It did not last long; the Communists wanted everything, and were contemptuously indifferent as to whether or not Li Tsung-jen agreed. They gave the Nationalists an ultimatum: either they accept the Communist terms before April 20 or the Reds would cross the Yangtze and carry on as before.

Li would have given in, but Pai Chung-hsi finally turned against his ancient comrade and would not assent. It was within the Vice-President's power to go ahead anyway, but the habit of years proved too strong. He listened to Pai and agreed, however unwillingly, that the war must continue. On April 17, three days before the truce expired, he sent the telegram to Fenghua that Chiang had been awaiting, politely asking him to come out of retirement and take up the burden of fighting once more.

The Generalissimo, it was reported, had been enjoying his rest and living like a quiet country gentleman, taking walks with Ching-kuo; talking over old times with family friends; refusing to as much as see government officials, let alone discuss affairs of state. According to Tong he made one exception and received a general who was an old friend, who sought to please him by telling him an interesting bit of gossip. Mao Tse-tung, said the general, had declared his willingness to strike Chiang's name off the list of war criminals. Tong says "the Generalissimo greeted the announcement with stony silence."

April 20 arrived before Chiang had made up his mind. The Communists launched an attack on Nanking's neighborhood from the south bank of the river and crossed over within a few hours of the deadline, cutting in on the south side so that the city was simply isolated. With no slackening of speed they drove on toward Hang-chow and Shanghai. Chiang could wait no longer; he made an appointment to meet Li Tsung-jen at Hangchow, and two days later the meeting took place.

No one had been hopeful enough to expect a peaceful reconciliation and so no one was disappointed. In spite of the common emergency and the necessity for quick action there was a row, a big one. Li Tsung-jen was irritated because Chiang had stolen several marches on him during his country retreat: the General-issimo had arranged for the nation's gold and foreign currency reserve to be carried over to Taipei, the capital of Taiwan, and had also managed to ship a considerable amount of American equip-ment and war material to the same place. Li wanted it all brought back, and demanded a general reorganization of affairs that would give the Kuomintang less power. The argument showed signs of settling down to one of the old-time feuds. It would certainly have developed along those lines if anyone had had the leisure to pursue the ancient path, but the Reds were closing in.

During the last months of Nationalist presence on the mainland Chiang in his capacity of Generalissimo (not President) was con-stantly on the move. He flew up several times to Shansi to confer with Yen Hsi-shan, hurrying to Peking at the last minute to direct operations from there, visiting Honan and Kiangsu, always under pressure, always under strain, yet remaining calmer than any of his underlings. His years of austerity served him well: his spare frame at the age of sixty-two could take a lot of punishment. Now he went to Shanghai, still uncertain of his status. He had not yet decided to resume the duties of President, and Li was willing that the matter remain unsettled as long as the Generalissimo directed the final stand they had agreed must be made at the great treaty port. The in-evitable retreat could then be laid at his door, where the Vice-President was convinced it belonged.

Li continued to write to Washington, criticizing Chiang and begging for support of himself. He knew that the Generalissimo was taking a last look at Shanghai and the coast, planning against the day he was convinced would soon come, when the Nationalists would rout the Reds and come back as a victorious army and fight their way across China, freeing the country as they went. Like most

of the generals, Li was not inclined to be as hopeful as all that: it
had been his urgent recommendation that Chiang give over such
pursuits and bend his energies instead to something really constructive; a trip to Washington, for instance, there to beg in person
for the help that had already been refused to Mayling.

No, said Chiang, he would not go to America, above all not just
at this time.

Shanghai fell on May 25. "If we do not retake the city in four
months," said Chiang, "I promise you, I will commit suicide."

He was making a speech in Taipei, addressing what remained of
Free China. It was a routine visit: he had lately taken to commuting
between the mainland and the new bolthole. He could not really
have been so sanguine as all that, but in a nation's darkest moments
somebody has got to act hopeful.

Over in Canton the generals were shuffling and reshuffling, still
quarreling, resigning, accusing, and intriguing. Nothing had changed
except that their foundations were sliding out from under. Chiang
was better placed for constructive thinking. He had found a mountain top outside Taipei, on Yangmingshan; the air was clearer there,
and he made plans. Why shouldn't other countries of Asia combine
with his remnant to face the Communist threat? He thought of
Southeast Asia, the Philippines, and Korea, and then he got in
touch with Quirino, President of the Philippines. Taiwan is only a
few hours by plane from Manila. The Generalissimo flew down and
conferred with Quirino. Later he visited Korea and interested Syng-
man Rhee in his plan. In the end the projected Pacific Pact was to
fail in the light of Nehru's disapproval, but it kept Chiang busy for
all of July. He also found time to drop in on the mainland and make
a speech at Canton.

"I feel ashamed to be back . . . in the present circumstances
of retreat and failure. I cannot but admit that I must share a great
part of the defeat. I am appalled at the existence of gambling and

opium smuggling in Canton under the very nose of the government. But we must hold Canton, our last port."

The famous White Paper on China was released in Washington on August 6, 1949. It was a blow to the Nationalists to be told once more, especially in such impressive language and at such cost in labor and paper, that they were corrupt and incompetent. But except for poor Mayling, who was there on the spot, no one suffered any extra embarrassment. Washington had already made it all too clear that the State Department was opposed to helping Chiang directly at this delicate point. To Li Tsung-jen, however, the White Paper acted as a shot in the arm. If not Chiang, why not himself? He would prove that he was a far better leader—not corrupt, certainly not incompetent. For one thing, he would revise the Generalissimo's plans for a final stand against the Reds. All he needed was that reserve, in men, ammunition, and currency that had been spirited over to Taiwan. He pelted the White House with cables.

Then Lanchow was lost to the Reds, and all of Suiyuan. North China was gone, the Northwest was gone, Szechuan itself would soon go. Chiang would have lavished preventive attention on Szechuan, perhaps, and held off the day of reckoning, but he determined to concentrate instead on the far more dangerous province of Yunnan. If Yunnan went, the way was open to Canton, and the province was, as it had always been, shaky politically. Chiang flew alone to the capital, Kunming, on September 22, had a talk with the governor, and came away that same afternoon. Yunnan's lease on Nationalist life was thereby lengthened for several weeks. But all this, helpful as it was for the short run, could only postpone the end.

Li Tsung-jen now devoted himself to a campaign to remove the Premier Yen Hsi-shan from his second post as Minister of National Defense and put in his place his old crony Pai Chung-hsi. The final weeks of the Canton government were given over to this struggle, which, according to Li and Pai, was crucial to China's fate. If they had the exclusive handling of affairs, they were convinced, America would come to the rescue at last. The officials were still hard at it, like Tweedledum and Tweedledee, when the Reds swept in on October 15. Bitterly arguing about whose fault it had been, they were forced to make tracks for the interior.

They went to Chungking. There Li yelled for Chiang, but by the time the Generalissimo had arrived—and the Reds were well on the way—the Acting President himself had gone, this time to Nanning. During the next month he had one last try at overturning the government. He could not come to terms with Pai Chung-hsi about it, however, and Chiang kept telegraphing him to return to Chungking. Li replied that he was having stomach trouble and couldn't possibly face the trip back. Suddenly he came to a decision. On November 19 he wrote to the Generalissimo:

"My stomach ailment has become much worse. I am very tired. So, I have decided to leave for Hongkong today en route to U.S.A. for a thorough checkup and, if necessary, an operation. In view of the grave situation, I shall come back in a short time to take up my responsibilities."

Li got stuck in Hongkong, for he had no passport and the government refused to issue one. In Chungking his associates were shrill with indignation. His abrupt departure had left them without any President at all, either real or acting, and Chiang refused to take on the responsibility of the title. He said it wouldn't look well.

In any case, Li in Hongkong wouldn't commit himself. Half the time he said he would resign as soon as he should arrive in the States. The other half the time he said he wouldn't, claiming that he would need the vice-presidency in Washington in order to arrange for aid. Finally his colleagues relented and gave him a passport, and he chartered a plane and took off forthwith.

Pai Chung-hsi had already given up and fled with his troops to Hainan.

Chiang's farewell to the mainland should have been dramatic, and if it is ever put on the stage, no doubt it will be. But it is not in him to strike attitudes, and he does not accept finality in these matters. To him leaving Chungking was a necessity for the time being, that was all, and he went about it characteristically, with deliberation. On his last day in Chungking he inspected all the military offices, and early next morning, on November 30, 1949, left for Chengtu. The Communists had broken into the city before his plane took off. No doubt he was humming.

Chiang stayed in Chengtu ten days, discussing the chances of a last-minute stand in Yunnan. This showed itself as unpromising to say the least; a conspiracy was afoot to nab him in Kunming and turn him over to Mao. He therefore gave Kunming a miss and flew on to Taiwan. It was as simple as that.

# 16 THE END?

Chiang's associates made their way to Taiwan according to chance, from wherever their fortunes had deserted them. There were two outstanding exceptions; Li Tsung-jen, who was in America, and Feng Yu-hsiang.

But Feng for a long time had not been a genuine associate. He was showing a fondness for the cause of Mao Tse-tung. He had gone to America and stayed there for some time, attracting much admiring notice with his rough, picturesque appearance and outlandish history: there he seemed the epitome of the mysterious East in our time. In the Western mind, the Confucian sage had gone out of fashion: Americans had learned to admire the age of the common man in China, and Feng filled the bill admirably. When he declared his abhorrence for the venality and corruption of the Chiang Kai-shek regime it was remarkably effective, and he returned to North China the happy possessor of a special invitation to visit Russia. Feng had a passion for moving-picture cameras, and in his luggage he carried an immense amount of undeveloped film, souvenirs of his visit to the States. It is said that he was aboard ship in the dark room, developing this film, when the fatal accident took place. The film caught fire, the whole room flared up, and Feng died in the flames. Like many stories put out by the Communists, this one sounds somehow fishy. Perhaps they were just tired of the Christian general.

Many others had joined the Communists: their list of names was still headed by that of Madame Sun Yat-sen. But the hard core, including Yen Hsi-shan and Pai Chung-hsi, and of course Chen Cheng, stood by Chiang Kai-shek. When "the dust had settled" and the various outlying posts had given in and the troops had reached the island, something more than two million Nationalists were there.

Two million newcomers, still without an Acting President. During the first frantic days it didn't matter, but after a few weeks things sorted themselves out and it was agreed that the affair of the presidency must be settled.

Taiwan houses were crammed with exiles. As each ship arrived at the island ports, more soldiers were brought in and quartered on the Taiwanese. A good deal of hasty screening had to be done in those confused days, and sometimes whole shiploads were turned back for fear they carried Red malcontents with them. But in general it was not too frantic a business; barracks had been prepared beforehand. It was the refugee civilians who found it hard going, as civilians always do.

Rather noticeably, Li Tsung-jen failed to come back within the month named as the limit of his American visit. Watchful Chinese in New York reported that he had taken a house in Riverdale on long lease. On February 21, 1950, the Kuomintang Committee sent him an ultimatum cable; he must return within three days or relinquish the presidency. Li did not return. A few days later, on March 1, Chiang Kai-shek resumed his office.

Argument raged in Washington. Britain had recognized the Communist government in Peking: should not America do likewise? Some voices were loud in urging it. Taiwan would inevitably fall to the Reds soon, they said, and if America was still backing the Chiang government there would be more complications. It is possible that if the Reds had not immediately taken up an inimical attitude toward the United States, Washington would have followed Whitehall's lead. But they were inimical, and that settled the question. Economic aid was extended to Taiwan, and in spite of Communist protests, the Nationalist representative retained his seat in the United Nations.

How long this state of affairs could continue, however, was a very moot point. The Reds were building up a tremendous force along the Fukien coast, preparing for an all-out attack that would at last close the troublesome chapter of Chiang Kai-shek in their book. There had been one determined battle for Kinmen Island (Quemoy), lying between Taiwan and the coast, and in spite of all the reports from the mainland about mismanagement, famine, and general distress, it was clear that the Reds were consolidating the country at top speed. Fifth-column activity in Taiwan had been pounced on and practically eradicated, but the menace from outside was drawing closer and closer. Early in June 1950 a rumor swept the island: Chiang was getting out of it. He would make his escape quietly, by way of Manila; it was said that he and Madame (who had returned early in the year) had accepted an offer of asylum from America. But he did not go, and the rumor died down.

On June 25 the Korean War broke out. All attention, including that of the Communists, was diverted to the peninsula. Taiwan was off the front page.

"Chiang is so obstinate," said one of his followers in Taiwan, "that you would not believe it. He is so obstinate that——" He broke off and thought for a moment. Then he found the words he wanted. "He is so obstinate he won't even stop hoping," he said.

What Chiang hopes for is to return to the mainland. If during the attack to attain this he should lose his life—well, that Bushido spirit he toasted in water, long ago in Takata, still holds good.

# BIBLIOGRAPHY

Berkov, Robert. *Strong Man of China*. New York: Houghton, 1938.

Bertram, James. *Crisis in China*. New York: Macmillan, 1937. *North China Front*. New York: Macmillan, 1939.

Brandt, Conrad, with Benjamin Schwartz and John K. Fairbank. *A Documentary History of Chinese Communism*. Cambridge: Harvard Univ. Press, 1952.

Chang Hsing-hai. *Chiang Kai-shek, Asia's Man of Destiny*. New York: Doubleday, 1944.

Chen Tsung-hai, with Wong An-tsiang. *General Chiang Kai-shek, the Builder of New China*. Shanghai: 1943.

Chiang Kai-shek, with Madame Chiang. *China at the Crossroads*. New York: Doubleday, 1937. *China's Destiny* (with notes and commentary by Philip Jaffe). London: Dobson, 1947.

Eldridge, Fred. *Wrath in Burma*. New York: Doubleday, 1946.

Feis, Herbert. *The China Tangle*. Princeton: Princeton Univ. Press, 1953.

Hsiung, S. I. *The Life of Chiang Kai-shek*. London: Davies, 1948.

Hudson, G. F. *The Far East in World Politics*. New York: Oxford, 1937. *Questions of East and West*. London: Odhams, 1953.

Hughes, E. R. *The Invasion of China by the Western World*. London: Black, 1937.

Isaacs, Harold Robert. *The Tragedy of the Chinese Revolution*. London: Secker & Warburg, 1938.

James, Cyril L. R. *World Revolution, 1917–1936*. London: Saunders, 1937.

Kent, R. H. B. *The Twentieth Century in the Far East.* New York: Longmans, 1937.

Lattimore, Owen. *Solution in Asia.* Boston: Little, 1945.

Linebarger, P. M. A. *The China of Chiang Kai-shek.* Boston: World Peace Foundation, 1941.

Linebarger, P. M. W. *Sun Yat-sen and the Chinese Republic.* London: Century, 1925.

Liu, Shao-t'ang. *Out of Red China.* New York: Duell, 1953.

Martin, Bernard. *Strange Vigour.* London: Heinemann, 1944.

North, Robert C. *Moscow and Chinese Communists.* San Francisco: Stanford Univ. Press, 1953.

Romanus, Charles F., with Riley Sunderland. *Stilwell's Mission to China. (The U.S. Army in World War II.)* Washington, D.C., 1953.

Schwartz, Benjamin. *Chinese Communism and the Rise of Mao.* Cambridge: Harvard Univ. Press, 1951.

Selle, Earl Albert. *Donald of China.* New York: Harper, 1948.

Serge, Victor. *From Lenin to Stalin.* London: Secker, 1937.

Sharman, Lyon. *Sun Yat-sen, His Life and Its Meaning.* New York: Day, 1934.

Sheean, Vincent. *Personal History.* New York: Doubleday, 1935.

Smith, Arthur H. *Village Life in China.* New York: Revell, 1899.

Snow, Edgar. *Red Star Over China.* New York: Random House, 1938.

Stilwell, Joseph Warren. *The Stilwell Papers,* ed. T. H. White, New York: Sloane, 1949.

Sun Yat-sen. *Memoirs of a Chinese Revolutionary.* London.

Tong, Hollington K. *Chiang Kai-shek: Soldier and Statesman.* London: Hurst, 1938. *Dateline: China.* New York: Rockport Press, 1950.

White, Theodore H., with Annalee Jacoby. *Thunder Out of China.* New York: Sloane, 1946.

# INDEX